COLLECTED SHORTER POEMS

Also by John Peck from Carcanet

Poems and Translations of Hï-Lö
Argura
Selva Morale

JOHN PECK

COLLECTED SHORTER POEMS
1966-1996

CARCANET

This edition first published in 1999 by
Carcanet Press Limited
4th Floor, Conavon Court
12-16 Blackfriars Street
Manchester M3 5BQ

A CIP catalogue record for this book
is available from the British Library
ISBN 1 85754 161 8

The publisher acknowledges financial assistance
from the Arts Council of England

Set in 10pt Palatino by Bryan Williamson, Frome
Printed and bound in England by SRP Ltd, Exeter

CONTENTS

from the 1970s and 1980s

from *Poems and Translations of Hĭ-lö* (1991)

from *Selva Morale* (1995)

9

ACKNOWLEDGEMENTS

Shagbark first published by Bobbs Merrill, 1972; *The Broken Blockhouse Wall* first published by David Godine, 1978; *Poems and Translations of Hi-Lo* first published by Carcanet, 1995; *M and Other Poems* first published by TriQuarterly Books / Northwestern University Press, 1996.

Grateful acknowledgement is made to the editors of the following, in which previously uncollected poems appeared: 'Cussewago' in *Salmagundi*; 'Let Us Call This the Hill of Sotatsu' in *American Poets in 1976*, edited by William Heyen (Bobbs Merrill, 1976); and 'A Weaving from the Zollbrucke, Zurich' in *H.D.: Woman and Poet*, edited by Michael King (National Poetry Foundation, 1986).

This collection of work from the mid-1960s to the mid-1990s represents what I stand by at the moment. One book appears entire, *The Broken Blockhouse Wall* (1978), as does most of *Argura* (1993). I have aimed at composing books rather than collections; from *Poems and Translations of Hĭ-Lö* (1991) to *Selva Morale* (1995), each book dovetails work from the immediate past with poems that had waited, in some cases many years, to find their berths. The uncollected poems included here now enter into the design, while the long poem *M* (1996) awaits a later gathering. The last two of the uncollected poems complete a suite, seven poems of which figure in the first section of *Argura*, all addressed to Termia, whose name one could translate, in a lightsome mood, as 'the buck of inquiry stops here'. Her identity is finally interior.

I have excluded a number of translations from *Hĭ-Lö*, and have replaced one version of Ion Barbu with another poem by him. On a few occasions I have newly supplied an epigraph, and also have added some endnotes while augmenting a few earlier ones.

I owe thanks to Michael Schmidt for instigating this collection, and to Reginald Gibbons for making suggestions about an earlier version of it.

Brattleboro, Vermont, 1998

from
SHAGBARK
(1972)

VIATICUM

Shedding ravines
And mist shoaling the cirques
What we were has come with us
What we are hangs back
The sky waits for its thunder

Padded sticks at the temples
Our only rhythm
Then our guides calling
Small wishbones caught in their mouths
Gill pulse through a pine wind
That sucks at lichens and our names

Next they will raise their arms
To the last cols
Doors in this termless morning
Sills, thresholds
And the firmness beyond

And then we too can shout back
Towards the windlost faces
Ears waiting
Through involved porches and the blood within
Beachless interior
River and drum

Dust runs after the deer
Cloud prints the mountain

THE WATCHER

On the far edge of a plain,
As on white flats of Kirgiz,
A muzzy grey edge of men.

It moves in my direction
Through wind that keens.
An old anxiety
Relaxes, and I wait.

White-booted and white-coated
They approach over snow
That caves beneath them.
Their legs lift and plunge.

I am not seen as they near –
One speaks to another,
Confident, precise
Under white, fur-lugged headgear –
His language is alien
But I can see that he is
Confident, precise.
In my secrecy,
In my inaction,
I admire this.

Then with his trained eye
He turns, squinting above me
Into pines over my shoulder –
A flanking shaggèd wall
Over depths of forest.

His rifle goes up –
I follow its sighting
To a bird that perches, waxen
And with eye of dark berry.

As before, the wind crooning.
As before, a calm
Unaccountable, a moment
That continues to fill.

18

I do not ask, will it end;
But am aware of sky
As of scud over harbors –
Sheeted and stretched above
The snow poised on that bough.

UNDER VIRGO

Farther than grass
might I go
listening

but for the
field's edge –
crud of gold

rubbed deeply
into the heavy
frame. There

rises the woodlot
and its other
whisper, its

browns and blacks.
Compost thick on
its floor – tasting

of brass warmed by
spittle, horn
pressed up to

distant lips,
embouchure of
praise, fat with

hope of harvest:
give it, bellower,
your high, firmest

19

tongueing, spin
the leaves into
dry light –

for they
forget you already,
the air has

gone shut
about them and
they curl, fingers

from cool hands
pendant along
secret flanks.

DEATH OF A STALLION

Where malady has winnowed him already,
Sinking over the ribs into transparence,
He nourishes the foetus of symmetry:

Crupper and taut withers subside over bones,
Tail sheds the spent wave. But on two hooves he would
Fly, foreshank rising, rear shattering its prance

To cleave the grass of a gone summer. His head
Stoops, he studies the hoof he would lift higher,
And the hoof he cannot lift at all, beside;

Caught fetlock, the conundrum itself a door
To clarification. His separate eyes
Protrude to gauge it, his ears slant down to snare

Or brush it in passage, and they frame that place
Where the ball has entered cleanly. They would shut
Trim as the leather lip, they would shield those eyes

Budding like horns – incalculable velvet
Of the next moment, whose furlongs he has seen
Already, whose grass he has felt simmer at

His knees, running into that shadeless season
He would crest once more, rearing beneath lightness.

THE SPRING FESTIVAL ON THE RIVER

Crowd fear: blown paper and uprooted ferns,
Down newsreel streets, down spillways,
Hands at random over me, cold pork,
Sweat runneling down my back –
Then the bridge:
Like carpet bulging up, it heaved the bodies
Wedging above the river, over barges piled
With cargo to the edges of their curious roofs,
Hulls squatting low into the water, swaybacked,
While on the bridge the heads bobbed like balloons
Between shops perched on either side –
Women holding their children high
Out of the surge, awnings snapping.
Where have I seen that other ashen whirr of images?
The public stairs at Chungking, after the air raids, after
The stampede crush – mothers as if asleep upon
The wide stone steps, their clothes torn back about them
By panic force of feet, their arms
Serene over the tiny bodies.

I cannot reach you now, how shall I find you?
Out of the back windows of shops quick with hands
Burdock and mangoes spill, the looser tiles
Like pebbles tumble off the eaves, and no one hears
Their sputter as they splash. Then, unmistakable
As bowstring past the ear, the whuck
Of separating cable. Massively,
Swarming with rucksack figures stabbing with long poles,
A barge piles out along the wharf beneath us, heeling

Into the current, its bow sucking fast;
The polers thrust, their mouths go wide, their arms rise,
Water spins its tons under sharp snailshell eddies,
The fine lines of that ink, how wet, how ancient.
Craning off the bridge, whole torsos
Lean down, grabbing stupidly, with knothole mouths.

I cannot reach you. Now it is I watch, farther along
The bank between two hulls, some boy oblivious
Who hunkers down, playing in shallows with a stick,
Picking his nose, poking mud into clouds of acid.
Now it is that dust motes, boiling into light,
Spin heliographs, but to what date, what hour?
The hills beyond the city: was it them I saw,
Glancing and running? Red, then, they were,
And silent: the bright and the clear –
Slabs of jasper, crystals of mica.

                                        (1969, war in the East)

section three, THE HOBBIES

Old clearing:
Grass flaking to spikes of sun now,
Nostrils flaring with heat of that packed space now,
Weight of return that crowds
The fading trace of an unfound thing now.

With her it is an eye
For the first orioles
Distinct as dice,
Or for the hobbies, raptors
Of the agile swifts –

With her it is that rip
Of the air's jacket,
Bladefold of wings against the slategrey back
And plummet smack against the smaller bird,

22

Gripped now against
The black spots upon the white belly,
Tangled among the red ankles,
Folded tightly into that single sound.

HUNGER-TRACE

Turn, let your nakedness reassume
The sun's body, let weight stitch your arm
With sleep: through you and under you, time.

Sand whelming dune grass, gritty flurry
Burying the small shoots to the knee –
Panic seeps from your body slowly.

And gull pivots seaward, steadying
Then yielding. Blade and wing hang planing
The one idea of wind too long

For the eye narrowing, tiring – these
Are receptacles, surprise gathers
Into them tense against vacancies,

Waiting till you wake. For then the low
Sound alters, light is newly hollow,
And the eye's quick lift its own shadow –

And the wing over you no reining
Hawk or falcon's, but greater, cupping
You in its air, freezing you how long

At the center, fresh crumb of darkness
Licked at by light: see the hunger-trace,
Fanning through feathers in a faint slice,

Slit of glitter left by lean feedings –
Waiting to strain, break clean and crippling
In the stroke downward of that still wing.

23

INVOLUNTARY PORTRAIT

'Bad news,' you said, and let sun render
The letter you unfolded brilliant with
The indifferent irony of natural splendor.

But then you turned, scribbled some plan
Across it, fixing fire in dead wine, writing
In time's teeth, as the unbaffled can,

Yes, countermarched whole seasons in your war –
Made spite and justice somehow both your friends.
All this I have admired, and more –

Yet, when you ask me to approve,
To foresee victory, I see instead
Your figure strangely set at great remove

Against a headland, posing there
Before my camera. And as I watch,
The focus will not hold you, and the air

Works changes like a fantasy:
Starts a scenario I cannot stop,
Gives me the island exile by his sea.

Fat sags along his poster jaw.
His eyes twist vacantly, regardless still
Of curlews overhead that wheel and call.

The cliffs march on the combers, deal
Their dull rebuff, and wait. Deal it and wait.
The curlews in their volley call and wheel.

And as he turns away,
The swift, high-angle shot of sentiment
Throws him steep upon the hill's flank –
His greatcoat slowly creasing grass, and bent
In the slightest parabola of blank

Intention. He ignores the road.
The crest might not be there. Below and always,
The slope-heaved billows stupidly explode.

LINES FOR LEIBNIZ

The hothouse flurry of the academy
Drove him to select life deliberately,

To let the carriage window's fluid landscape
Form his eye's garden, frame his singular grip

Upon the manifold – he would jot his notes
On whatever road sped the duke's business.

Those notes lie now in Mainz, Hanover, Berlin,
Ungathered. How long, in wood walks, had he been

Fretting retrieval of Substantial Form
Only to lose it to the leaves? – though in time

They gave it all back to him, newly perfect.
How many designs he left to execute –

Wagon wheels that plowed themselves out of mud, and
Nails whose tiny spurs lodged them unrepentant

In the wood, and a museum that would house
Dutch sail-wagons and Chinese wind-carriages.

But it was this gift of tongues made into hands
That fated him to build in the Harz Mountains

For the Duke John of Hanover's silver mines
A windmill pump, to keep tunnels clear of rains;

The delegation came for its inspection,
And that day the wind died out of all heaven.

The wind died out of all Europe while he wrote
To hold its unity before the breeze, set

Full above the signature, *Pacidius*,
To yoke schismatics once more in the embrace

Of dialectic, strenuous, with small spurs.
What years dwindling to carriages, those letters –

Yet, the acacia boughs outside my window
Do not sway in fantasies of knowledge now,

This time their disarray holds their uphill slant
With an old, unforeseen advent of poignance:

The fern accuracy of each tiny fan
Hanging from the haphazard inflorescence

Finds place in some unguessed scheme of completeness,
Though still I feel little toward this locust, this

Thorny tree of Egypt.
                              Morning: he embarks
on *postes 'portefeuille* for the petty and grand dukes,

Taking with him on the quick trip by carriage
The *I-Ching*. It is still morning, the image

Fashions him kin to us, yet remote as well,
A profile accurate and sentimental

Looking up from the series of charmed guesses
At nothing in particular, beyond trees –

He forsook religion toward the end. Only
One came to his funeral, his secretary.

CIDER AND VESALIUS

Like a fruit wine with earth
  Clouding its sweetness, color
    Of day's end, this cider
Collects light from the window
  Of October – I scan
    Vesalius the surgeon's
Woodcut anatomies
  Sliced and prepared for the eye's
    Terminal erudition:
This solvent ruddy earth,
  Chilled, is best commentary,
    It tilts the wings of bees
Into refraction, wings
  Already numb about
    The body of the queen
Who dies: long live the queen –
  Bright milkweed drifts about
    Her dozing combs, the eye
Burs, rinsing her blind hives.
  We want no other gloss
    On this vivisection,
Yet want the litany
  Of fear transmuted, need
    The slow insinuation
Of spirits through our glance
  At knowledge.
              Look again:
    It did not move, it stands
At ease, it rises well
  Above the horizon, dressed
    In half its muscles. These
Dangle loose here and there,
  Rags in the white air left
    Motionless by the blast
It heard with ears it wears
  No longer. Now it waits
    Attentive toward the bright
Still landscape at its feet,
  The streets and houses empty –
    Its arm crooks in the quick

Arrest of intuition,
Its finger lightly bent
Toward a zone haloing
The smooth cope of the skull
Whose back is all we see,
White, blooming suddenly
Out of the sinuous stem
Sheathing the spine. Now, soon,
That silver sound again –

These streets are some real city,
No Hieronymus Bosch
Weaving his figures here,
Arguing brutal and
Sophisticated joy
Behind the passionless
And naked faces, through
Steel wires penetrating
The body pinioned by
The harp in hell. Threads tensile,
Demons reaching to pluck
And stroke them into music,
For we sing without joy
Or knowledge, bone against
Muscle, muscle against
Nerve and vessel.
The young
Student went from Louvain
Out to the roadside gibbet
Late at night, and he pulled
The femur off the hip –
The bones were bare, still joined
By ligaments – and then
Each night thereafter, piece
By piece, till finally
Only the thorax hung
From its chain. His desire
Was great: he clambered up
And yanked it off, and made
His first articulated
Skeleton. Then he said
Discreetly that he'd bought

The thing in Paris.
                    But
        The first plates that he made
Were thumbed so avidly
    That they disintegrated.
        And all his woodcut blocks
Were lugged across the Alps,
    Over half Germany,
        Outliving half a dozen
Publishers. Now it rests
    With us to speak the sequel
        As if to his portrait, where
He holds the malefactor's
    Dissected hand, each tendon
        Strung out in demonstration –
We must tell him the hand
    Has not changed, it is still
        The malefactor's, and
It is alive. The pale
    Tendons have reacquired
        Occulted vigor, slipped
Back into place, and bathed
    In blood again, that blood
        Which in all innocence,
At freezing altitude,
    Required the flier's glove
        Of fur and swarthy leather.
Over the skies of Munich,
    Through searchlights sweeping cloud
        And flak flowers, that hand
Squeezed its release, and all
    The fine grain of our shape
        Graved deep into your blocks
Of oak, the arteries
    Feeding back to the great
        Aorta, *toti corpori*
vitalem spiritum –
    All melted in the sudden
        Flame – *naturalemque*
calorem.
        This is the
    Last glass, spinning its lees

To hellswirls out of Bosch
In silence, emptying
   Its far end, tunnel of spirits,
      Bosch's ascension panel –
Inexplicably yours,
   Who wait there with the other
      Suspect seekers for escort,
Angels handing you on
   With your face passionless
      And final toward the mouth
Of the high tunnel, till
   You travel where the shapes
      In little pairs waft lightward,
Mount through to the other side.
   With us you leave these other
      Figures, diagrams
Of unwilled ecstasy,
   Sinews drying to ink,
      This glass drying to stains
Of cider, while the autumn
   Milkweed lifts into air,
      Silk wrinkling in wind,
White inchworms draped from trees
   At loose in the loose wind,
      Fouling whatever moves,
Squandering transformation.

COLOPHON FOR CH'ING-MING
SHANG-HO T'U
   *(The Ching-ming Festival at the River
   by Chang Tse-tuan, 12th Century)*

The woodsmen yank their donkeys
Heavy with cuttings
Out of the misty wood.
The hamlet sleeps, empty as the crows' nests.
Willows stain first light with celery tips.

Through them a family entourage
Returns from the ancestral tombs:
The foremost horseman leans
Outward in gallop, catching
Sight of the city –
His cries would leave his mouth
With the clarity of vision
Were not his form rubbed clean away by time.
The others lope behind him
Even sedan carriers
Jostling sprigs of willow lashed to the cabs.
They do not see, beneath them,
The peasants slanting back now toward their farms,
Wives twisting on their donkeys
To watch the city as it drops behind.

Barges begin now: the canal
Curves upward from the lower margin
Bearing a deckhand stretched in sleep
And a cook who fries fish.
The shops yawn open in air hazy with breakfast.
Four stevedores lug wheat from a barge –
The overseer disposes
His bulk already on the bags,
Waving his arm egregiously.

But soon the rainbow bridge, seething,
And one more span above a moat
To the great gate, while the canal
Loops outward to the upper margin.
The wines, cheeses, incense,
Rich fabrics, fortune tellers,
Medicines and samples of calligraphy
Decamp from the interiors,
From carts and quayside barges.
                              Always the barges,
Navigating with their spatula rudders
Or roped tightly to the bank each with its own winch,
Draw deeply, gravidly,
Bringing it in, all of it –
The ten thousand things
Arrange themselves upon

The hundred diagonals –
The brush strokes are strong, all of them,
Deep distance, penetrable space. . . .
Inside the vacant tower on the great gate
Hangs the alarm gong brilliant
From its leather braces.

Supply, provision, engorgement –
A triptych waxing on the sun's gradient,
Even as cart-wheel rims, foreshortened,
Stand wider at the tops than at the sides.
The eye that noticed this
Cannot be found in the ten
The twenty and the thirty versions
By all the bastard and the well-paid sons;
Chang dressed his customers and onlookers
In the rich sameness of prosperity
So as to drape their singleness of gesture.
Carts wallow multiple as noise
Passing the temple door
And cool stone feet of the Buddha
Lodged in the midmost of the shops and stalls.
In that finesse of the Constructive Art
He was not imitated.
His focus ends at a crossroads, at high noon;
He leaves one to imagine
The Imperial Palace
Farther on into late sun,
Canto on tiered canto
Bodiless, whole in splendor,
Picturable
But not pictured.

IN FRONT OF A JAPANESE PHOTOGRAPH

A sentry and a ladder mark the wall,
But shadows only, on the open wood.
Its paint was burnt away, though not quite all:
It stands yet where the man and ladder stood.

Sun making second morning at ground zero
Had photographed them, silhouettes on white –
Matchstick rungs and the flat outline, no hero,
Of the single human shape, erect and slight.

He might have looked into the glare, or not.
We make out only, once again, the wood,
And shadows cast by nothing at that spot.
And looking, that we stand where he had stood.

POINTING

Old mortar powdering from older bricks:
I chiseled chunks out, heard the seated bone
Twisting on gristle after long disuse,
Consistency of stale bread, knife stuck deep.
Take out the old connective tissue, let
Air pack its ice around your buried gums,
Work till the evening like a soft eraser
Smudges the inessential: brick is rice paper,
Fishermen take the shore path into sky
Fogged limitless, T'ao-chi spread it like mortar –
Jade blades up to the midriff, over the path,
A gate half open; dusk dissolving creepers,
River village under the moon: dogs barking,
Fishermen file home, torches in their hands.

PEAR

Tithes, swags and filchings from the dark tree –
What have you thieved from your own body,
And by whose hand? Heartwood stiff already

In the stunning light, hardness is wise –
Slowly it trims distances with eyes
Rimming old prunings. They do not close,

They watch the boy's hand dart from below
For fruit, eyes to which his yet may grow;
Leaves fingering through his hands also,

Silk whispering shy of his ear's face;
The hand reaching would test nothing less
Than evil in its felt weightlessness,

Its perfect vacancy of motive –
So young Austin would have it, would have
The act itself smooth as an olive

Caught and stopped growing in his hand's heat:
Else he would have foreseen the panicked
Stirring of leaves he feels taking root

In his breathing, his eyes, his running
From himself or whatever new thing
He is: rings ripple, bark breaks, and hangs.

And the hand falls. Slowly, as you would
Shroud a child in sun-sleep unshielded,
Your body swims into wheat, toward shade

Of that tree forgotten, the theft so
Long forgotten; and whatever you
Have taken, it will precede you now,

Grass there will stoop in salutation,
Wind mantle you with it, worm glisten
With it; for only you have not known.

34

FOR THE ENGRAVER

Shall I say your thumb brushes my thumb,
That together we are thieves of time
And time's pieces, bending over them

With styluses, prying to possess
And reduce each of them to riches,
To make leafy the atomic rose?

The accomplishment of burglary
Lures us to the same scene unwary,
And we find, lifting the sash freely,

That the darkened house we penetrate
Is our own, and we our own secret,
And on the wall, dim, our own portrait

That hangs – we must take it with us now,
Our skill vague in our hands as shadow,
New stealth grainy as our lives, and go;

And, as the young Kathe Köllwitz did,
A harsh lamp near her head suspended,
Shadowing the tall jar of acid

And westering moon of her small face,
Turn a dark eye darkening toward us,
And then an eye blind with light as ice.

Her back humps into blackness, her hair
Draws back into the taut dark nowhere
That floats her table and composure

Around the focus of her calm hands
And the etched figure that burns there, tense,
Lifting up blackness in a black dance.

LEAVING THE COAL CELLAR

The wind lisps from its belly
Rehearsing the immunity of its names,
Slipping through nets of what is
Like shoals of small fish turning
With one intelligence,
Brightening one moment down
The million coins of their flanks,
Then darkening through weirs
Of the trees, leaving only
The tapering long wheeze of the recovering lung,
Cloud tumbling through it in a frieze of attitudes
Unfinished, hurrying toward completion –

I store another season's tools
Beneath the house and climb
Through sloping doors half-folded back like wings;
Emerge with cobweb face and hands
Into this wind laced suddenly
With the old hint that blood sacrifice
Of a young girl can raise wind again,
Out of death wrinkling the mirror
Silver to the sea's rim,
Lift canvas like these trees, humming again
With that swarm of bees death tunes and dances,
Oars leaping hammer-speed before the storm
Into their raid, then homeward with the wreck
Of pollen dangling in a favoring wind.

TURN

Your neck, coiling to your bare shoulder,
Pulled itself tighter beneath warm hair –
And now that tension, like my future

Meeting me momently, advances
Its edge toward the still net of my gaze:
This is how recognition seizes,

How the patterns of obscure ruins
Reveal themselves to fliers, faint lines
Rising printlike through the grassy plains,

How war comes, blowing torn cloudshadows
Over the waking face of land, as
Suddenly the shapes of small countries

Shrivel like puddles under bald sun –
While, lost in time, slopes we might have known
Fold to wings of the rocked, sleeping tern,

Wedged at ease deep in the green day, where
Mushrooms drink the earth's secret color,
Steeping in the lòng noons toward summer.

QUIET

Bent to your legs, undressing them,
Your back bends the light with it,
Warmly down and along
The spine's rivulet.

Then flexes it out to less than sheen
With your rising, gathering
All to contours, with the open
Secrets of odor.

Later, when the night rain has laced
Air with earth, grass, and the mixed
Pungencies of stone, there sounds
A patter, relaxed.

Warm void on waking, benevolent
Silence of this room becoming
Tiring-house to gestures,
The day's turnings

37

Idly wrought to the pitch of amendment.
You turn away in sleep, animal
Languor, a waterfall's smooth head,
Or hopes quieted –

It is hours until light arrives,
Lifts us out along some radius
From this hub, into the balanced
Exchange of lives.

Sleep, while off toward terminals a thrumming
Crosses gaps in the night wind –
The lean of whistles, not breaking,
And then, broken.

VESTIBULE

All day our paths had crossed, I'd missed you twice
Or three times – then, had come home tired to find
Your sweater on the couch, your shoes kicked off,
The coffee still warm in your waiting cup –
And lightly called your name, only to hear it
Measure the silences; then felt my eyes
Stray back across the sweater's rich abandon,
The shoes more delicate for lying empty,
The porcelain zero of the cup – but then you called,
Upstairs and far away. Your voice brought back
Another room we entered once together,
Catching our breath – bare benches where the Shakers
Sat quiet after field work and prepared
To go together to the larger room.

DARK ON DARK

Fireflies heavier after rain, gold
Flaring green, god and mortal mingled –
Come, look with me over the whole field,

They surround us, swinging and lifting
Apostrophes on dusk, while words hang
Shy of speech: *those you love will live long* –

Presences through haze, needing no voice,
They widen through our wake in wet grass,
With hid roots tug vanishing at us –

Leaving touch as our child leaves us – as
Even now strength sieves and the light goes
As to a strange place. Yet it shadows

Some familiar experience,
The way pages half possess our hands,
Filtering through fingers till sense thins

Into that large hand round us, dusk full
Upon the whole unremarkable
Mask of memory, air threading cool.

Where odor interleaves with odor,
Dark on dark, there you wait, your finger
Marking place while the head lifts once more,

Soft cone rinsing inward, and inward,
Light spiraling in dregs round the slurred
Center – the recognized, retreating word.

from
THE BROKEN BLOCKHOUSE WALL
(1979)

LETTING UP

The meander of my walking, and through it
A sun that swings to go with me at each turn,
And sweet fatigue that remains childlike because
    It works at nothing.

Push aggressively enough at the stout weave
Of what is, appearances we must take as
Being at least what they seem, and you tear through,
    You come stumbling out

Where the bright warmth sealed behind late windows seems
Miniature tenderness and stale fury, seems
To dwindle with cold speed as feet find themselves
    Running now, fleeing,

Carrying a stick figure who cannot let up.
This, too, comes to me from my walking, the one
Map of it that I have, unrolling between
    One step and the next.

When the gray infantry broke through at Shiloh
They found campfires, skillets over them cooking,
Sunday breakfasts laid out, and swirls of steam still
    Coming off coffee.

Communion that seems an end, fleeting, factive,
Must begin somewhere. They stopped, ate and drank, snooped
Through tents and read letters from girls. And they were
    Lost to the advance.

FAMILY BURYING GROUND

Dry walls through second-growth
Meeting at scruffy angles,
And the stooped fitted death
Of the mason unrenounced
Where brush from three tracts mingles
Man-high. A new road clears
The granite outcrop, houses
Follow. And now I hear it:
Measure that has advanced
Sure as the pulse's ferret
Through flesh, stone for the city,
And how that cadence fills
With dust spun from the body
Which, dragged around high walls,
Inscribed a bitter plighting.
And picnickers sit aptly
Among the graves. Horns grating
At an intersection spill
As if to mesh remotely
With the lark's gapped music
On an ancient scale.

LUCIEN

Were those flares new to you,
Still their pulse downriver
Would spill at the same tempo
As your wants and their heats,
Their sure guesses: something is being poured,
Something fused beyond trace
Of any former shape
Or life, puddling to magma.
Only the face itself
Of yearning would seem strange,
Though spores of it now gutter
Down afternoon, powdering

Over the obdurate
Skin of what stays, warehouse
Mill rail steeple, grit spurring you
Irrelevantly to turn
The pronoun's lash against
Yourself, *you* and then *you*

Until in the street's eyes
It is your own that jell, the maze
Familiar,
The bridge alone letting you
Watch the late summer front
Shred toward storm, and there is no damping
The quiver underfoot
At midspan (or the flash
Of a fin tucking under),

Cables muttering
Their chill life to the hand,
And colder if you hold
In the same gust that floats
The pigeon every lunge
Of the ranked spans
And their lights threading homeward –

Lucien, your fury still
Veins with the muskellunge
Nudging at locks; and while
Your own breath blown from you
Augurs the focus, some projection's
Pure point out there at last
Churning to rise,
The channel scrawls its white
Flawed cursives. Evening waits,
And the swimmer toward the moored barge
Rolls his stroke without haste,
From his lean arm the veil
Splits evenly across
His flowing face.

Skirting screen walls that glass
Their own lines of force – rigid

Telemetries – the flicker
That endures whirls dirt over tracks
And settles. Once more grasp,
Once more refine that grasp
And it all spins without
Touching: gunships that once
Slid through your little fists
Gripping this rail until
Bloodless (you hid
Simple delirium),
Shipbuilders' flags
In that thin amber of fever,
And now the equable
Hiss of small prows that stir
Sandy scurf among towers, flecks
Suspended through the dome
Of the gem, with a rust
Drum that flames, bannering
An abutment with soot, two boys
Chucking in rubber –

And the space cleared in you
Glazes, that some fissure might sheer
Up through strata, insinuate
The full torque of its ice,
And cloud seem less far
Where it luffs tugging the glared
Half-coiling river, and the hid
Spindle rides, hub of your gaze;
That your forearm, Lucien, might twist
Beneath silt where the fires
Burn colder and the lost
Turn more urgently, to grab
That column at its base
In murk, rotate the profile
One notch, another world
Shine through –
                    But the front masses
Elsewhere, . . . and if spasm
Clicks into place behind
Your eyes, it is because
You turn too quickly, you pivot

Into the trick: the car
That nearly hits and then
Shuts you into its speed,
The night driver whose mirror
Stripes his eyes, and leaves molten
The high slope of one cheek
Charring through: he has yet
To come, that messenger
Whom you wish, obscurely, to touch –
Indifference that survives
The crossing, the change of suns
And a cope of stars altered.

REFINDING THE SEAM

Near the old path the self-same smolder
Vents from a dead gallery at hill-crotch
Where no man has yet built his anonymous house.

The mines of Nero and the ovens of Frick
Double back at this boreface, at its buried
Stinkfire which, unabated, leaves

Hill lines wavering in shimmer, clearest
Through shutdowns, the strike's dry clair-obscure
When a pigeon dislodged by footfall

Can raise dust puffs with his maroon wings
Meaning Arcturus and the bear
Will not go unattended that turn through heaven.

AM ABEND DA ES KÜHLE WAR . . .

In evening, when it was cool,
Give me, I nearly said,
The corpse of all that light
Which is still living,
Which cannot be set out
Into its unmingled portions.
Spoken to no one, then,
Yet spoken: lend it to me
For keepsake, which may not
Be kept but which may yet
Keep me, green branch brought back
And profiled in the beak
Of the cool hour.
               For again
I am obscured along
That bright way which is neither
Simply there nor simply
A way, route toward
The world in common,
                  that shows
Signpost of angled stanchion
Enlarging down the arc
Of movement, pitted paint
In fugitive arrest
Of that plunge,
             and drives mass
Floating beneath each jarred
Persistence, a dear head
Exhausted in the car,
Space lifting it unshielded
Against the bessemers
And blown gas flares,
                  and is
Finding myself in that space,
Waked by the humming car,
Cheek pressed on cold glass, eyes
Clean down onto close water
To see a chuffing tug
Warped to its pier, the little
Waves flattened into place,

And a man leaping
Fòr the stern rail,
The surface under him
Gripped in a workmanship
Of sun and shadow, opaque
And flashing in that cleft.

BOUNDS

If I had delivered the morning paper
To the mine manager in his hill house
    In West Winfield after

The October revolution, in slate dawn
Prepared for mortal shapes of newsboy feet
    And files of the first shift,

Might I have been inept enough to ask
The new housekeeper why, when she called her daughter,
    Her words molded strange music?

She, then, off-guard, might have blurted to me
That her dead Count bought steel here for the Czar,
    Before the chairman of steel

Who owned those limestone mines had placed her there
After her jewelry had given out.
    They remember her voice.

When a man jabbering with colleagues lightly sideswipes
An older woman gripped to her shopping bag,
    Odds are he fails to notice.

Odds are that no one interrupts them, either,
To isolate the gesture, lift into view
    What had been on their minds.

No provision for that, no salaried
Questioner, for having gone that far
    One has usually gone farther,

Or turned the furrow crookedly by looking
Over the shoulder. Custom, that thin humus
    Of the law, ridged and rutted.

De Tocqueville interrupted Elam Lynds
At the Lynds hardware shop in Syracuse
    And heard this former builder

Of Sing-Sing, innovator in the prisons,
Say that he found the whip best – more humane –
    And deemed it necessary

To break men to passive obedience.
Securing thus 'a constant habit of work',
    He had eased old abuses.

The questioner, of course, continues; that
Is his art. When that gadfly questioner,
    Among powerful sons

Of the powerful, ambling and gesturing,
Alluded to their city's walls, the logic
    And compact we have dispersed,

He took them at the same time through the gate
Into the half-formed, along the ravelling
    Lifeline of his sentence.

Rope of twined lifetimes, of allegiances
To salt and the grape's candor, oak and stone
    And the grain of linked reasons.

To wind it back up, though, is that to take
The same way back? Through genial dusk, to follow
    The party of long talkers

Threading each district, and the limits, then,
Scatterable. . . . A hobo holds his head
　　In both hands, cooking coffee

Under the railway viaduct's smoked arch.
A questioner is worth his augury,
　　As when a swallow streaks

Up from the warehouse roofline, or erupts
Clearing the noon glare of the careful fields,
　　Sensing already a changed air,

The shape of other weather in its climb
And dizzy spinout. Scrawled intelligence
　　Of the turn.

GROUND OBSERVER CORPS

The Warsaw refugee
Polishing round bronze
Had said, 'This Galahad
His hair like a lion's
Was modelled on the head
Of the young Paderewski.'

Paderewski! – that mane
Flowed whitely in the picture
Snapped at his recital
At the Hotel Ryder,
Oiled hardwood sheen
Long since burned on its hill.

Down from that hill, our yard.
On a clear day my eye
Spanned the flat French Creek valley.
Blue blank north. . . . A boy
I sat alert or bored
For hours, tallying

51

The planes across that corner,
From a shack telephoning
Sightings in: prop, jet,
Direction. That was one
Exercise for the learner,
Reader of the dull quiet.

The maligned 'fifties closed
In with their simplest lesson
Redundantly. And where
The softly curved horizon
Met it, something buzzed
Minutely, and trailed off.

Toward evening pencil beacons
Marked Erie, where the lake
Lay out of sight, enormous.
Winking toy vigilance!
And the lion, from pale Wilson's
Dying hand, had got Poland,

Poland, and Chopin's house.

FOG BURNING OFF AT CAPE MAY

Vaguely at first, then firmly,
The beach extended west
Of our sandpit. That point, then,
Was not the last.

A mile more and we found
The broken blockhouse wall
From nineteen-forty, arm-thick
Firing cable

Shredding into surf.
Oddly archaic, those
Batteries untested,
Greenish fuzz

Bearding the rifle platforms
Offshore, concrete stripped
And draining rhythmically
In the tide's beat

While the line floated one daub
Of zinc white over slate,
The Cape Lewes Ferry sliding
Cleanly from sight.

It was our idleness
Slow as that whitening day
That held us. But through haze
Burning away,

A fat man being tugged
By his paunchy dog, and tanning
Women finding sleep,
And our girl running,

These held through more than distance,
For that shore was a shore
No one can now extend
To any future,

The margin that had gone
Unfired on, the last edge
Behind which houses waited
Without damage –

World to which men returned.
Archaic, it cleared through air
And we had walked into it,
Whole. We were there.

MARCH ELEGIES

Lightning. And wondering if dark would fold back
With full weight
       following some close bolt
Or float headily, still scattering,
    I felt or half-felt

The concussion, an acrid charge, sweetish,
And saw nothing
       in the excess of light,
Thinking: of course, that is how it seems,
    Blasted clear of weight.

Fragrance not frail, tensile, from a clean blow
Suffered cleanly.
       And any reckoner
Vaporizes past laughter, toward
    The unwit of nowhere.

If I must watch like a French peasant
When the last
       of the rear guard has gone
And the bare street grows strange waiting for
    Columns to come on,

May I hold such blank punctuation
As his hand
       might cup his window frame,
Posted experimentally one
    More time, light in time.

*

Splattering of rain on the splay barn,
This the old Finn
       had lingered over
Telling of his wound, the hiding, the healing
    Farm by the river –

Dry sound that rain made on the sagged roof,
And the power
        a scythe had to obsess,
Moon's curve hung on the far wall among
      Discarded harness.

Meals brought in secret, not that pale myrrh
Suffused through the body
        Of Sarpedon,
Meals brought in secret and the water's
      White repetition.

His wound whole again, the partisan
Crouched in nets
        shawled for the crossing
While his boatman dropped rhythmically
      On the glistening

Pole that propelled them, scanning just past
A rick of wood burning
        off the forked bow,
And dragged into the shore-riffle, holding
      Against its flow

While the form of a man trailed its own
Bent shadow
        into impasse, blotting
Into pines uncut by the terse flare –
      Which itself drew off

Into velvet exhalation, brands
Jarring loose from it
        to drift in the Tornio
Breeding smoke with a low sound, slowly
      Less and less.

                 *

Down the sandpath I had watched mica
Spin hints of wet,
        studying that fire
As a river studies itself. I was
      Younger than the war.

Mother set table and ate nothing,
Knowing of that death
           before word of it,
Her brother in my recollection
      Withdrawing from sight

Even as that path turned, rough brown arm
Folding into
           the foreknowledges
Of small hills, leaf litter smelling
      Like uncut apples.

Fire that dreams the dangers of bright things
Tarnishes
           to the black gold of water,
And a mind early from sleep bears them
      Lightly together,

Their life the temperature of cold leaves
Smoking under
           a boy's clear spurt, stains
As if from the glazed throats of apples
      Streaking those burnt sheens.

With the photograph's buttoned tunic,
I could fit
           his jaw's curve to my own
And have no questions. Innocence can think
      Of meridian

And live there, even as she did once,
Playing hooky
           from a Lutheran
Hill school, door wide in dry heat, and she
      A dot in the field's noon,

Declensions carrying unbroken
Over barley,
           lieblich liebliches
Drifting down half an acre to where
      She sucked oranges.

His jaw's curve fit mine, and on his ring
Two leapers sail
      through a bull's horns,
Their legs slimming over his neck's burl
    Into sleep's ease.

So then: the Hungarian machinist
In his yard, scrap-hoard
      near slag hills, wryly
Holding out his stub finger for me
    To verify:

'Well, it grew maybe a little this week.'
At evening hoppers
      were shunted full
From open-hearths, pouring orange down those mounds
    To the pool's sizzle.

*

The cleanliness of profusion comes
Renewably.
      Yet fogs through spring woods
Deterred one companion, whose captain
    Had burned huts in raids.

Where purslane invades whiter rue
Along the first hill
      where this trail bends,
Smoke recedes from me in a dead lake
    With griefless, small sounds.

And then a cupped place: someone had plunged
From that drift of whites,
      his sleep still pressed in –
An imprint not of meditation
    But of blind action

Which my own blundering had triggered.
Sharply that body
      hollowed in starred grass
Sets the first term in an argument
    Without end or egress –

57

Still there, he is elsewhere, even here
In my own skin,
            and between? Between
Falls that wide field crossed by everyone
        And held by no one,

Sequence, and network, and maneuver.
And Grace? Grace follows
            that chancellor
Who ordered cavalry to rebillet
        Away from farms where

Clans pressed olives – he wrote of choked barns
But also
        :   of 'young women who would be
Made uneasy by your soldiers'. Thus
        Machiavelli.

                              *

To find room, and again to find room,
Yet make that need
            less than criminal.
Kings on their islands were far always,
        A spacious exile.

The temptation, the believable
Illusion, is
            that significance
Falls into place under one's need like land
        In its spread fullness.

And rather than an uprooted man
At last taking root,
            it seems that one
Is a cross-country runner for whom
        A third wind comes on,

For whom also the terrain opens
Its entire scheme
            as he cuts through air,
His momentum quickening as though
        He were the planner.

Could he then meet a storyteller
Going the other way,
          he might hear, 'Brother,
It was you running that last highway,
     And you were those others

On the tow path, and down the post road!'
But that witness,
          that friendly ambush
Would not slow him, he would continue
     On each road to thrust

Toward the felt center, his blood's onrush
Accumulating
          veins, high junctions –
While, already, planners have squared out
     Great intersections

And rayed broad avenues toward étoiles
Not to string out
          park vistas at large
But to draw rioters down those same routes
     Pouring to converge

Inevitably, past this or that
Loved angle, past
          the builder's scaffold
Drifting its web against a wall's bulk,
     Until all are spilled

In on the aim of massed regiments
That have been waiting
          at parade rest,
And behind them the attentive cannons
     Eager to speak first.

                    *

Through profusion the clean path turns
Bewilderingly
          hidden. The young
Immigrant shoemaker ancestor
     Spilled by rout along

Bull Run gully, crept down at nightfall
To wash secretly
           his beshatted drawers.
He found one more squatting at that task,
     And then, further, blurs

Through the stream's haze, pale evidence
Of a congregation
           intent there
On those same duties. He did not say
     If there were banter,

And the black run of course showed no hint
Of the blood
           joining it not far off.
What he held to was cold wet relief
     Meeting his frank want,

And loosening in him a weeping
Quiet and wide-eyed,
           alien joy
Prickling his skin through the weariness
     Then lifting away.

                    *

And if naked force hypnotizes
So that even
           to the veteran
It remains unimaginable
     In weight, drift, outline,

How it resolves into aftermath
May elude
           every myth of ending.
Weathering the skull's travels, two skulls –
     Speaking and unspeaking.

And for each man who comes off a field
Unable to discern
           the action
He has walked through, is there another
     In isolation

Projected motionlessly, unseen
And yet stonily
          exact, one man
Whose being focuses that strife, mute
          Point that draws the cone?

Against that fantasy, an ink scroll
Puts five colleagues
          at their squared game board
In a mountain nook, one of them shut
          In on himself, hard,

Set to one side in his remote mood,
While his neighbor
          exults, arms lifted
In the shape of a cliff-face that tops
          The enclosing wood

Which finds its own echo in the sleeve
Of the third fellow,
          draped dopily
Across his pate, baggy with chagrin.
          Though they sit wholly

Preoccupied with their toy warfare,
Their forms go out
          into the brimming
Repository of forms, they spill
          Toward no one thing.

                    *

Believable illusion, as mist
Before whatever
          unshifting stone.
But mist itself plays the revealer,
          Condensing each outline,

And I cannot will that disclosure.
Circling, a man may
          retell the story
Lived by another because neither
          Is in that way free.

Kokoschka had set a fresh portrait
In his host's boxroom
            to dry. The host
Had brought home the Easter lamb, and asked him
      To remain as a guest,

He could stay the weekend. And the painter,
Looking at the dead
            eyes of that lamb,
Proposed suddenly to take the skinned
      Thing to the boxroom

And *do* it. If he began soon, there
Would be time enough
            before Sunday.
This man given often to foresight
      For once in no way

Summoned that penetration (the war
Not far off
            and the wound it offered).
He found what he needed: a tortoise
      And light-shy lizard,

A tame white mouse and an old oil jar.
But still missing
            was some final touch
For the composition; as he poked
      Through the great house, each

Thing took light from his desire and flared
Or failed to crystallize
            the ransacked
Compilation. At last on the maid's
      Windowsill, erect

In the pale phosphor of its full bloom,
One hyacinth.
            Although its odor
Was a dead child's whom he had painted dead,
      That did not matter,

62

It gave scale, focus, the obscure sign,
In the way a story,
              overhead, comes
In upon life at hand and one says,
       'That is how it seems. . . .'

*

Imponderable authority
Of the gift stroke
              or random onset,
That is an overmatch for all save
       Those who live for that,

Who hold themselves, inconceivably,
Open to each thing.
              The lance, the break
From one level down through another
       May or may not strike.

Stuff's first convulsion, through all of space
Equally, leaves
              an old simpleton
Stooping in the street for a rumpled
       Glossy magazine,

But leaves Eustace also, that hunter
Who found a great buck
              waiting for him,
His hounds casual at its forehooves –
       In his blood the hum

Steadied, as he made out between points
Of the bone rack
              a small figure who
Hung crucified, saying, 'Eustace, it is
       I who have hunted you.'

The opening, a path blocked. Strict width
Of that gate
              claiming size, story
I cannot read for being part of,
       That reframes its raw

Elocution: each first time, it tells us.
To him dismounting,
          kneeling, his free
Worship was a thing unstudied in
      Death's repertory.

Hands framing air, and his hounds patient.
No, not held open
              to everything, not
With the fable as it grows solid
      Or with him who meets it.

TO THE ALLEGHENY

Sweeping in from a grasp
Of the horizon, to the cool rim of drink,
To the fleck of autobiographical concern
Buoyed within it, one still may not
Arrive at what is nearest.
Between those scopes, as between
Banks variously eroded, the fixed
Renewing flow:
What cannot be held
Comes closest, keeping us.
And that hunter
Screened in the draw down which deer venture
In files toward the river, huddles
Like the worker in the comb
For less than that full measure
Which comes to him. But do we think of him
As turning away? He stays also
That he might not lose hold
Of himself. Flow smolders through the cut
In braided rhythms, but one only
Unravelled with those crows
Scattering from the fawn's carcass
Stumbled across, a boy's ribs
With the head of a dog. The unripened

Instance disperses stillborn
Into correspondence. And the gatherer
Binds dower unto homestead
With the mouse's tooth. And space,
In the interval, maintains its lattice
Crystalline and griefless, open
To anticipation. Eggs tumbled
In readiness, stones of the bed
Furrowing the film that roofs them, glow through
While the lithe bulk swaying
On impact to go crashing
Down, goes down within
The lodestone of the will.

Air is clear pollen, and the bee's wing
A forest of small hooks and spurs.
The sunned oxbow likewise, that slows
Toward the ungated and retarded ponderings
Of my own nature in its fallowness,
Then slides toward straightaway
Whose allure, phase crowding phase,
Progression pouring, comes
Like Céloron sweeping from the bend outward
Paddles glinting, to plant
Lead plates at creekmouths for Louis Quinze,
A white volley through stillness, the zouave
Smoke of the possessor. Unquilting,
That puff drifts a chill loveliness
Whose last elegance is that it passes.
Yoked in, however, compacted
To an earth's color, it tastes
As speech may of a world's future
And persists as the world's salty continuity:
Layer over layer, stone gliding
Beneath its loose mantle
Resumes through pitch and split.
But taking hold even there,
Regime of the extreme Scythian
With grip lithic in the mound,
Unshatterable in remote permafrost,
Against what any place
Tilled by frail stewardship

Can hallow: fully accoutered,
Attendants on their mounts
Slaughtered in parallel, the great one
Gone with his retinue into death
To seize every known thing there also
With linked victories. So provisioned,
They would extend a present
Colossal and opaque,
The metal glittering
Where a pick dings it.

But whoever looks into the implacable
Growth of that dominion
May stand back, or rest in his understanding:
Gladly will he do without the full secret.
Having found limits
Where none were set, he will
Be able to return.
And opacity will go with him
Unmenacingly.Where creeks marry
Allegheny or Monongahela, and, lower,
Where spills of stone shelve
Into bends of the Ohio, carvers
Have grooved out shapes of the wild turkey,
Turtle, man, fluid otter,
And one panther with tucked forepaw, volts
Staggering from his forehead. His eyes
Declare no memorial. And were the hunt
Somehow to resume, would we call these
Efficacious? Swirling in one spot
On each broad outcrop, tangled and overlayed,
They draw each other unto
Themselves, even as the first carver,
By working there, made that place
The only place. What begins again
Is the uncomprehending stare which, returned,
May carry its own future, that look
Given the familiar. But to begin,
And then to wait, should also be
To resume and to continue.

REDEMPTION

Rain-soaked rocks bulge
Against the freshly inked
Birch stand, that were inert
For Orpheus, that could not bounce
To his twang. And over them
Lichens distill worlds,
Asking no knife for such
Big loaves botched and abandoned.

Invisibly among them climbs the imprisoning
Glass mountain once located by a girl,
Though she had lost the bone
That would have freed her changed brothers, the hapless
Seven ravens.

Bird's leg for a pass-key,
Gift of a star's furnace, it grew heavier
When brought here, and fell from her hand.

Severing her finger she fitted it
Into the spelled lock.
And that was in no far country.

The easy thing had slipped
From her grasp.
                As it had to, foolish girl,
When you came once again into this place
Where your brave makeshift
Was the sole measure left, a price
Written from the beginning.

MIGRATION

Not swallows volleying,
But swifts, two dozen in a kettle
Over the square-sided mill stack
At fading six o'clock –
Forty, fifty in echelons
Funneling to that flue. With morning
Their outthrow seems more rapid
And less visible, when the air
Pulls muscle tighter around the heart.

In short bursts
Scattering, they sally
Into the grainy, dispersed hectic
Of betterment. There is no other way –

Terrible because equal,
The lunge into those rounds
And the momentum for return
Filched from the treadmill.

Even the tendons listen
In the violinist's arm
Slowing toward the peak of its arc.

Make out Bernard again on his cliff edge
With bent wings, master of the hive
Preaching crusade at Vézelay,
Drift of banners over armor,
His voice above them high as a bow-shot
And inaudible. Nonetheless they turned
And as one man massed toward havoc.

At the high edge of the far wall
Of transparency, impenetrably heavy,
Being resumes its plunge,
The gulf sings from that rebound –
Distantly inmost, as the body sprints
Humming from its crouch.

FROM THE 1970s AND 1980s

CUSSEWAGO

If this twilight
falling in the same way
soothes, now as then, first the witch hazel
and through hemlocks
drains the last thrush, its trill
lingering in my own throat;
if these boughs
sifting the low early star
sharpen the same waiting
for her girl's fall of hair, that red
once more out of leaf blur while ferns
measure my thighs;

then it becomes narrower, this interval
between forefinger and loose shale
where the trilobite lays its pressed shell, aeons
as moth or angel
cooling the palm, the boy's hand
reaching within my hand;

it becomes steadier, this pallor
braiding from the wrist, chill
Cussewago –

and I can tell no longer
if the red coiled on the shoulder
of the current, the slow
tawny unravelling, advances
from that other summer
for it bleeds also with birth's ochre,
nor can I know if her neck
turns there to revise
all grain of previous touch,
air molten over silt, minnows veining
its skin with their late risings

or if these in one temperature of flesh
fuse where the gnat grazes
or yet if the ball of her finger
would set milk's promise in my hard

71

still virtual breast, or if the wells
of her temples cool my own:
                              oh woman
ripening elsewhere, is it you thinking in me now
of junipers towards evening,
first trees that seed their field;
is it you lifting their scent, their compact darkness
sucked up from grass shadows
as wax flecks migrating towards the wick?
From behind, forest
wades through earth, and I know that some hand
has passed whole through these dark
first breaks of flame, air alert now
to the branching possession that will come, the leafy
orders, their mingled capitals.

LET US CALL THIS THE HILL OF SOTATSU
   (circa 1970, war in the East)

There is, finally, the cleanliness
of profusion. Basho and spring roads,
profusion, fogged dawns, walks among huts
        smoking after raids;

purslane's invasion of whiter rue
along this first hill where the trail bends –
smoke as a dead lake up to the knees
        and griefless, small sounds.

Big drones already busy, and now
the declaration stands one week clear,
rue anemone takes hold where large trees
        stand off the younger

and some fugitive has plunged from that
drift of whites, his sleep's curve still pressed in –
otium tense in *negotium*,
        the meditation

contained already in the action.
And when *il Signore* Chancellor
orders cavalry to re-billet
    away from farms where

they press olives, he writes of choked barns
but also of *young women who would be*
made uneasy by your soldiers. Yours,
    Machiavelli.

Profusion and spring roads, emergent
delicacy still formulaic,
and beneath it all some great stone head
    overgrown – Olmec

victim relenting, crannying into
flower and asking no dreams of us
(our lust, ire, righteousness never more
    than such in this place),

nor intent on tasting some root blend
of moss, honey of the great mastoids,
and the narcotic pulse of rain, sun,
    rain: the cleanly odds

of blank regard jaguar-helmeted,
light once each day through chinks light has bored,
mineral distillates foreknown in
    taste not yet savored.

A WEAVING AT THE ZOLLBRUCKE IN ZURICH

Bending the current, pillars of flowing rust
where a yellow derrick splashes them down to lay
lanes for the S-Bahn: sons of Brutus and Ion,
paid by the sons of Tell to slosh in white-wine
shallows, muddy the swan-scoured aisles
with crude ferment, tilting plates into place,
drunk with their work.
                       Kibitzing from the rail
with unblinking businessmen and one little girl,
I follow the water. They are rerouting the channel,
regrounding walls around the seventh city,

toying with them for a man's reasons,
noisily for man's boyish reasons,
but even so Helen has not been forgotten
(of course she is forgotten, the drama discounted),
her windows down the lake's curve sink and shine,
where they gave her the best care, and maintained
their own ways of understanding her. She
who was never there! (but of course she was there)
on Nile-bank rather, waiting for Achilles
no longer the sulker, boyish skulker (who they say
never came), in order to hold and to heal him

and he to hold and heal her,
and that is the later story,
extravagance as humble
as homespun and the needle,
and a luminous clock dial
piercing the small hours,
tall white-gowned air.

Desire re-frames the prospect of desire,
and holding to a fable is to take hold with certainty
of consequences that cannot be foreseen.
Gods like shrapnel or pursuing seeds:
winter wheat and the fine
crenelations of towers
thrusting from the kernel
under cold rains, spear-keen

74

veinings of the light at Troy,
winter wheat in a spring mind!

And so embers re-frame the fire, raked and blown
in breast of woman. And the Helen dying here
in Reform's acre, through the watery chime
bent and re-bent, was scandalous
yet unimpeachable,
a strain-straight insatiable
novice of the cowled
air-belled anemone
that rolls the hysteria
of sunned stones high up the beach.

Ditched with snow in the furrows,
pooled with March in the hollows . . .
for the torn pine branch
had long since brindled the snowbank,
resinous lizard soaking up the sheddings
of high fires, the shape of its nature traveling
deeper into the drift, enlarging there.

Pines in wind call for no truces but lash out
low responsories, freaked with sea-floor sheens,
and narcissus massed under rain glows more than yellow,
acceptances by the dead in that bed's motion.
But sons of – and what shall we now bravely call
the fire-bringer? – march down into metallic forest,
keenly rethinking gate, portal, the entire house
in its lived interlock, along with the deep courtyard,
out onto mortal stems; or else, meandering through ruins,

we paw for the fulcrum between a hawk's rise
and the pulse's rush, between wild violet and recollection,
and so feel guiltless and renewed as the full
weight whelms out and bleeds through the broken bowl.
Miss? either way missing the chance to yield,
being brash agonists in some medley,
and that was not the way even of Helen
who, though she invited them, underwent the charge
and the curse and followed past shadowy Karnak.
Pooled with March in the furrows! For, long since, the pine branch
bored into whiteness and peasants dragged fir trunks

out onto the ice and fired them, smoke tunneling up,
until they could net their lines
in baited webs across jagged black water.
Long since! yet one cone infuses four walls
with coded combustions of the daystar, and sooty
columns tower from the heart's floor longer
than hickory tangs perch or the hook-jawed pike.

So the later story, as it did with her, presses claims:
past the last gate and in a far place, yet home,
stranded, carrying the full load yet weightless,
focal yet swept to the margin, still waiting.
For what should we do in Rome? Over again, new hurts,
carnal alchemies in five wounds none dare invent,
in summit-deep swevyn of a lake, window swinging
into one room, stilled wing-brush, a clear page,
totality in the petal, lightning from age to age.
For what should we do in Rome?

They have come, gone, and so return, the edge-on profiles
of pursuers, kindly or killers, even in uplands
etching the tide-swings of their arrivals.
Not with girders in the shallows, but at the station I felt her,
and now as then it is meet to name her who came there,
H.D., American, where I'd not thought to look: in the impulse
to meet each familiar as if a stranger, with the unvoiced question:
Have you gone where I have? and watch the space
between each and the tracks for a white flash,
the badge, that tell-tale of breakage and then mending:

if valor is the near downstroke
of some far, still dangerous sister,
endurance is the warrior
submitting to her, the submitter.
How many have shown that seal
when they have come?
                              But of course
only you told us you had come this far.

from
POEMS AND TRANSLATIONS OF HĬ-LÖ
(1991)

Stopped by a woman
at the gate of a strange town,
I implored, 'Let me pass, I'm pacing
just to keep going back and forth, because
I'm afraid of the dark like anyone else'.
And she said to me,
'But there is the lamp, I left it burning!'

– Vladimír Holan, 'Encounter V'
c. 1943-48

The writer and translator of these poems is a Chinese intern in psycho-somatics who worked in Zurich during the 1980s and used his writing as a way of adapting to the West. He returned to China just before the Eastern European revolutions of 1989. The anomaly of a Swiss situation was eased for him by the historical resemblance it bore to the ministate administered by Guan Zhong, compiler of the *Guanzi* and a model for Confucius, which had to exercise cleverness in order to survive among more powerful neighbours to the north and south. Both the anomaly and the cleverness, in a formerly peasant culture turned affluent beyond even its folktale dreams of wealth, were further eased by his taking stock of Gottfried Keller's prophecy that there would come a day when 'a great deal of money will find its way to our country which we have neither earned nor saved, and then truly the Devil will get his teeth into our necks, and the fabric and dyes in our flag will begin to mean something'.

To the voluminous and inconclusive speculations in the West about the significance of the East, Hï-Lö's efforts do not pertain, unless as a belwether trotting alongside Dr John Wu's contention that any syn-thesis of these opposites would take place first in the West. Hï-Lö's own notes are rather sceptical about any such synthesis, however. Across one folder he scrawled, 'It does not add up' – a folder con-taining oriental lyrics and epigrams by Peter Huchel and Johannes Bobrowski, but also the ethically questionable Heidegger's Lao Tzu,* and quatrains by the political theorist Carl Schmitt, whose ambiguous career during the Third Reich does not leave one thrilling to his testi-mony that 'a holy man from the East led me through the saving gates'.†

Since Hï-Lö's parentage was mixed (a Japanese father from the Manchurian invasion, with an American missionary as the maternal grandfather), it comes as no surprise that he did not wince at the con-tortions into which he bent oriental traditions, or at his adaptations of Western practices, or at his resort to languages of which he had no thorough knowledge in order to make music for which he could supply no living context. Hï-Lö remained the child of his age in this, that he

---

* 'Ethically questionable': Heidegger himself treated the 'questionable' as a pre-eminent category which included the unpleasant extreme of *Erschütterung*. The strenuous conversation among nations which he urged but for which he receives little credit in the current questioning of his record was of course valued by Hï-Lö, who counted Heidegger, in spite of his errors, as its most reflective recent spokesman.
† The line quoted from Carl Schmitt concludes his post-war poem, 'Song of the Sexuagenarian'.

followed the pack into this peculiar territory, and pitched his tent in their desert. From beneath its flaps his shepherd songs dispersed among the circumambient ditties of Berber herdsmen, Siberian shamans, Zuñi initiates, and Aztec priests.

David Gascoyne has observed that poets writing in English still compose homages to their cultural predecessors, as a form of iconography carrying forward the impulses of Eliot and Pound in what Mr Gascoyne construes as a salvage operation. Pound, however, argued that 'shoring' things was one matter and 'shelving' them quite another, the shelf providing no salvage post but rather a stage for new alignments. While Hï-Lö was no theorist, his sense of renovation (witness the fragment from Liu Xie) assumes the force of that distinction, and his homages have as their reverse side a frequent impulse to satire. He saw no allure in Western mystifications of silence, whether from motives of experiment or historical guilt. Perhaps like renovation in his tradition, silence is the equilibrium of a steady hum, just as presentation, in his version of an archaic source, is statement. The renovation he most valued in twentieth-century European poetry flew no flag at the head of an advancing column, for instance as with Jiří Kolář's orientalizing 'Ars Poetica of Master Sun'. It was the attempt at a new Christian metaphysics in the late prose poems of Oscar Milosz, in a statement of findings that assumed the priority of changes other than those of style, and which Hï-Lö knew lay well beyond the translatable reach of his compatriots. 'This elixir will suffer no rebottling,' he scribbled next to verse 81 in *Les Arcanes* (the translation is by Czesław Miłosz): 'Here, in this tool bag, O king of toilers, you will find the cross, the scepter and the crown of the world. But I must tell you once more how the ancient King became blind.'

After the democracy movement died in Tien An Men Square, Hï-Lö returned to practise medicine. Scattered notes indicate his awareness that the manuscript he left behind elegized a European era which had recoiled into memorials and cenotaphs *pour mieux sauter*, whether with mindfulness or amnesia it remains to be seen. The farewell taped to his bicycle combines part of Tristan Tzara's 'Sagacity Dance Number Two', written in Zurich, with a stanza of his own: 'Thickening fog from unexpected fans / impassive high-voltage arc that fastens / corridors spine of roofs and smoke / degree of wind that rips the washing', and then, 'A shaken excellence / T-squared from Homer by Pythagoras / and sprocketed to this circle / whirling below? / "Of foot, of fighting, of mind".'

80

FOUR ANCIENT POEMS

Between the life mask of Jefferson
          nearly stifling him
and the suicide of Forrestal
slides a breath held indefinitely
          and a face evaporating to phantoms.

Ballads dissolve to utterance
in the browns of rivers, *megalopolitans,*
in loam and bran chaff and oxides of alloys
scampering through the slow strobe of sun.

My horse drank from little caves in the Wall.
          For miles, bones littering moonlight.
And who will judge the guilty? Thousands
stipple the field, naked stubble, and my mount
          takes her way, treading the shadow's edge.

Between utterance and river
stands, it seems, a lone speaker
          tided by multitudes
streaming from then through now, streaming.

DITTY FOR MAYOR FU OF FREIBURG IM BREISGAU

Bronze yellowbill by the lake,
fat Mayor Fu,
you told us, venerable drake,
but who told you?

Clamorous on splayed feet
clacking, flapping,
announcing the black bomber fleet
a full day yapping –

old *b'iu b'iu,* your din
left you the lake's premier citizen,

81

of waters mirroring hour after hour
cloud drift and the winking
darkness and your nephews cruising unblinking
across the spire of the tower.

But our head-down diviners trudge now through glitter
turning over in the plage
bent on believing that art, even yours, is no transmitter
of messages,

and makes no claims, reaching
indeterminately, never quite beaching –

while this shimmer, your home, extends from shore to shore
about which connection
they float few inquiries, no detection
being called for.

When you dredge up gobbets from the depths,
occasional diver,
and spit them among piths
of the surface, both arcane as ox liver,

and we resume our query, old bird,
that question rummages
the attics and cellars of its own word
long since they rebuilt over the ravages.

And the present you will be drifting over,
pintailing its quiet,
will ripple its wide discourse of moved and mover
while we go on trying it:

'Who can be in stillness and, out of it
as well as through it, move a thing
onto the way, so that
it will come into its own shining?'

FORGED HEART BLADE

His son dead, Meng Chiao had to put aside
the bow of mulberry and six tumbleweed arrows
shot by an archer in the four aimings at his birth.

And then refusing to eat the carcass abandoned by winter
he proscribed the knife of his own kindness – for on its point
his virtue would have stunk like dead meat.

Between the thing suffered and the sacrifice
stretch the snow ranges with their soundless
dead glare at storm lull over the last crossing.

Yet they are here, keen under crudded mantles
and sheathed in the beds of high lakes, here they
shall rest, swords heaved by priests and chieftains

into the ooze at dawn or sundown, and abide
in the protection of valleys they protected,
arduous to fashion, unblooded, of highest worth.

TALLY STICK

    'A bit of sea' –
Joha waited a lifetime to hear
    this commencement
in a round of renga
so he could say 'Mount Osaka!'

        Ford Madox Ford with fellow officers
        at *bouts rimés*
        in a dugout between bombardments:
        contested realities.

'A little birth' –
the other meaning, the overtone,
        Joha waited in vain
to catch from his partner, so he might
come back with : 'words at the wedding'.

                Pericles after the action
                upright in his utterance,
                upright, in its matching separation
                from the remembered action.

'Even in
an age gone
rotten
song's way goes
right on . . .'

                Even in the days of the magpie
                when the pen flies winking
                and the easy wind fattens many wings –
                even then the voice of the tortoise paves the long path.

        A bit of sea
a little birth
        Mount Osaka!
words at the wedding: indeed,
to hear these speaking each other, to the end.

A SASH FOR WU YÜN

O dropsical Augustus, your tuner the Great Woz
has outlived his time –
yet the Tao I studied begins, through cold hazes
of necessity, to spell its name.

Name! Soundless, not to be manipulated
by the clack-mongers.
So the administration was not impressed, being still delighted
to drape parrots on its singers.

My apologies, Li Po, I got you into that stew –
no way out but the ladle,
with old Cow Leasher, castrato, chief of staffless
ditherings and twaddle

lifting that spoon, pouring us out seriatim,
landing me in this hut.
But the Tao I aimed at begins, beyond even drums
of the rebellion, to show what's what,

and the cock I owe you shrieks its red silence,
and the rue I owe guards it,
and the honor our masters have tread out in obedience
wends towards it.

Who owns the thatch he must reclaim from sparrows
and bring his sky under?
Sidney and T'ao Ch'ien, the bow for your two arrows
bends in thunder gardens.

Prehistoric fellowship of wine, grain, feldspar,
anterior loves,
flares coiling into the void that floats our star,
are what, beneath quiet, moves.

Are what in the red cast of the stone head
and in its shut lids
and in the curves of its mouth, intimate the dead
coming to life in the gods.

Yes, hell is populous with administrators,
and deities get demoted,
and *communio sanctorum* swarms with agitators,
the ranks bloated,

and now they tell me that at White Cloud the Prior An
was incinerated
by his monks. From the Republic to Tien An Men
smoke drifts unabated.

They have plucked leaves from our Book of Great Peace
to fan those fires, but
the realized mind does not smolder, I take notice
in order to forget.

Yet, to serve as fig leaf over unwieldy parts,
can that be good
even for the leaf? A sage application disconcerts
because easily misunderstood.

Let them use us, but then let them build
on the brash diamond
at rough in the heart's flaw, and have its world
gyrate through the clan, and

have the whole spinning thing meet the infinity
of suns under and over,
all in the effort at hand, that quantity
set midmost, our mover.

Let, let . . . and let stoppages of thought
meet the solving rains,
let bookstores carry at least one world map, and let
the city clear the drains.

Sun bathes in the white east and that gorge seethes,
then couches in the long valley,
but its steam has purified how many worthies?
and which one keeps tally?

When the palace wing burned, virtue cried arson
but stood there without water.
A thrown chair folded itself into a picnic fire
where it fell, but not one person
showed any appetite, the daughter of Senator
Beautiful on Twelve Sides lay severed by a smoking rafter
and sold no tickets. Slowly it came to me

that all my affairs were present, and that the moment
was on fire. I sat down
before those embers, no one
paying me any mind.
Mei Bo got sliced and pickled, Ji Zi pretended
to be mad, but Wu Yün discovered
that alchemy was concrete and consequent
and every bit the roasting he had feared.
Each movement in the compound
I saw from a hawk's brain, and heard the full
orchestration of wind, men, and holocaust
note-perfect, while the hells
unravelled their aeons within minutes? Seconds?
When I looked up, the living sheen on her blood
had not yet gone glassy among the braids.

Fire sleeps in wood, only to be wakened
by the slumbers of men –
air wants to darken, in a bituminous
dream of the earth.

Let us pronounce benedictions over the wedding
of oxygen and chair stuffing,
over the transubstantiation of scholia and curtains
let us swing incense.

(May they not hurry the celebration, that filmy
entourage of breezes,
nor the eunuchs usher us, nor the best man be
Zeal of the Land Busy.)

Thereafter to this place, and my second hut,
the original a sacrifice
to lightning from the immortals, who will not let me squat
like some *perfectus*.

Standing in the ashes I saw monks sweating
up a hill road
with a wagon of bricks, joists, and tiles
for their monastery,
like the friars under Fra Leo
hauling stone up to San Francesco, to keep

87

the negotiable bones in place.
On my shelf near the classics, your letters,
and warblers past the threshold
I gauge by the acceleration of Aprils
timed by the plits from my eaves.
The summers becoming embers, I begin
to lose track of my poems on the histories.
The scrolls no longer beguile me,
not even John of Winterthur
totting up legends of the Emperor
who was to rise up from mincemeat
and scourge all baldpate instigating Franciscans
'who will smear cow dung over their tonsures
to hide themselves', while he harries
with a great host to Olivet
to yield up all empire at the dry tree –
now that would make a resounding ditty, but
it does not suit my mandolin.

Beyond the blood mists of force, I see ancient hands
go rung over rung
out of Climachus, the amor of Mozartean masons,
and smiths hammering.

See ancient faces float from the years' dark
in the eyes' brief dark,
shaping themselves as seeds not yet planted,
the quickening of work

cast back by dragons unwinding
as they tear me away –
cloud rope, hold me tight – and I watch my own steading
of earth burn beneath day,

the cyclone stilled, welded, in more than a dream of earth.
The palace has surrendered
to a web spun through one night by revolving fires,
and Merlin has wandered

among them, shedding their spell, speeding
past the defective ear
of Arthur, through gnats over a streambed in August,
shat through power

beyond the last throne, though he condenses to all those matters
he is meant yet to speak –
sun and moon, let me go – and at last mutters
into the glare, the break.

THE DEATH OF YURI ANDROPOV

In snow squalls over this hill, on a bridge, Lenin,
    in rooms above it Solzhenitsyn surrounded:
    'Your socialism may be as bad as you say
    but our socialism will be good!' Here Brecht recited
    then slyly exited, coordinates chalk the wind,
fifteen seconds to bundle them off the tram,
    handicapped herded by a few teachers –
    the prettiest woman, childless, wheeled a boy
    who laughed No! or cried out No! meaning it
    under Ignaz Heim in sandstone, Friend of Folksong.
Realism binds a spell around the matter
    obsessive matter incompleteness of the matter –
    balloons bobbed the drabbly Tennysonian
    locks for his centenary marked months late
    in the streaked mothy air No! they slanted
higgledy-piggledy up the High Promenade
    No! over a signed Cocteau unsold and oranges,
    Yoruba womb in ebony, smoked glass bank,
    and coffin in a tram keening down the cut, white cross
    floating on the sedate blood rectangle,
and hop-skipped as English Rock wailed
    from her radio No! while slowly into
    the barren woman a slim hull of colors
    berthed itself among quiet throngs, their pier
    bannered under scud low and sweeping.

Negation the first gesture, affirmation
   therewith a follower, this may be
   experimentally confirmed, yet it does not follow
   that choice has yet been born, only that
   its powers have at last seized on the clutter.
Crooner cut off, the boy's boots No! kept on
   flailing the beat, then snowy strings, 'Pathétique'
   No! No! No! archepiscopal burble
   'Chairman Andropov passed on today in the Kremlin'
   lenses swelling his pooled eyes, flakes holding to them,
mittened girl whanging the wire fence among
   Yes! cloudy strings resuming, and under glass
   the brightness welled out; down his mottled cheeks as
   all drove white and one may begin to imagine
   her tears at last coming No! Yes! No! Yes! Yes!

RHYME PROSE THREE: CHAPTER OF THE NINE ROCKS

One aspect waves under the water face, it rephrases the tilts of
   her mazy phane, it is bearded with her shifting tints. Its contrary
   rears above such propositions, splashing, judging the flux and
   her agitations, denying with stance and essence that judgment
   begins on its own frizzled pate. The unitary aspect is no longer
   at hand, having been small and uncomely and shagged by an
   urchin into the offshore brightness, vanishing. But from there it
   imposes its terms, there it abides.

Drifting me into being, the heavens of water.
   Pouring from my brow, water's chevelure.
   Sluicing mind, the roaring intellect of water.
   Altering mind, the molecular zero cataclysm of water.
   Presiding over my undoing, the long hands of water.

Blasted to pieces, disjecta, together with my ancestors spread out
   abiding, yet from us the iron rim, the black tread, the bare heel
   of a child draw tone and rhythm. We sing.

90

I am tied neither to approaching totality, ecstatic concept, nor expanding view. My mineral horizon, such is totality. Here, now, the golden age.

In hot necessity my mother conceived me, in metamorphosis she brought me forth. Hard in thy hand I am, in Him am nothing.

To be poured out is not my prayer, for I have been, but to occupy space as the correspondence that can inhere only there, and all that it can be there. *There* even your great Kant swerved on himself, mind not on but in the unity of object, for there is a coercion involved. There is here.

The larch splitting my side sentinels the stream cooling my fury.

My white mantle shrouds a removal from history which lets me assess it. And this is what you marvel at: not the icy carapace, but the crystalline discipleship.

The one finding his way to me will uncover in my cave the skull of his first similar, and the trickle of saving blood rusting its sutures, and the onset of storm, through eclipse and down-breaking flashings, in the twelfth hour ever approaching. But he will find too that the crown of my hill presages alterations with the breath of browsing deer I seem to remember from before time, auguring a last great change. He will find the exiled path of the stone.

'VEGA OVER THE RIM OF THE VAL VERZASCA'

Vega over the rim of the Val Verzasca
and a mountain heaped from night with house light in it
      make a vast cave over man.

I have mislaid Rome, and the long house of Greece
has slipped my grasp, I am motionless.
In the eye's cavern, in the ear's dripping chamber . . .
      hunters brushed at wet space
      arching them overhead:
      endless, those recessions.

And on a mountain, where the last evening
      trades fuzzy dusk for totality
and stone ledges are everywhere our door,
      and we are set free in the house
to run, loll, knock over the ochre pots
      where bloods of gift achingly flower –

      yet as it was with the commanding
         Florentine, so even now:
         the color of all this
         has passed when I feel it come home,
         and even it, while it speaks,
         has not yet witnessed the end.

CLAM SHELL WITH HUNTING SCENE

Resolving autumn, and by Rhine flood
vine-hung bunkers kneel among shore ripples.

      Lather and branch lash, white tail tuft

Where the hunter, still and then leaping, is renewed bloodrush
paced by the ever-valving and shuttering deep iris.

      Quarried companionship, pursued gift

Justice with headman's axe slides among shades of
justice with sashed gaze and all-bearing shoulders.

String longing for the shaft

Ravenous paws of the maples scooping, cuffing at
the chance wing, arrows from the water, quarry from the heart.

No rehearsals, the act has begun, is swift

Spot weld by the missile caught side-on running, there is
no leakage of the message fused by flesh into mind,

A value fugitive and feeding, the dripping pike gaffed

spending itself in the breech nova, the shell empties
so that emptiness may take hold in matter's long wall.

Cliff its seam, vein its rift

Variations in the constancy of union
recalibrated where ten arcs crossed and the bronze rested,

The gone heft gaining weightlessness

but thrust beyond motion at one flicker by the meaning
no beast anticipates and no man does not.

weightlessness at the top of its loft

Bronze edge, lead ball, steel borer and splayer, heart's harrier,
shall you weave coats from the storm to cover a stranger made
welcome?

Hammer, stone, eye and eye, warp, weft

But the last miniscules I cannot make out, the great hand hurried
them,
O Father I am small, and through long watching may grow, but
not larger.

Fifteen stars fence polar fire, the moated wall mirrored them,
songs from that palace have not yet found the tomb,
but now our body is a ferment, many where one was,
its form stretches beyond sight and will know no ease,

the sinuous line of the violin pushing alone
into the next spaces, darknesses up and down,
married not implausibly to the mourning, hammering
clubfoot of the great drum.

Shouting matches between Buddhist and Jesuit,
mind's fountaining fire against mind mirroring it,
shatter. Where that glass was, night's acreage
spreads to meet returning light and labor's dull rage.

Into spring fields, to turn up flint bits of first man!
But one must wait for rain to baptize the worked stone,
yes, wait for the plough, then for downpour, then go
head hung forward through fragrant furrows.

What were their hopes? To build a house for the ages.
The four provinces of time a stone seat for judges.
Their ship of feasts was keeled longer than a fortress,
splinters from its ribs shine up through this loess.

Where lines between watchfires crossed they laid out our themes,
as a bird through night's dome again and again aims
through origin to destination. What has pushed
their themes upon ours? Flint flakes, the soul is not finished.

SORTING STRAWS

A crystal into the salt swirl . . . and it begins
where there had been nothing
between light and the eye, ladders springing
over whirlpools to hang

anchored among handclasps, those glistening
scaffoldings that turn
into structure, acrobats cartwheeling entire from
the homunculi of pattern.

But realignments have invaded death, catalyzed
by crime past the scale
of speech that held it, beakers shattered and the wave
carrying off the wall.

So that speech itself has asked itself to fall quiet.
And with it duty,
knowingness flapping like a loose tarp, each pirate
taking booty –

but do these have us wait for the doe, her grassy jaw
pausing as the eyes lift,
who waited for no corps de ballet, her step
the unseizable gift?

Duty quiet still knows ashes sifted with generational
sands of the river
and the pine branch it reset for a hammock to attune
some last cover,

duty looking beyond quiet looks to unlatch
a gate opening on
that high bridge conjured over the tumult by each
tenaciously held tone.

Lan or thoroughwort is no orchid, but 'orchid'
is what we get:
rough word! Pull up hawthorn roots and you grasp thornbush,
leukakantha thrust wet

into contests of candor, whiteness outdoing white
in the brutal swings
of renovation, or in the prickly savagery of ideas sniffing out
the staleness even of things.

Yet shades of that noncolor: what shadows them
burns farther than away,
as the spring's root and the wind's mouth stem open from
le dieu caché.

If they orchestrate 'monkey's tube trouser tatters
codpiece drying stain'
while lenses veer towards the dead moons of Neptune, craters
dilating the screen,

there still oozes from all this some physical
or metaphysical sepsis
which they only half-credit, a putrefaction nine times
their own encapsis

of the required art, for more than their knives now
addresses the corpse
plump or bony, smooth or hairy, scalpeling whatever
in the soul usurps.

The soul too can be false, charmer incapable
of sweating long enough
to distill pure potions, or of putting them
surely to the proof.

Novel histories of the passions flutter decayed pages
and so, that day no further,
that year no deeper and that lifetime no freer of the rage
dragging the groove or taut tether.

In wheelchair limbs banked coals break to embers,
but shall we then know
the anatomy of loves bent past our reach? O Herd Boy,
there are galaxies to go.

On his knees before a deer, a hermit has proposed
creature to creature
neither devotion nor daftness, but attention, and she attends
though he will never teach her.

Were they to follow my hand through its brush tip's
elixir spreading
into hair, raven's cry, parting at morning, would they
still dispute while reading?

The within of the immeasurable firms, and I have
touched you at last,
and this warmth signals from lastingness, even as you give
form to what has been missed.

'AND WHAT DO THEY DO . . .'

And what do they do when they are lost in themselves?
Sit on benches, stand in grass and watch sails.
Stare forward, elbows on knees, at hells revolving.
Is this in a garden, or out in the blown waste?
From a hill the resting soldier saw plumes of earth.
The hermit asked, 'What are they doing down there?'

Day has advanced. And to one turning back
in inquest of the day, as did Holbein
Skull son of Skull, to claim his father's brushes
and scaffolding and the gold paid in fee,
they will say, 'The cloister has burned down.
Go, if you wish, dig gold from the ashes.'

Day leans forward. The babe of time in his brain
pings with a small hammer against the wall
tick-tick. Soon peasants will come heaving torches.
Yet how the father's hand rewets and smoothes
powders of berry and bark on the groined curves.
And cowled singers file in to take their stations.

97

HAZELNUT

Instead of perfectly evading us
the power swole and burst like a hazelnut
set in the fire, all the while holding shape
in his mind, as he wrote to his father Leopold.
So it can be. And so then came the unfolding
through sketches during the hot carriage rides
towards after-dinner card tables, the Prinzessin's,
to improvise among the unhearing. But once
the Landgrave set down his ivory toothpick,
staring at nothing, taken by the modulations,
the fragrant stink from his ceramic pipe
in trilling swirls, the musketry at Salzburg
and Amalia's hair long ago. Those also
smolder, also delay within the broadcast
efflorescence not wholly held in score
or serially decaying minds of those seated
in curved rows to listen, there or here
or in future, no more than in one stab
of the sky zigging down between cool firs
rimming the slopes he scanned from the swung carriage,
he has been telling me one thing all this while,
or in reedy whine of shrapnel off stone
at the bend of that road when another brain flared out
to sink like his unregistered in the field,
hearing – it enters between the shoulder blades – the river
of cloudy light, wet granite, and starmoss dirt.

FANTASIA FOR DU BELLAY

Fevered a second time, going farther under,
I saw the rooflines of Rome drifting above me
on the early walk to work, no
others in the streets, a holiday.
Foreigners with foreign boss miss the privilege.

And then saw priests and prostitutes and felines,
those permanent residents, trailing home through
still empty prospects, tirelessly
themselves, and timeless in the light that wrapped them,
Du Bellay's century with Pasolini's.

But cursed and honored first by the young Frenchman,
one hundred lines for a cat! So there it was, then,
from one in the cousin cardinal's
employ, that hairy tailpiece for proportion.
Yet the fire hadn't finished with me, I waited,

carried at first, then winding through Italy,
threading frozen passes, thus now the Frenchman,
and lodged at a mill, the darkness
torrential, timed by the thudding of a great wheel,
France not far, but chills eating through gunny sacks:

to that poured rhythm, shapes of France's future
swam before him, and of the church's also,
though in that hour staying
only to sear the satirist and forsake him;
and then a woman's voice, foretelling his deafness.

OSIP MANDELSHTAM IN THE GRISONS

   Wings sickling meadow frost – were
harvests along the way to his 'hills of mankind'
this urgent? So little time to prepare
     that long meal for the mind

   which, though they stole it, he could rebuild –
plow-spill, honey, or blood's gold under the skin,
the soul's abysses craving their arches, filled
     by cross-ribs groining in.

Sceptics claim that he never went,
anymore than he ever mastered German.
Italy! Clearing through hazes, ocherous tent
        for the spirit's Europe of Russian.

        There are the eyes of time
            the time never has,
        and there are colors brought home
            from wandering in the gaze,

    but it wouldn't be long before high ice
was Russian murder, and binoculars
in one's helpless hands, powers of the Zeiss,
        reached out for other powers.

    In looking towards the high sluices
of a dry stream, reconnoitering advance
alone up its bends, there was the sibilance
        of waters to win, real voices.

    Laughter cascading from below,
pressure for days in the chest easing in speech,
the builder's mute heave and balancing, all go
        through us and out of reach.

    Through, but that passing makes the span,
the architecture, the materials,
and the thing bearing their crushing weight is man,
        a slight thing in their scales.

        There were the eyes of time
            the time put out,
        there were colors of time
            the time did without,

    and it wouldn't be long before mountains
of a steel man pyramided the skies –
but like Goethe refusing any lens,
        Joseph used human eyes.

100

The art of peoples? If that's your horse troop
of insomniacs churning the earth to war
or poetry, there's still the swallow's loop
    and the quarry it twitters for.

WIND UNDER SASH, VAL FERRET

Night-stuttering glass, a brisk hexameter
    as if the shade of Rudolf Borchardt passed
self-refugeed again, not singular in that honor
        yet alone out there,

carrying on his back the evening purples of the Mantuan
    and the ladder cliffs of Alighieri
back into Italy, back into the dishevelled, shaken
        atelier of the villa,

not as gods in his rucksack, nor the images of gods,
    not as *lares* but as the icons of men
carrying them, themselves carriers – for the clouds
        raked by the peaks

admitted only the most portable pieties
    and promised cyclone over anti-cyclone
of our new rain, saint clown seer duke *bona fides*
        of the types of the peoples,

amazon skull-smasher demoniacal berserker
    social democratic emperor
sculptor manipulator-of-masses-in-bulk worker
        plunging to the far plain,

paladin pastor pathfinder toppled out of the human
    to the primaries of a pre-world –
but trekking down, there was a German and a man,
        his paces still spacing them.

    As if the shade of Borchardt rattled the sash:

even before the fist of the subjugator could squeeze him
        onto the roads, he numbered all the hands
to be hacked off, and went, not giving in to his doubt
        that the rope he would rappel onto

might have been jerry-rigged over that jumble down there . . .
        and in that moment let me suspend him
as the fist of the folk did, not alone though singular,
        rhizome dangling in the unrooted.

RHYME PROSE FOUR

The infant is buoyed by black smoke. And whose bairn is this?
    Lashed in green swaddling across a plain board,
    attended by sweatbright cradlers of bronze blade, by puffers on
        tusks of the ram or mammoth trumpeting through pine web.
    For nurses he has hyenas licking themselves, prowling,
                                        cosseting fleas,
    he bawls for no breasthold nor do his eyes blur. And he looks
                                        out at us.

And who are his protectors?
    Kindlers of fires here in the glade and there in a village,
    their skins ruddy, ashen, oily, varieties of one species,
    three who sought no star and waged no journey, no gift-
                                        bringers these,
    though they celebrate, crouch-prance, cousin him around among
            slouch and whinny of sly pelt, the far wood no refuge.
    They are nature moving towards blind completion,
    he is completion's pip thrusting back into nature,
    and the dominion twisting one of their mouths senses the curb
    of that law, grazes it, hovers. Towards us the small one stares.

And his hopes, his chances?
    Their kin he is, yet is not: unnumbered in the childermass,
                                        wilder.
    Crystalline forms of these his companions glitter in furnaces,
            shine in caves of punishment and lack. Therefore

he floats mast-lashed to a papoose rack, the smoked abiding
                                                        seed.
The chemical pleasures farmed in this our garden corrode
visibility but not vision: wayfarer of the miniscule, already you
                                have budded from Krakatoa
and I am learning to ferry you through the lid's wink,
to beach you on the slopes of your assaulted growth
where a troop of demons rings you in the equilibrium
demanded for your balance, your intact pirouette.
They will kneel to you, blowing bubbles windowed with
                                      towers, treasuries,
piping you, from their illimitable embouchure, cap and bell
                                        and hunting horn
and roistering lordship, surpluses of safety all
evaporating. Pook! while the scene that already had appeared
                                                        stays:
oxide of expectation tints none of its recessional blues, it is not
sulfate of fulfillment exploding among those walls, nor do the
                                        cindery pillars
climbing out of them, layering dusk, sift chaste flaws through
                                        future ambers.
But from hiddenness something has come, has anyway arrived,
                                                is what
looks out at us, and so from a phosphorous I glimpse edge-on
                                        and not always
a child peers out along the slow fuse of continuance.
I, Ernst Georg Rüegg, have seen this in the thirty-fifth year of my
    age et in pars fecit anno domini nineteen hundred eighteen.

They say that once each cycle
        all of the gates open,
the under-gates, country wide – – who could swing them? –
and high crystal fixities, pivoting:

and even the wall wanderers,
        those unburied ones, interrogated
but released into non-meaning,
        even they swim through and speed on –

and all the replays, didactic
        insistencies in slow motion,
lips intoning, and eyes
        rewinding the unrepealable,
cease when deer bend at the pool's edge
        and look across to the man reading
not from a book but his own fiber,
        from its grain wherever it has swung
on the small hinges of action –
beginning to read, that is,
        long after the pratfall
he managed in blood and inefficacy
by listening for the grindings of hell in the distance
then trying to haul back his mother's damned soul –
long after he got up
        by pressing against the dust
and then readjusting his robes
        before making a cloud exit:
all that comes before his looking into the living text.

•

When the Wall came down in Berlin
        the orchestras performed Beethoven,
letting the wind bands in the villages
        be heard, and dances, in the villages.
There is the unity from below, unstoppable.
But of the misted union
        between dead and living,
unsearchable, we may
        still ask: does it sharpen

at the behest of the living or the dead?
And we must ask: what of
                    prolonged suffering
cancelled at a stroke by the gates opening?
Among the dead, they say,
        it lifts in purgation.
But among the living?

                        •

The man who read under the deer's gaze had taken the tonsure,
formerly the boy known as Turnip, and he was a good boy
but he also wanted to go on a journey, so he went,
yet his mother only pretended to feed the poor, and so
came to wander the hells wailing for sustenance
gliding like reflections in stuffed shopwindows, famished ghosts.
Turnip was a good boy, but he rolled around on the ground.
'Get up! Set out bowls heaped with rice, pine nuts, roast fish'.
Thereafter the king stipulated that his ministers
bring from the treasury platters of agate
brimming with red petals, and amber with greenwood.

Therefore at moonrise
        the older hills climb out of clarity,
therefore the fields are taken in
        from the spent ground and folded,
at dawn the mists lift from them
        over a battalion of shadows
                sliding brighter.

                    •

The ford of souls ever
        was a tricky passage,
even here the king's nephew chooses white water
        when he stabs his king.
                        Even under
improved conditions there is something
        disconcerting about this transit.
When the revolutionary fallen were to be reinterred
        at the column, Place de la Bastille,

'Entrez, sublimes victimes!
gloire et triomphe . . .'
Berlioz framed the hearse bearing fifty coffins
with a wind band of two hundred
and wings of massed voices and strings, 'Something
they can HEAR',

but twenty-four horses pulled raggedly
and the hearse swayed and tipped,
the procession stalled and they all cheered
Louis Phillipe on his balcony,
the clarinets paled unless trees
happened to reflect them,
and the strings lagged,
and at the climax
the Legion of the Guard stood dropping in the heat
and the sergeant major in his mercy had them step off
to fifty unmuffled drums,
blotting out
the choral apotheosis.

●

Richard Strauss on the podium
under a dome's oculus,
night pantheon of the swooning ear
and organ pipes in phalanxes
behind the percussion –

therefore the Reich's filmmaker, panhandler
of the cavernous, the swimming,
panned to a blond gaze and low bodice
as her eyes valved shut
over her own image of those pipes;
overlayed it with her beddable face *in exstasis*,
each bourdon, each stem of vox humana
towering in perspective,
lacking only the fins to home them in on their hits.

And her eyelids darkened with blood shadow,
                 young matron of death,
         while the old sorcerer led them
under the night eye of the dome into one rhythm,
         pantechnicon smoother of the long beat
                 in the ongoing
         convergence of the arts,
     snowy-haired Strauss on the podium.

                        •

Carnevale trombones blatting down their arcade:
at the focus of the Piazza San Marco
         maskers heaped trash and torched it,
exceeding the scale permitted by regulations
and so drawing gendarmes to the perimeter,
         yet there are also regulations
traditional with the Most Serene Republic
setting the time elapsed before its gendarmes
                 may move against bonfires,
said fires having their privilege at this season,
         but the enforcers stormed the piazza
before their stopwatches stipulated it, and so
                 halfway out they hesitated.

At which time the maskers, attired also
         as gendarmes, bolted from their pyre
but froze in mimicry,
                 the two fraternities
standing at impasse
                 while the blaze towered.
         Rippled column of air,
arcade and roofline swimming as the heaped visibles
         twisted towards the invisible
from the crackling of an era swiftly rumpled –
         from the focus of stalled choruses
                 crouching mirrored
around climbing flame through flame climbing.

                        •

And the fires in this sacrosanct foolery
        thrust aside altar candles
or yardarms and radar nibs
        sparking the storm's tooth, corposant,
or the burning inside Daigu, Great Fool
        when the mother whose boy he had buried
asked, 'Where has he gone?' and he stood speechless
        then left for the tracklessness of the high places,
or even the fire set by a warlord around monks,
one of them blurting, 'Where is the eternal?'
        with his master answering, 'Right here,'
and the other pressing him, 'But what IS it here?'
        and as the flames rose, 'If you have done your job,
coolness will climb to you even out of this fire.'

                        •

When jubilation crackles from those whose fathers
buried their crimes under a parking lot, this
        is a tone in the teeth of the wind.

Early today in the villages
        bandsmen stamped in the squares,
breath white as they moved out
under a baton towards the base line of hills
        where Sirius, or Sothis, or the dog
notches over, timing the gait,

the first star that we found with its dead twin,
        presiding jointly over flood and sirocco,
Sirius and its dark partner in dance
not themselves listening, yet gauging
        whatever in us may be listening
                for the living.

108

SPRING HOUSECLEANING

Flares from Beirut, North India,
and the West Bank
through one more May
of pink candles and white
down the chestnut avenues.

Pebble blossoms, paved
before the shut calyx
of the madhouse door,
red geranium
petals blown over them.

Kneeling at matins on one
good leg, one peg leg, a man
tamps cobbles into sand,
and it is not the stones ringing,
it is his hammer ringing.

ANTI-DITHYRAMBICS

He only wanted to sleep, that wakeful
professor among the ridgey pastures,
        he only wanted to lie down
    and snore like the hired hand sprawled
wholly this side of a searing command.

Through the car's headlights, a grey crone
        pushing a milk can on wheels:
    what Zarathustra caught in his high beams
was at first merely an old man of the woods
but at last the greybeard voltage that sizzled him.

    Under the sweep of headlights
        the flank of a red thresher
still chewing across the dark field:
behind, virtues churning sightlessly,
ahead, the massed clans of black grasses.

The inconceivable marriage was here consummated:
  the lonely one with his thunder eggs
    and a milky wraith off the peaks.
But their children are not our lame wolves in lamb's fur,
their terrible bairns do not clamber back into old forms.

A GROSS OF POEMS LINKED IN THE MIXED MANNER

1 Cubical interferences in clouds of summer,
     steel rod angled off the pole
   clasping the flap of red announcement.

2 Foam over the rim
   after a fast pour,
   soulful advice that smacks
   of promissory notes.

3 *Ein Blick ins Chaos*
   and that would be the sound of it, too – looking towards
     the flash over roofs, years,
   past candle and Nicholas soaring
   over sailors in their swamped boat.

4 Brecht, who never stayed anywhere
     very long, stayed
   in Herrliberg, with radio and ashtray
   and a Chinese painting on the wall
     that could be rolled up.

5 July haying under way
   on slopes of a valley
   opened only in this century,
   men pitchforking heaps
   and riding them downhill

6 while a red medical helicopter
   thrumbles far below
   carrying off a man
   who failed to jump
   fast enough from his tractor.

7 No plaque, 'Goethe slept here',
   for the street musician
   with orthopedic frames
   and garden swing rusting
   on his filthy back.

8   Between inscribing
   Pontius Pilate our abyss
       and Christ the human future,
   Lavater looked up to see his young fan Goethe
   skinny-dipping in the Limmat, chased by police.

9 With top hat, velvet frock coat,
       and gilded stick
   a personage forges through morning fog on the Minster Bridge
   but even he comes after Luther, and so cannot
       secure a General Dispensation.

10 If there be Unnatural Thinking,
   it follows: there must also be Natural Thinking.
   Infamy of the court painter, Piero di Cosimo:
   he let the grass grow in his front yard.

11 In every chartered street I smell
   Arabia Deserta's oil,
   high tree withers, avalanche gathers, and down toil
   ten thousand villagers
   into every chartered street.

12   The one-man band,
   seeing the cop draw his sword,
       exercized
   that capacity known as
   the Science of Absence.

13   Wagnerian businessman, puffy
          black velvet beret,
      gets a measuring sidelong glance
      from the Kabbalistic gardener in
          compact blue tam.

14   Thus Celan rebukes Brecht
          for chromaticism,
      obvious banging of the intervals,
      reproves him with spare leafage held up
          on the pruned limb.

15   While it all goes, still
      there is sequence: the School of Storytellers
          was the first to disappear.

16   'Tell me, Jung-chi,'
      asked Dame Macleod in her West Sea castle,
          'Is God naturally good?'
      'No madam no more than a wolf.'
      She in a low voice: 'This is worse than Swift.'

17   'L'homme qui médite est un animal dépravé.'
      Vera Figner studied medicine in Zurich,
      returned to Russia and agitated,
      was run out of her practice, and steeled herself
      to serve as one of the Judiths

18   who offered up the Czar Alexander. Back
      from the casino, Dostoyevsky had stared
      into his mirror and shuddered.
      On Kant's wall, Rousseau,
      'the Newton of morals'.

19   Through a midnight street
      under a sun umbrella, a cyclist
      straight down the center,
      between bolted villas
      trailing his signboard: VOTE

20 Herr Hadlob, Minnesinger and
          migrating goose,
      were you distressed when Herr Bismarck made off
      with your hand-painted book? The bullfinch pecks at your sill
          and I doff my hat to you.

21 Gunning it in neutral,
      the trucker hauling away
      tons of newsprint –
      everyone must have 'views' –
      fumes while the blind man crosses.

22 We live
      with our own hells
      about as long
      as the fly lights
      on a burning light bulb.

23 A mother pointing to the ant
      knows her boy may
      or may not crush it, and waits.
      Gnomon, finger in sun,
      in the firestorm love's index.

24 Here Hegel eased his Geist.
      Here Joyce and Musil, neighbors, never met.
      Here Mann climbed Pisgah.
      Here Canetti learned to love cities.
      Hier Heidi war geboren.

25 We are not here to judge.
      And so there is the American author
      lurching through alcoholic slush onto tram tracks
      CLANGCLANG whom I yanked back into literature.
      'F--k 'em!' fist flailing, "Nam again!'

26 From one year to the next Charles Péguy
      in the stall for thrown-off books
      in the Minster's ballistic shadow –
      'The church can never reopen the workplace without paying
          the price of economic revolution for eternal salvation' –
      for which the scholar laid out 720 *petits sous*.

113

27   Here Heidegger dragged out his seminar.
Here Wagner conducted his affairs.
Here Steffi Geyer brought the strings that untuned Bartók.
Here Max Ernst scuttled seriousness.
Hier Ulysses war geboren.

28   'The Gold Card? But anyone
can get a Gold Card.
Mine, mine is Platinum.
The Platinum Card
is a matter of divine election.'

29   Scratched out
on the billboard, the eyes
   of the fashion model.

30   Bourgeois marriage's last hymn
was inscribed by Beethoven.
Must one lack a thing to praise it?
At the eaves, five knobbly-necked sparrows,
future Leonoras, challenge the violins.

31   From the high oriel window
   of an alley
at sacrosanct midnight,
the fluid madness of a ballade
   by Chopin.

32   Russians on forced marches
to outflank Buonaparte,
and the Polish draftees straggled,
lugging their twelve-foot Madonna:
'Let's just stay here at Rapperswil.'

33   In the lake castle, glass cases
with blurry linoleum-block
money from Solidarnòsc
and plaster casts of Fredéric
Chopin's hands.

34   'Nothing means more to me
     than the Italian resistance!'
     but Silone stared in disbelief
     at his future wife:
     an Irish spy for OVRA?

35   Roar of the fighter
     'star web on the sword-sheathing lake'
          trailing the sight of it
     while a noose flies over the piling
     and paddle wheels flailingly reverse.

36   Girl in braids and a pastor,
     a Persian and his mother,
     officers on the deck
     as the wing formation goes over
     'Look up and are not fed'.

37   To the wide bow wave
     a gull flies closer, a turtle
          bequeathes bubbles.

38   Sturdy, hearty appearance,
     children and old ones gazing
     into the hotly glistening
     pit of red pistons, brass valves, as
     the big ship takes them away.

39   Ugo Foscolo fled Buonaparte
     and came to live with the chickens
     in a vicar's backyard
     in Protestant Hottingen.
     'Send me my Dante.'

40   Foscolo fled Zurich for London
     where he bought a garden cottage
     but declined to teach Italian
     to the ladies. 'Send money,
     in this country it is a sin to be poor.'

41   If a man's illegitimate daughter
becomes his housekeeper, then
Mnemosyne looks kindly on him.
Foscolo's commentary on Dante
in the misprinted English version

42   netted him four pounds a week,
but then there were the creditors,
and the roof leaked on the *Inferno*.
Pastoral Zurich! Six lines of Homer a day,
boiled meat, and stinking soup.

43   Polytonal Furtwängler
at Berlin's end in Switzerland
fine-tuning a radio:
'They say X is dead, and Y,
but where is the one I'm waiting for!'

44   Inside the bookshop window
the local product lay wrapped
in prefaces by Sontag.
The scholar stared: 'I have not
fled far enough.'

45   Haughty rider on the road
from Baden to Sankt Gallen
is a papal secretary
with a fine finger for scrolls
rotting in monks' privies,

46   thus Poggio toting a Quintillian
in his saddle bags,
leaf shadow in his sleep,
and on his tongue phrases

47   about muslin shifts on the women
wading into the baths.
And when they burned
John of Prague in Konstanz
he raged and wept.

48 Alpine self-interview
on a terminal moraine
among Fallen Erratics
in voce profondo?
Goes without saying.

49 Merry music of street work:
flame-hissing mouth, then spewed stone
and tar, then pounding steel –
O animula, parvula,
how to make your way.

50   The rippled pianola of Liszt
and stage melodramatics filled the first flics.
     Old wine! And still
when the waiter uncorks a classic bit of cellarage
the customer narrows his eyes with pleasure.

50A And this is not my pleasure.
    'I watered my horse in cavities of the Wall.'
    Fire's cool void in the fingers, wind's flame in the gaze.
    A mess of still pools, slavery drawing down, ditch and shov-
    el.

51   Back in my province
a flag hung out of the window
     signified a sermon,
a moral fluttering in the drafts of paradox.
This city too preaches and preaches.

52 The apache has his poetry
in Baudelaire's Paris, Apollinaire's New York,
while the fleeing jongleur of Zurich
refurbishes the gait of the ragpicker.

53 Mist rubs a hole in the mountain, loopholes
     siphon value to the vaults,
Baudelaire boasts about shoes plugged with paper,
and the console-wired graphomaniac adds zeroes
     to the sliding sum.

54   Let us praise Archilochus,
     Old Testament of the Id.
     'If you can't f--k it, and
     you can't sell it, and
     it ain't Greek, kill it.'

55   Let us compose our variations
     upon Goethe's satisfied epigrams.
     'In the coolness after phantom
     lovemaking, out of the power that blooded
     your thing, you make some other thing . . .'

55A Ditch and shovel, still pools down the tunnel,
     fire-voided fingers, flame-rippled gaze,
     and this is not my pleasure.
     'I watered my horse in cavities of the Wall.'

56   In the tool shed
     the shovel wobbles, indoors
         the lampshade:
     young metals of the mountain are speaking
     to the coathangers of the heart.

57   'Here Wrng Wei hangs up his wooden hay rake,
     and his round-sided ladder,
     and the brace for his spine,
     and incense in perpetuity
     to Sung-lin, Nurse of Peasants.'

58   The Bank Habib
     has abolished fixed interest.
     Brochures from the Bank Habib
     are piled up in Zurich
     every Sunday and burnt.

59   Teacher swings
     a laughing malformed child
     around the street corner,
     redbird sinks through branches
     to the clamorous nest.

60   Stone arch over the torrent,
     Romanesque chapel,
     quarry in the hills
     over the stone museum, and the wheezing
     attendant with stone lung.

60A   Fire's cool gaze fingering the void, inflaming
       the tunnel mouth, a fusilade over pooled ditches
       so that 'I watered my horse in cavities of the Wall'
       and this is not my pleasure.

61   Orange raincoat,
     blue hat, black river of hair,
     white gloves knifing up,
     and a queen's ankles
     separate fast traffic.

62   A bent alpine farmer
     piles stones from his meadow into cairns
       along the hairline paths.

63   'You are not inclinded
     to survey the visibilities
     of Zurich and its adjacencies?
     Mais, Monsieur Lenin,
     have you not come here on an annuity?'

64   The cement basement
     of the Muse's house: puffing steam pipe on a wall,
       irked visitors searching for 'works'.

65   Fuming steam pipe
     on a relentless wall, patrons of the Muse
       lodging protests.

66   The nuclear engineer sojourned
     seven months in an ashram.
     From his ring grinned and waved the guru.
     'If you are lucky he will
     materialize one for you.'

67   Is it any worse, this
    stink of state rockets on a holiday,
          any hollower than
    the snap and ripple of massed banners?
    What I have mislaid is

68   the wet light under mushrooms, the sound
    of streams far under a plank bridge,
          the transparency
    of the wing that has just passed and
          flashed before the beginning.

69   A sikh clasped his white-muslined companion
    in the rushes, his temple
    burning behind him,
    while a green light
    blinked on and off at the landing.

70   'What We Are Fighting For':
    a pope gesturing benediction
    while dropping his penny
    in the Red Cross cannister,
    followed by a Swiss general.

71   The Wheel of Fortune
    is a roulette disc.
    Voltaire is a bloodied bust
    inscribed *Candide*. And a canny
    Ghandi waits in the wings.

72   Candidly Kokoschka painted it
    in London in 'forty-three.
    By 'eighty-three the flood had beached it
    at the Kunsthaus. Thus the Sheik's doll
    glances at it in passing.

72A Boats at their June moorings slapping companionably,
    muteswans dipping their necks singly or in pairs,
    belling their wings out to dry while peonies and the Tree Rose
    vie for evening honors, magenta against blood purple,
    early summer in the ripples, antiquity quickening in the
    moon,
    swans resuming their patrols, singly or in pairs, the Tree

73   Met a frog
         at the bank:
      gulped, blinked, and squatted down.

74   Saw a frog
         among the swans:
      looked the other way.

75   *Brek yo nek,*
      advised a frog in the forest.
         I slowed my pace.

76   In white coats
      bent over black holes, over proteins
      and the brain's Mariana Trench,
         ears pressed
      against matter and the scrolls of the Vedas –

77   while sun imprints
      the lintel of a hut near the high pass,
         route of armies
      and strangers: *God save us*
      from Storm, from Avalanche, and from Terror.

78   Frog chirp is, but no Four Legs
      dawn reflects in the pond
      where no sun burns, no water spreads,
      and the path curves up from shoreline
         with no walker.

79   Raw and ancient April,
      the baby warbler repeats
      his instilled melody.
      'Returning with the years',
      everything at stake.

80   Bird tune beating the leaves,
      wind beating at the pane,
      moon beating on the yard.
      Dr Johnson clung to each, trying
      not to lose his mind.

81   Imlac gestured broadly
from the roof of the Burghölzli.
'For five years I have restrained
the rage of the dog star, and mitigated
the fervours of the crab.'

82   In forty years
the tempo of Beethoven has slowed
      by one third
while semiconductors, encoding a fat *Logic* and a Psalm,
draw from them one tone untwisting among overtones.

83   Thus the language of the world
hums alongside the speech of the sage,
a whipped top that rescues
gravity into dance,
no loves, no quarrels, no deals.

84   Thus in poised lucubration
behind shut eyes, thinking whirls
to the annulment of massy thoughts,
as all anew weightlessly attend
to the History of the Prince of Abissinia.

85   Shadowfoot, king
among the one-leggèd,
sallies forth like a sprinter,
and on a July scorcher
kicks up his sunshade.

86   Hail, speedy Shadefeet!
Isidore's praises
and Aristophanes'
merit rehabilitation.
And lend us now your cover.

87   No mystery at all
about the former legionaire
pinching soup cans into a biker's helmet
under the lantern jaw of Savonarola.
That is Richard Savage.

88   And the fellow bowing vibratoes
       on an abstract violin
       while two Guest Workers smash up café tables
       as the girl watches?
       Rameau's nephew.

88A   Three tailored American blacks in predawn darkness
       ranged through a hotel courtyard
       like a team deprived of its hoop while the hotelier watched
       from his stone porch, plump and bored.

89   Bottled waters promise island holidays.
       Blue moons envisage cheese and surf.
       But where has that man
       gone with his lantern, looking for man?

89A   Through a streetlamp's cone mist streaming as one turned:
                                  HEY MAN
       HOW DO WE GET OUTTA HERE!
       and he blessed them with his RAUS! and a stubby
       skyward forefinger

90   Come scratch my back,
       blackbird, as when I left
       your island brother and came here.
       Bring my scrolls, and bring
       that green sea of leaves.

90A   While Neptune on his greasy wall fountain slid to the tune
       of dribbled plashings,
       forking trash aside from his foam-spewing thoroughbred,
       that beachhead a tidied crashing.

91   Ten years ago
     with alpenstock roaming these tables
       the last man from his valley
    to speak that dialect, stalking the wedding guest
   under the iron sign of the peacock's tail.

92   In the morning
       setting the bedbugs
       on fresh paper in sunlight,
       at evening
       replacing them in the cot.

93   The Writers' Association
       got a German Jewess deported
       back to the Führer: she published
       without getting her green paper. So who says
       that free expression is meaningless?

94   Two men in their fifties
       striding side by side,
       yes! identical twins,
       growlly, all business,
       each talking to himself.

95   The tank-like wren
       hops, gobbles,
       then delivers himself
       of interviews on the ever-
       present crisis.

96   Will no one listen
       to the swollen marsh tit?
       His grandfather was a pastor
       and his cousin has reformulated
       the global organization of production.

97   Testing air-raid sirens
       as the watchmaker
       closes for lunch
       and the fruit seller
       resorts his peaches.

98   Danton roars in the sleep
       of Monsieur Lenin
       next door to young Büchner's walk-up
       via Wells's time machine:
       the decay of rhetoric.

99   Aquinas at the gate of the end
      fell silent. But then there is
      The Customs Inspector: 'Mr Lao Tzu,
      if that's what you've got in there, then
      put it all down on paper.'

100   And so Frisch read Brecht's exile poem
      on how the *Tao Te Ching* came to be,
      from a windflapped carbon
      while standing in the street:
      'Copy and pass it on.'

101   Here Walser was a houseboy.
      Here Walser clerked in a bank.
      Here Walser clerked insurance.
      Here Walser addressed envelopes
      in a *Stube* for the jobless.

102   Grey doric columns
      carrying red carved beams
      carrying the green vine
      into ramparts, pasture, cloud.

103   Here Walser clerked at a long table
      in a sewing-machine factory.
      Here Walser set out on fleet foot
      for a factory in Winterthur,
      where he stretched elastics.

104   A Christmas evening graveyard
      sheltered by mountains from the wind:
          hundreds of cupped red candles.

105   In the ancient barn, canned music
      for pigs who never see daylight,
      on Hanged Man Pine Tree Road.
      So once there grew a harsh light, where now
      dark meat fattens for the dark-minded.

106   The lady offers to buy them
both a cup of coffee.
Seated, she says, 'I'm hungry!'
The scholar pays for both platters. She:
'Next time I'll tell you about my socialism!'

107   Walser to Lenin
in Spiegelgasse: 'Do you also enjoy eating
this Glarner Birnbrot?'

108   The headlines part to disclose
Yevtuschenko in folksy shirt
premiering his filmy childhood in Venice
('Eternal Venice sinking by degrees
Into the very water that she lights').

109   The sidewalk spritzer advances, twelve
nozzles sizzle,
order drips in their wake,
while the plastic reservoir sloshes
seas, chaoses.

110   (Mark it well, managers and soaks,
cheats and charitables, you wise
savers and reckless go-for-brokes,
whether it came or went: it dies.

111   And whether you hoard your thin life,
Midas, or richly squander it,
Duke of Chin, or cannot get enough,
Faustus, death writes the final chit.)

112   'Space is not what they say,
and then there is *le Mouvement* . . .'
Oscar Milosz
threading a cowbell angelus among
mists on the Rigi.

113   No Roman death mask of Brecht
over the Bechstein grand
polished by late sun
high on the Zurichberg.

114　A muteswan heaved itself up onto the quai,
　　　rolling and unrolling its neck, galoshes
　　　slapping over the stones. *Clackclack* went its bill above
　　　the birdbook, wing stroke enough to break an arm.

115　Nearsighted scholar and messenger of heaven
　　　gazed at each other for a long moment
　　　in Orwell's target year, the Year of the Rat. Winter fogs,
　　　and 'in *The Spring and Autumn* there are no righteous wars'.

116　The street musician shrugs and packs it in:
　　　two whores grin down
　　　from their breasty window,
　　　radio still blaring.

117　August heat, night window wide,
　　　the world breathing where
　　　a man under a lamp near his radio
　　　sits naked to the waist,
　　　his arm timing late Mozart.

118　'We filed out of the woods' (militia)
　　　'and there in the meadow, a hut
　　　with lamps and pictures on the outside,
　　　the old man and goat inside.
　　　And the village still called him their own.'

119　Having clambered to the top of his field,
　　　he owns a fifteenth-century house.
　　　A magnet hangs in the bathtub,
　　　another hangs in the mineral water, and the little
　　　clincher hangs in the orange juice.

120　　　Sparrow my alarm clock
　　　to aerate my slumbers in the house
　　　　　of Paracelsus.

121　In dialect the Frau shoos her goats
　　　　　among cowplates,
　　　a young intruder barks Deutsch to his
　　　　　radio-controlled jeep.

122   In the Swiss monthly
      for paraplegics, athletes
      wheelchair down a sprinting track
      among paintings of cherry pickers
      toppling out of trees.

123   On the truck flatbed, a stack
      of gleaming sheetrock,
      in the air the musings
      of Monsieur Mallarmé
      while they lift and unload:

124   *Uno*
              per
      lor-
            o,
      uno
               per
      il Signor
       Diavo-
               lo
     e uno
           per
               noi!

125   Silone's window looked out on the mountains.
      So did Brecht's window, but he was not
      interested: Brecht was interested in things
      that could move. And Silone's fugitives, no movement
      left to them, vanish into the high snows.

126   Swansdown
      and junkies' needles
      snared in the hurdles of abandoned weirs.

127   Leapers around a bonfire before
      the emeryboard Opera House Extension
      while masked extras beat their shields
      with nightsticks in the wings.

128   Each night during the youth riots
streets were hosed and vacuumed.
So the morning shift still dozed, fathers
looked past their children, the powerful
blow of life swung wide.

129   The Roman baths have been resurrected.
But at the swimming complex designed by Frisch
workmen sliced off a hanged man at the knees,
refusing to widen the excavation
on his account.

130   Just listen to that one-man band:
unfolds like a harmonica,
opens himself like a drum hole,
and through it he goes up,
free from grief, free from snow.

131   Fleshy crosses of clematis
trellising the city mind
one mid-May moment
with country mind.

132   Lakeside restaurant:
it is napkins in floral sprays,
and a portrait photo that says
that here you'll not go in want:
it is the owner's face, and the owner-wife's, and it is Richard
Nixon's.

133   'No phosphorous, no thoughts': thank you, Doktor Professor
Moleschott.
Driving against pilings, the surge bursts into boiled
cauliflower,
each cluster melting at impact, somewhat overcooked, the
tailrace
a swirl of inedible disjecta. No moonlight, no phosphorous.

134   'Pine's waist thin jade now,' sang Wu Wenying
at the hetaira's grave
while a jay grieved for the tree.

135   Lake gulls follow the tractor,
      settle in swirls
      over fresh furrows,
      but the worm startles them.

136   Startled, touching her hair, the widow
      blows a kiss to her dead
      while flowers deepen and shine
      under sudden rain, row
      on garden row.

137   Blasted to the isle of Ufenau
      by Erasmus, syphilis, and the Curia,
      Ulrich von Hutten laid down sword and pen:
      'One lives off the countryside, the forest,
      each castle keep . . . Haggard peasants. . . .'

138   One sail up the lake,
      one sail down,
      one bomb in the blue, one
      in the sea, one in the ground, with our
      little sun between.

139   Perfected waves
      smoothing to nothing, teaching
        the unperfected.

140   Artemidorus and Jung-chi
      co-laborers of a morning,
      with Synge and the gull he watched
      through a long morning on Aran
      trying to break a golf ball on the rocks.

141   Only a return summer visitor
      to her wild Aran shores, you are,
      yet she sits at your knee, Psyche
      of the living tresses, to see
      the photos you brought back.

142   Hand-carried from a Nile cliff to this lake,
      the sayings set down by Judas Thomas:
      'All of them sozzled and no one thirsty, though
      they came here empty and will have to leave that way.
      Blind drunk, for the moment. But when they shake it off . . .'

143   Unearthed by monks at Einsiedeln,
      Mechtilde von Magdeburg's love cry:
      'I want the unmingled wine!'
      (After the ceremony they poured their best vintage,
      but most of it trickled through my beard.)

144   Halfway up the black Adlisberg
      a woodsman came down shouldering a golden log.
      He asked, 'What are you doing staring at stars
      through stripped beeches in piercing December?'
      And I asked, 'Why are you hauling that imponderable
      treasure down into the dead city?'
      Before we could speak further, lake mist rose and belltowers
      blinded us with four luminous strokes.

from RHYME PROSE SIX

Johannes Bobrowski was marched off by a millenium in the
making, past Novgorod, where his comrades chose to spill the
cloister bells into snow. Past villages in the north, 'no one will
learn where we were,' the better to retain the lineaments of
Sarmatia. ÓndraŁysohorsky took shelter in Tashkent-Kuibyshev,
then in Moscow. His nation, younger than he was, had been
crushed back to the peoples who must send forth both raven and
dove. Qu Qiubai, nation-hunting, went to fledgling Moscow, by
way of rotting in Harbin, hallucinating enlightenment in the
Manchurian boondocks. A Czech and a *nabi* from Shanghai con-
verging on some hidden territory perhaps of most ancient name
perhaps stretching new boundaries. Bobrowski found in certain
plain words a hidden territory nearly, ah nearly impervious to
the long guilt of the raven. This he hid beneath his wing, this he

carried towards Sarmatia. Lu Xun did not move; Lu Xun scoured bricks with acid as the new walls went up around him, perhaps to the good, yet remind us, Boethius, that in your cell you fingered no rosary, but rather the rational beads of *amor quo caelum regitur*. In the end Lu Xun had to dispatch Lao Tzu through the last outpost again, into the blown wastes of the northwest, having him tell the guards, 'The nameable names are not the names that name permanence.' And the copyist dozed, his brushes cascading to the floor. Qu Qiubai made it back to Shanghai, electing the mystique of foundry sweat. By the osprey he was devoured. Łysohorsky returned to his Latchik miners, saving for them and their children the ikon of Saint Francis. Him the fledgling hawk lashed with its steel beak. Bobrowski was demobbed into moldering internment, along with his Christ of Memory, and Proserpinal psalms brewed from a second Buonaparte's muddy folly, their *Selah* breathing out ever the word 'bird', and a map he was refining with the aid of that bird's eye, a map of Sarmatia.

Dear friend, from this window
the path to the end is clumped violets
turning sun into moist lobes
that exhale the undersea and night past Arcturus.
The black mirror stays real.
But enduring it, good hands
make gardens.
          Where
the arbor ladders shade
floats a stair, sliding if you gaze at it,
and that is the ascent, old friend:
our climb, the stink of it
with the weariness, burning ledges
contoured to each corrugation
of those ephemeral
radiant leaves.

HILL COUNTRY BALLAD

Bowee, boweree,
went through this gate in a high year, but remember
clearly only the great weight falling away,
bowee, bowdowneree,
as bass at evening flash over brazed water.

Bowee, boweree, bowee,
lies of the time and my part in them, inertly
manifest in these crystallographies,
bowdowneree,
part of the crucible's intricate walled peace,

bowee, boweree,
where snare drum riffs among the pumpkin lanterns
bobbing on sticks as children to the clock tower
bowee
cleanse the slow lattice of each interlock,

bowee, boweree,
but the rash return, devout feet memoryless
troll me to my knees, hands cupped in amber,
bowdowneree,
and the fresh catch torn living from my side.

THE CELLS AT TUN-HUANG

Where now hangs the saddlebag of pointless zeal for Yen Hui,
where lies the road to dark Wei and its dictator?

Where has it blown, the sandtrack to dissipated Emirs
for barefoot Francis, where the fire that englobed him?

Where are they, the left hands of Mucius Scaevola, charred,
and of Colonel von Stauffenberg, mangled but willing?

133

Where scrapes the trench shovel of Musonius Rufus,
where rock the lever and treadle of Simone Weil's drill press?

Where is it shelved, the parchment of first entitlement,
and where has he gone, the man who recognized it, reading its
    blanks?

'Then who is it standing before me!' bawled the emperor.
'I cannot tell you!' barked the wayfarer, and walked off.

Into grey mosses bearding a blue cliff.
Into the blessing before battle, in the mass sung raggedly
    afterwards.
Cursèd be he / they/ we! This too shall pass, but not adroitly.
In the psalms of the man pulled from flood by a stag, and
    therefore
in the emperor's lust for the stag, that his horns be turned into
    wine cups,
in the saved one's betrayal of the deer to the throne-holder,
in the eavesdropping swallow's flight, for he told all in time,
    and in
the stag's rebuke to the emperor, for this in turn
made the wretch confess to his ruler, who demanded:
'Shudderer, stutterer, where is the golden one who spoke here,
where has he gone, who gave you your useless redemption?'

Into the air past your portals, O great one,
not the air but the earth stretching away, magnificence,

not the wide but the red earth, high one, reddened
to cochineal by petals of the mango, eminence,

where they have fallen, majesty, and blooded our ground,
there one may pursue him, the foregoer, the horned knower.

*

HONAN FOLKSONG
(sung to two-string violin and wooden-plate drum)

Uphill and down and again uphill,
   he takes hill after hill
   and will never get his fill,
upridge and down and again upridge,
   he takes ridge after ridge
   and high edge piled on high edge.
It lines out and winds on,
   the venerable, improbable
   vine of the araconda,
and the hesitant pheasant
   shoos off in a tattoo that his long
   tail flails *whang whang* –
a big python writhes on the path,
   with a sliding push to the bush
   slithering thither
and singing honky-tonk
   the apprentice monkeys
   go go go up the pine trunk
and everywhere the invisible note
   of swelling elegy from the nigh-
   tingale's yellow throat,
where all you see is
   cloud and more cloud
   and mist swirling past,
mountains a whiteness
   and whiteness where the lines
   of the pines were:
hid in that wood
   a temple, and in that temple hid
   a lone man and good.

from FOLKSONG *I.ix OF THE GREATER ODES,*
THE CLASSIC ANTHOLOGY

Gong and drum boom,
stone and flute tones hang clear,
and in good grain there is ringing,
let clanging ears of it come.

Real work pays off. Our empty
cups have filled us with wine,
fortune forever greens
and returns with new grain.

MENCIUS VI.1.viii

Where the cypresses of Ox Mountain lie axed
              the rains bathe them,
         shoots sprouting from stumps –
but each day the cows come
              to nuzzle them clean:
the Ox lies stripped bare
              by his brides, even –
yet in the windless forerising
              day buds from darkness:
let the pale tips
              answer to mists now and dew,
let great Ox stir through his felled shanks
              and green dawn over him.

SINGLE SEAL QUODLIBETS

Rooftile and shield rim:
    shielding the house
and roofing the warrior,
    two seasons of shelter
over one head surviving neither.

    Stagecoach footstrap
easing me down out of battle
to approach with measured step
the cleared space, steadier
    in my grip
on the outstretched bowl
    held low, held level.

To begin is to make offering,
    take, present it
lifted up, be lifted and so
raise the bowl and begin –
saying it is furthering it:
to further it, say it by moving it
    along, get it en route –

that is the whole record, the all
if you take the bowl and begin:
    give out the lifting up
and be lifted in the bowl of the beginning,
for that making is a way-making
    in the bowl so taken,
the beginning cupped in and raised up:
    presentation.

TWO AND THREE SEAL MEDLEY

The river is the law

even though you are bound to your land
as the comet is wound around its orbit

And of course if you drain the marshes between mountains
and lug lead from the mines at Yen
and float it on scows to the south
the river is the law

And then, too, if your door
feathers itself in fire,
if the wing of the flame bird marks your passage
and your wicker threshold is for burning
law is the river

Law may be the measure
for measure is the fire
renewing and furthering
the heat and sweat of the job
such, surely, has been the law

and a man standing
straight and unblinking in his rank
may well be the lance shaft of the law

but even so and ever
law is the river

AGE OF GOLD

The huddled egg breaks open,
new leaves move on the tree
            for Lord Lucky –
      his cup runneth over
bearing out the big-bowl reading of happiness

. . . but let us rerun that sequence:
      blind trust
beaks through the warm shell
    while fear trembles the tree –
      for Lord Lucky
a claw slices down
      beside the hand
cupped around his child.

Of what use plunder
    to prisoners of war?
Hemp dangling fruit by the outworks.
Across a wide famine
      birdcatchers
    drag at the wind,
men try drumming
    bream to the surface,
their rafts adrift on a fast current, O Lord
      Lucky!

        Mayflies
thronging the air.

BAROMETRIC READING INCORPORATING
SINGLE GRAPHS

Remembering
    has gone the way of soft speaking
yet much chatter animates
    the Lucretian quanta of danger –

garrulous
    cliff after cliff,
and a wind like three dogs barking
    or a dog coming down
like a wind with three toothed howls in it –

a loop of furry risk.

But in the pauses of it,
    grain hushing,
wheat standing quiet.

LIU XIE, WENXIN DIAOLONG ZHU, 6.521

Writing alters
    and therefore abides.
Braiding rope
    it makes fast to adequacy.
So go where the day leads you
    and finish what it began.
Grasp chances, grope
    through openings, fear is a phantom.
Keep your eye on the event
    and give back its strange contours,
ask the old ones: learn from them
    how laws came into being.

DAWN IN SHIH-CHENG
Lǐ Hö

Moon is setting over Great Dike,
Lady and Herd Boy ford the high river –
where is the lane not washed by havoc, where
    is the one place?

Streaming time, the ten
cauldrons of the unborn are pouring
their northern surf as we listen for
    their boomings.

Marsh tits harry the cygnets,
I have dropped my scroll in shore eddies,
come January my labors will
    lock in the pond.

Gull after gull breaks open white day,
a girl, weeping, has turned into wing flash.
Stroke your zither no more, Nomad Boy – a bronze bell
    hangs brooding in the cloud forest.

from TWENTY-THREE POEMS ABOUT HORSES
Lǐ Hö

1   Dragon spine fluttering with money,
    mint-issue hooves trampling the mist white,
    but no one weaves saddle flaps of silk brocade.
    Who will cast him for a gold pizzle whip?

2   Midwinter grasses, sweet roots, and in boulevards
    of the capital snow bunches like salt.
    To see if his mouth is hard or soft
    take him in hand first with a bramble bit.

9   Shu of Liao's boy died in a hurry,
    no one any more can feed fire breathers.
    Night deepening, frost leans on the stables
    of thoroughbreds, west wind splitting their hooves.

11 A court dandy's mount given over to his lady,
    silver trappings pricked with piebald bitch unicorns –
    and at high noon above the salt cliffs
    it scrambles for footing, drained, against wind and dust.

13 Whose son is this gentleman of jade rings?
    They say a knight's bones are fragrant – sun, barley, and
          long time –
    and he has heaped out gold for the bones of one horse,
    setting them on the road with King Hsiang of Ch'u.

17 Iron glinting into grain still green,
    millstones dribbling grass in a fine scatter –
    today's crowd is set on narrow-necked fillies,
    and the big outfits are wary of long teeth.

18 Po-lo once looked this horse over,
    noting his credentials, hair swirls along the belly.
    Now they feed him white grass and give no interviews.
    Which sun will he leap with over Blue Mountain?

WEEPING FOR YING YAO
Wang Wei

Stone Tower Mountain
home to tombs
home to the tomb
we have taken
you we have taken
up the tower
the peak death
have gone with you
home
and now we
lean down
through cypress, pine
carriages and the hearse
we have set your
bones among clouds
have seen you
home
no more
never again
setting among clouds
your bones
and now
down go
carriages leaning
pine, cypress
never again
no more
what stays
are the torrents
shooting fixedly
white water
mindlessly
this is what stays
only this
stationary
spilling

tomb, tower
death the mountain
mindlessly
down to men.

WANG YANG-MING

Emptiness at ease is not the great void,
brewing within it, a balancing stirring in the first mortar.
What does it hold
                    lacking which we are at lack?

When high feeling has passed, air clears to the last ground.
Action inheres nowhere in remembering or refraining.
Flawless, the hiddenness of metamorphosis –
and who else will pursue it with me, if not you?

THE PROEM (OPENING)
  Parmenides

The mares pulling me with such force kept on thrusting
as far as my soul could go, once the women at the reins
had gotten me on the way that the Goddess lays out,
road of seething mind tracked through speech and story,
that carries the undeflectable man on course, aiming
his thought straight. This was carrying me at last,
I could see those horses of unmappable mind
tearing along it, straining, steered by those women.
The hubs of the wheels shot fire and shrilled the pipe's high pitch,
spun forward on both sides by the whirling metal
which those priestesses, daughters of the sun,
shoot into motion when they leave the hall of night,
as they did with me, and, throwing their scarves
back over their streaming heads, make for the light.

ORPHIC FRAGMENT

Close to the dwelling of the dead,
                    on the left you will find a spring.
Near it towers a white cypress.
Avoid that source, do not
                    even try to approach it.
It is the other spring that you need, surging
from the lake of Mnemosyne,
                    a cold torrent.

Before it stand guardians. Tell them,
'I am the child of earth
                    and the starry regions,
but heaven is my home.
                    You know that already.
Thirst burns in me,
                    I am dying from it.
Let me taste the coldness
                    gushing from the lake of Mnemosyne.'

And they will let you drink
                    from the divine source,
and you will come into dominion
                    among the heroes.

CHRISTIAN EPIGRAM, PALATINE ANTHOLOGY L.59

Egyptian woman,
hidden infant,
and close river –
these are the human
early current
in the Pattern-Giver,
see it who can.

from POEM ON DIVINE PROVIDENCE
  Orientius

The bulk of these years is already gone out of mind
    because your page is inscribed with no verses.
What conditions have made such silence your product,
    what anguish has squatted on your glum genius?

                .   .   .

If the wide sea were to rip broadside into Gaul,
    surging toweringly across its tillage, surely
there is no beast of the field, no grain or fruit or olive
    and no choice place that would not turn rotten;
no plantations and great houses that would not be swept
    by storm crash and fire blast and be left standing blank and
sad:
like shouldering a landslide, going through this ten-year slaughter
    strewn by the steel of the Vandals and Visigoths.

                .   .   .

And then, too, you trudged among the wagons, eating dust,
    lugging weapons for the Goths, and no small bit of bag-
gage,
beside a white-haired commoner, ruddy with the dust of cities,
    driven the same way a shepherd goads banished sheep.

                .   .   .

So you cry over farms laid waste, courtyards deserted,
    and the flame-swept stage scenery of the villas.
How, then, not weep over losses that are truly yours,
    if you could peer into the trampled sanctums
of your heart, their splendors crudded with filth,
    and hobnailed swaggerers in the mind's cramped cell?

WALAHFRID STRABO

What enwombed the marrow now nurses a tree,
    a shin bone flowers – surely a good omen.
Amazing: the bark is not spongey, it's even
    tougher than the wood: such is the life in this bone.
Nothing, great king, shuns your service: you hunt the doe
    and a forest sprouts from her bones! Hail!

TRAVELLERS TO BROCELIANDE

This is the Book of thy descent:
this is the Book of the Grail.
Here begin the terrors,
here begin the marvels.
I, Ignavus, saw
from the middle of my hut
that book smaller than a hand
come from the hand of Christ,
come into the middle of my doubting
on the eve of Good Friday,
a heath in white Britain
holding us, that was in seven seventeen
and the book was lost, then found again . . .
I, J. Bodmer, saw
in the moldering pile *Parzival*,
here begins Wolfram
in the blackness of print, Zurich,
seventeen fifty-three . . .
But when on the third day he wished
to read more from the little book,
It had gone. 'Off to Norway,
the weird beast will lead you,
you must sweat and stink': and so
past a foul hermit and black fir,
battle tower, queen's lake, convent
and a fight to the end with devils
possessing a man of God, there came

146

to hand the little book
and so I have set it down here
on cloudy stone, on mists
shifting through the trees.
I, Wace, historian,
wonder-hunting, bagged nothing,
came back as I went, a fool,
yes, departed a fool and came back one!
It was damn foolishness I went looking for, and
          a damn fool is what I discovered.
I, Cologrenaunt, knight errant,
Chrétien's man, saw
the chapel spring boiling ice cold
by the pillar of emerald.
Grabbed the gold basin and splashed
that water over the pillar –
the sky blackened, flashes
fell with snow, rain, hail, trees . . .
but then calm, and in the vine
birds thick on every branch,
each with its own song making one music
that held me contented there. Fool!
A knight barreled down on me,
a roaring giant, ripped me
off my mount, flattened me,
stole my horse, didn't even look back.
I dragged off to my host,
but they all said no one ever
got out of that scrape before.
Exactly as I left, so I returned –
now that it is over
I see my foolishness.
And exactly like a fool
I have confessed to you
what I never wanted to tell any man.

GOUTY BRIGIT: EPIGRAM I.284
Janus Pannonius

Gouty Brigit lying in soft grass
        and a snake creeping
towards stricken feet.
Seeing its coils, she leaped
        from her blankets running,
painlessly doctoring
the malady medicine could not touch –
whether fear did it
        or the limbs themselves,
aid came from the Macedonian beast.
How rarely the meritorious
        get their reward!
The serpent-helper was clubbed to death.
In my judgment, bitch,
        it were far better
had you changed places with your benefactor.

MY COUNTRY WEEPS: 1636
Andreas Gryphius

We are finished, yet still
        they have not finished with us.
Brazen troops of nations,
        crazed trumpets,
blood-slick sword
        and the big howitzer
have devoured everything that sweat
        and diligence laid away.
Towers flicker, the cathedral
        lies roof through floor,
city hall sits in terror,
        our forces smashed,
girls defiled,
        and wherever we turn
flames, plague, and mortality
        pierce heart and spirit.

Trench and street are the constantly
                    refreshed conduits of blood.
For eighteen years now
                    our rivers have
brimmed with corpses, slowly
                    pushing themselves clear.
Yet still I have said nothing
                    of what vexes like death
and dips a lashing beak deeper
                    than hunger, pest, and holocaust:
that so much treasure has been
                    plundered from our souls.

THE COURSE OF LIFE
Friedrich Hölderlin

You too wanted more, but love pulls us all
   downward, grief more greatly bows us down;
      yet not for nothing does our curve
         bend back to where it came from.

Upward, or down – does there not still rule
   in holy night where mute nature broods
      on futures, rule in utterly twisted
         Orcus, a straight way, a law?

That is what I found. For never, from what I know,
   have you high ones who sustain all things
      led me, as mortal masters do,
         with care by a level path.

Man shall try everything, say the high ones,
   so that, fed by strength, he may learn to give thanks
      for all, and fully grasp freedom,
         to burst through, and go, wherever.

THE TOMBS (CONCLUSION)
Ugo Foscolo

> 'This prophecy Merlin shall make; for I live
>   before his time.'
>   – the Fool in *King Lear*

                    Palms, cypresses,
the day will come when you'll see a blind beggar
stray through your ancient shade, feeling his way
into the tombs to take the urns in his arms
and have speech with them. Those secret vaults will moan
and the house of death will tell the whole tale,
how Troy was levelled twice and twice rebuilt
in shining splendor over silent streets
only to burnish Greek glory for the line
of Peleus taking its last prize. The poet,
easing the pain of those souls with song, will make
Greek princes deathless in every country touched
by the fathering sea. And you, Hektor, will win
the honor of tears wherever blood is held sacred
shed for one's native earth, as long as the sun
shines down on the catastrophes of mankind.

RAWLINSON TWO-STEP
(Poems 4 & 12, Rawlinson Ms. Bodleian, and
'Die offentlichen Verleumder', Gottfried Keller)

Ne sey never such a man as Jordan was;
wente he to Gogeshale panyles.
A thief creeps out of his hole
to make his rounds, he wants
to snatch our purses, but makes
a little discovery, so now
he's after bigger game.
Ore est temps d'alier a diner,
ore est temps d'alier a diner.
Ore alom, alom, alom,
bele companie avom.

150

Arguments over nothing,
bankrupted learning,
tatters on the flagpole
over a flagging people.
Wente he to Gogeshale panyles,
ne sey never such a man as Jordan was.

Everywhere he goes
the vacuum of the times
Stondeth alle stille,
stille, stille
lets his shamelessness
puff out, and he prophesies,
climbing onto a rostrum
of stinking rubbish,
hissing his salutations
to a dumbstruck world.
Stille stondeth alle,
stille stondeth alle,
stille as any ston.

Seed hath found furrow. The earth
changes, changes. Millions
Bele companie avom
live shame and laugh at crime
ore est temps d'alier a diner
ore est temps d'alier a diner
and what had been fantasy
is now the case – the stalwart
bele companie avom
the stalwart have been scattered
and the stinkers have made their pact.

Someday, and it won't be soon,
they'll talk about these times
stondeth alle stille
as they fabulize over the Black Death,
school children muttering
through the lectionary of plagues
stille as any ston.
And the children will build in the field
a bogeyman out of stubble

to make happiness flame
from afflictions,
to torch radiance
from archaic horrors.
Trippe a littel with thy fot
ant let thy body gon.

A CENTO from VALAIS QUATRAINS
  R.M. Rilke

Like someone talking about Mother
and turning into her while talking
paths that lead nowhere
small waterfall

much shadow without doubt seeps in
threatened and redeemed
mixed from sweet evening, pure metal
wine: ardent comet

Wind taking hold of the land like the handworker
who knows, immemorially, his materials
a fine branch of terebinth
absent presence that space drank

Will the sky, in the gaze of shepherds and vintners,
held there, stay, this sky of blue wind?
Abstracted path, goats halted
poplar in place

Who, obeying summer
eternalizes it
submissive grey rose, trained vine
erased beneath these motions

Taking a long step back, the craftsman
holds his work up to the mirror of space
paths giving on nothing save the open and the season
until an appalling sun gilds them

Before you can count to ten it all changes
wind over tall stalks and the wide wave gone
unedited light beyond the range
menaced and saved

Stirred from evening sweetness the pure metal
we enter into its body
branch of terebinth that space drank
the open, the season

Ardent comet of wine
on another plane, higher
turning into her while talking
and the wide wave gone

Butterfly, sun's cousin
torn letter the lover was writing
even while the woman
was hovering at the door

NOVGOROD: COMING OF THE SAINTS
Johannes Bobrowski

Now
as day breaks, light
sets out over the shores, the lake
lifts into cumulus,
around its wings birds
darken and shine,

where the wood image
floated, green graining
and the dark face
of Nicholas, a wave's
green fingers pressed it
under the river,

153

and came Anthony
the Stranger, a stone
wafting him over the waveless
flood, bore the man
who stepped easily
ashore: he
had seen the city,

towers and roofs,
over mountains those walls
lifting and plunging in volleys
of dark and bright fliers,
and one turret inscribed
steeply against sky.

So be it. Across my way
a cross has fallen,
sayeth Anthony, a stone –

So, fool, you also, fool,
go, fools and holy babes
over the quivering bridge.

They pass on crutches, rags
flapping their spindly arms, ancient
windbirds out of the winters.

Down the road you come shouting!
Lift this stone for me.

HOUSE
Óndra Łysohorsky, 1946

Hatred makes this age, so I mean to serve
the man who goes beyond it. Look at this town:
    exquisite once, it is rubble.

A single house left standing. Rain, darkness.
A grain trucker is sheltering there –
    tomorrow he'll be far off.

154

That house is what I want to be:
ragged roof and crust of bread for the drivers
    who truck wheat, pushing on,

so that some day one of them, ending his run, will say:
There was a house down there, I stayed the night,
it stood in the middle of a field of ruins.

CENTURY
Ion Barbu

To shiver out the crests of birds,
emblems slicking smooth in flight,
hooked eagles haunt the studied
radiance while you gain height.

Sickles have flashed through the waste – call out
to the wild thyme, scorched wall, to fine
ring fingers from the blank ages
beneath silver in the blinded mountain.

THE LAST CENTAUR
Ion Barbu

. . . from sun which clasps cloud . . .

Fitfully, he squeezed himself to the last,
his head ringing . . . then smash, over stones gone green
the whole crown cup at one stroke splattering
all that thinking lofted within the beast.

Vaults have melted and poured the contrary whole. . . .
Flesh went off in freezing jags of mist,
in foggy coils, slowly, though a stripped heart
arrowed by fire winnows itself from night.

Plodding executioner, vast sleeve
with its trains, shadow dragged at the embers, axes
slicing into the glowing clod. And earth

tumbles to slumber. Nevermore centaur: the wild.
Yet under scorching trots at the stud farms, ringing
deep within piled strata, veins of gold.

YU-VU SONGS OF THE NA-KHI

Boy Dawn wind shining, and the silk stars
     fringeing your jacket meet my hands.
     Spruce beyond roofs, quick seedlings,
     we contrived no appointment,
     spruce shedding to earth,
     we made no arrangement,
     water finds its way.
     Gulley splices with runlet,
     the wind gathers, arriving,
     leaves loosen in acknowledgement.
     Bamboo roots tangle to one clump,
     massing to maturity:
     the day has twelve hours,
     which of them might have married us?
     Paper shreds into water.
     Your voice repeats the wind –
     Long Tail flaps off looking
     for his own singer, calling and calling.
     The day waits upon us –
     what are you thinking? Say it, even
     as the oak ladle, balancing
     the mounded barley, spills.

Girl Rushing words, meadow waters:
     you are testing my youth,
     the riffle purls, you wait for me to speak.
     And your own speech: should I listen
     as I have known others to listen –

his word into her stillness,
now you to me, yes, as you say, the two of us.
And golden rocks at the world's heart,
feel their light covering us – the mason
dares not cleave it, nor could he.
But your family is solid, with
great holdings, your father
sees in you his promise,
his esteem is your treasure. . . .
Whatever you mean to tell me,
say it now, heap
your ladle with the dust
of this brilliance.

Boy You only, word after word:
like the bamboo knife your voice pares me.
Everything? oh yes, I have everything –
the artemisia field back of us,
the field to our left rank with sorrel,
tilling, sowing, yes, a fine future.
What do they want from me, nagging!
I don't want anything
of theirs, not one pinch.
But you, an only daughter,
your mother has given you her bronze keys,
and now she brings you a husband:
house in the hills near Dsa-du.
Do you set these aside
for our kerchief of white silk,
for the speed we shall make,
our handful of syllables?

Girl The picture of me you feed, and feed upon,
scatters seed in swamps.
Crows roost on my rooftree:
I have waited with them
long, longer than you.
Keys to my own house, yes –
but what use are they in Dsa-du,
past lakes beyond the Snow Range,
no oxen, nor cattle; and I,
I am sold into that narrow place.

157

Needle and silk I leave,
already I have put them
away. Mint dies on the rocks,
let us go to them, to one of the high meadows,
the three meads of Yu-vu
hugging the crags.

Boy I have marked it with fir boughs –
a tree spreads for us in that field,
a boulder stands: I have
set our names upon it.
You can hear, under the glacier,
black water meeting white.
The silver that I hear clinking
in your sewing kit, let me
take it to Li-chiang,
the market there has silks and fine shoes,
without them I am only
a mouth speaking.

Girl But your words trail
like ink through water, spreading:
from your brush I feel it.
You have set our names there,
let us go, then – the kerchief
and whatever else I have:
yes, to the market at Li-chiang
while the day is ours.
My home dwindling in vision,
mind clearing:
hawk's wing on the arrowshaft.
Hurry, then. The elk
wears forks of bone,
curve into curve joining;
and you will find me here.

Boy And when I come –
the fourteenth, no, the sixteenth day,
moon not yet full, the auspices
holding (I'm yours, the cutting
lies severed) – yes,
the sixteenth, in the evening,

I shall wait above the village,
whistle three times, wait three hours.
Come to me through the leaves,
cup one in your hand
and whistle like Long Tail.
Now, turn back home
once more, go there slowly.

Girl I plucked the leaves as you said,
blew on them, I have worn out three;
but you didn't come until now!
That house holds you
as a jade thumb ring the bow.
Don't look back –
did either of us want this?
Yet here it is,
It is ours. Come,
water pouring from the cup
cannot be regathered.
It is ours now.

Boy Rest by the fire, there is
no buzz through this meadow.
My reed changes like the wind.
As I stepped across
the threshold, my father
stiffened in me,
and my mother's warm sleeve –
foot balancing on the oak doorsill
then into air: I ran, then I
turned back, but stopped:
eyes blurring, spilling into the dust,
she didn't see that, no flies
stir their wings here – there is
no one here but us.
The inchworm coils forward,
part of him spins back, arching –
but we are here, your eyes
are the same eyes:
tell me, what do they say,
what are they trying to say,
now you must tell me.

159

Girl Your foot sprang from the threshold,
your mother, the thought of her.
But she with all the others
at the pine's foot yellowing:
mushrooms die of a season, their colors
leave them, one day they are gone.
She and the others, do not
think about them,
nothing will separate us
after tomorrow, or the next day:
your foot will lift, mine fall,
that will be the way of it,
the one road, now and after.
The musk deer leaping for his cliff –
has he arrived yet?
And they will sing the Wind Ceremony
for us, nor are we the first ones –
mint over the rocks vanishing.
The evening, can't you feel it?
How can they touch us now?
Listen: at the foot of
Nine Mountains, into the pines:
stone pheasants calling.
Look neither right nor left,
the boar makes these ferns his bed.
Come, lie with me here.

from
ARGURA
(1993)

SAHARA FRESCOES, TASSILI

These were not guilty. Care was blind care
without puff-drift from a gouged acre
or ozone burnt back through stratosphere –

neither x-ray nor photograph nor
decodable fantasy nor sheer
index of the fleetingness we bear,

but a common trace on the high wall
of passage, milk and rock powder's full
shimmering caravan in profile,

as surf ripples along the dune's break
to a bound wave pulsing from each stroke
of the inner fountain, man awake –

bull's hump, elephant's radar-web ear,
delicate furred dong of jackal, hair
hive on the bride backlit by dawn's roar:

for when ice rolled back and sun strengthened
over the great middle garden, wind
herded our tribe chanting, drove with sand

through jonquil and blood ochres crushed in
shoulder blades, and led across the green-
abandoned advancing wash of stone.

THE CAPITAL, 1980

Between the Archives and Justice
the high banshee lisp of the riptooth
but louder still through the carpenter's truck door
We doan wan no ed yu kay shun
into the unanchored slant
of unrenewed definition,
where Whitman learned to sit the hours
of terminal love with his wounded
tempted in line of duty to play favorites,
and where on the outbound commuter
a man stood prating in the valor of drunkenness
about his colonel
                              'Don't worry,' he says,
*'I've slated you for the one-tenth
who ain't going to 'Nam'*
                              the car wobbling him
as a bell clanged without reference to the stops
*When that kinda thing happens
it kinda makes you think . . .*
slack-jawed under the dinging
signal too rapid to be fateful
and too slow to sound a warning.

LEAVING THE CENTRAL STATION

Now that my own was moving,
now that change was sliding in, quickening,
faces on the platform hinted things
striving to show themselves, to touch the fact
of weight unmooring into vague futures, blank –
but then I sat up and turned: *Haydn!* a sharp pull,
not the face but the fact of Haydn, that tug
part of the speed, colors beginning to run,
spreading out to take the name now, *Mozart!*
and it was no face in particular,
with sweeping granites of the retaining wall,

164

rushing bright oblongs for cigarettes, beer,
and scraggles of dry vine dangling between them,
militiamen under packs, bowed slightly
by their dark rifles, with two last children,
girl running a tight circle around boy,
a pressure no sooner stated than developed
spirally, crumpling funnel in the chest
engulfing those close strangers
                                    settling back
into themselves and reaching for something to read,
pale in plate glass we were forms for that pouring
and its planetary, nostalgic clatter,
with the two gentlemen and their activity
not gone therefore although left quite behind
dispersed and swirling, submerged after being found,
turning to the next idea and its pursuit,
going off separately though they knew each other,
deposited back there or below, each of them
humming and churning, while apartment blocks
thin and scatter and raw fields open out.

PILGRIMS FOR BENDIS

Like travellers from the last century
and staying only one night, none the less
they have returned in thin hours when fury
worked loose, landing again at ghost Piraeus

recklessly: coves were shooting white
against an undercliff, and there they moored,
scud beating in from behind. Unabated
the sea all night came heavily unfloored

and vomited morning through a coldly molten
lucidity in atoms. They filed over
a hill to the old fort, followed walls part way
to Athens, orating, shooting and roasting plover,

165

and dawdled where the Artemis of Thrace
had loped in deerskin, building on that beach
their evening fire. Racing for her there,
bareback riders had leaned with torches, each

a muscled glow along drumheaded air
pulsing and shredding over glinting hooves,
unlit smoke rolling behind them, skulls
socketing the flare, and then roofs

kindling along cornices, the city.
Sokrates, custodian of the chase
who came in order to see the ritual
done for the first time, saw fire wash each face

before he went back with his friends, saw flame
goading the sweated necks of horses, profiles
of new rhythm abstracted along dark.
Chines of tile shelving upward layed the levels

of inner gardens, steadily riding ship,
alabaster bloom on the slave's tree
maturing the anchored likeness, pruned and reefed
lemon and salt to the hand's tyranny

and a master who has just left her, stepping
down from his damp ledge thinking: He who died
was loveliness, but he who lives shall be lovely,
price and weight of time in a perishing head. . . .

So that head fading will have been supplanted
by itself, hounding itself down lanes of flame,
leaving its lover wanting all he wanted
recedingly, though assured, a fleeing same.

Bendis: that sliced shining of a mouth rifting
lip from lip over those keen incisors –
has it been said she murdered with her gifts,
spear offered in each hand? They were not hers

but theirs, both citizens and aliens
together students of the kill, who lit
their many flambeaux from the one, tensing
to flare them in the collodion of spit

gilding the drypoint tautness of her smile.
Their horsemen vanished where the jetty spins
spume from the breakers, glossily rolling speech. . . .
Between our dog-teeth hang the spade-sure twins.

INTERLEAVED LINES ON JEPHTHAH AND HIS DAUGHTER

Lawn at sunset, during arrival, before the visit,
   for having returned in pride the general turned father,
not a field for crossing, bladed with amethyst,
   greeted with fulfillment, when the voice sailing out
and crisp withies of hazel twisting through hawthorn
   was his own girl's as she ran towards him. No, not thee.
Lithe and strict, that gate of a green power.
   His pledge to victory was the first who should leap the sill.
For the invitation is to bring gifts to the feast
   the face of battle newly unveiled itself as hers,
though they could not yet pass the shadowing door,
   and the face of submission as the new face of battle.
Green at evening is drenched with the price and the consequence.
   For what should he do in some other place, with less wagered?
Emerald is not heartless, but a sunk tide of fire,
   and some other conquest, such could never be his,
jade is the pomegranate turned away, speeding past harvest.
   More than readiness unfolds the eddying sun,
unwithheld, unknotting against the remainder,
   not alone while it revolves there, nor unseen.

167

'FIRE IS ONE . . .'

Fire is one, and thrusting his right hand
into it the prisoner won a new name
from his captors, the would-be killer
now Scaevola, as they watched the flesh go.
He saw a different thing, that to go on
into that zone was to encounter it
as either the up or down, twofold ordinance,

and conflagration as either the not-yet-come
or the done-with, now a fourfold pivot,
and holocaust as flanking choices not chosen,
by now a sixfold counterpoint, and burning
as the unborn who tugged him down untravelled
compass-points, the twentyfold
                              dispersal
through false liberations from surrender.

He too saw the one thing, that he had not
lost hold of courage. But the power that saw?
More than the newly left-handed in him,
more than the right-minded, it was his full face
that turned towards fire and, though variable
and dissolving, vision finally at grips,
held that one flame as the only heaven, and lived.

ARMIN

It seemed an eagle, simple
turning and tall descent, the burnt dome ample,
undeniable. But what shot
        down was a shield

        and stuck in the marsh and turned it
smoky and depthless. Close by, still filthy,
rearing as a hot brass flower
        out of all size,

168

it made midday sullenly
rebound, and I thought of crouched Scythians
when bowl, plow, and ax plummeted
    among them, and one,

    coming to his wits,
grabbed them up
             and made himself their first king.
But here, only this reeking slab
    and my two hands.

    Though all will come to be born
of iron and Lupa, though over the race of men
the dome shall whiten, this my tribe
    will, of the other

    limiting downward eagle
bear memory and bear arms, no hotly squiring
mania ours in this pierced air
    by the bean field,

    by the mucked mallow pond,
under noon reasserting its bullhorn.
I was born near hills but shall fight
    in the marsh forest.

    Birth. Homelessness. Rome's wars.
January, plinth of two-headed winds,
gateway of spin-facing auguries,
    has opened on us.

CANZONE OF WOOD, PAPER, WATER

Convex lens of water
in a glass is sanity,
though thunderheads now totter
no less steeply within
that clarity –
drumming in along
the horizon they encroach
on its studious thin
sweat, their beat narrowing
or widening as I watch.

One of those gestures
of useless wonder, then,
sky-clear, while a speck whispers
and flashes, rolling dark
on the cloud wall again,
little fighter
learning to search and hurl
the muddy ball for work.
Balanced now, but lighter,
I feel his whirl

in my own head, slipstream
clouding a nerve, fine sluice
miniaturizing a scream . . .
and can be typical
in that, or find its use,
while between acts, between
shutterings of the eye
in the meanwhile,
I huddle down to glean
the given and not die.
Across the meadow, men
swarm over a new house,
denim against raw wood.

They tap in one more good
beginning, one more end
nailed to beginnings,
in storm light seeming sharper,

brighter . . . and like some power
bending over the torpor
of this prefatory lull,
they fill the hour
to its brim, yes, are
accomplishers of the cup,
and under contract. A full
draught of it, then, for
the encounter leaning up

straight into the moment,
however it spill –
the straight thing without easement,
where there drifts instead
a lacey sail
spread to the westerlies
by high spiders blown seaward,
newly refined dread
and shruggings. Westerlies!
Towards and still towards,

to infect every good
beginning with an end
starved, a limit understood
too simply, and breed weary
knowingness. Or a mind
casual in its tether
driven against the marl
slabs of vapor, the very
seething of that weather
its blindness, and the whirl

of scud crowding the line
its embodiment,
the century's design
at random: streaming men
in a wave unbroken, bent
wherever force drives –
emigrants towards the earth's
stunned colors, heaped even
in their own coats. Lives, lives . . .
testing the worth

of repetition. I want
this apparition blottered,
for it leaves driven and spent
what would stream back to the hives
of the unscattered –

souls as bees, who accept
each lost city, rumpled
where vine has crept
crumbling them, or the trickles
from a smashed temple –
preserving none of it
yet never losing the way,
meeting the cycles
at last, sensing that it
will all come again into play.

Is it such rhythm, then,
that draws those workmen up
the roof's tarpaper lean
shingling with tiny blows
that trail through the gap –
winter brings down the year,
the unfinished house will wait
where blond plywood glows
vulnerably, where clear
showers will sop it late

into next spring. I watch
longer than I'm aware,
their work ends. Still I watch.
What is aroused,
moved by more than their care
for the god in the detail?
Like a long drink of space,
like everything unhoused,
I bend towards the gale
no longer knowing the place,
as if it were uncaused –
has the long trail
of embodiment snapped here? –

and spin like Averroes'
impulse when he first shot
our form through space
spreading it flat there,
experimental thought
stripping thought away, then feeling,
and then each sense
until the burnt-out similar
turned and flared cleanly, wheeling
into light's far suspense . . .

but what I had felt before
and not confronted was
my body as one more
among those roofers, held
by hammer stroke and pause,
balanced thing
meeting pine's willing pulp
with bone the builder. Skilled
in nothing more, that swing,
earth's weight its help.

Elation in flung arms,
a dancer's drunkenness
in labor's forms –
can the expansive be
driven and drenched through us
so it blurs the cost?
If only we might pay
that simply, and go free
with that much, that at most . . .
if it were ours to say.

I have seen newspaper turning
in crosswinds down a road
dreamily skim the burning
lake on that blacktop, light
as protozoa or odd
hints of a fugitive
existence. Whirl and skim.
And Augustine, lifted out

of things, saw each thing live
with a fulness strange to him
and felt that he had not
existed in the same
measure. My own eyes give
the figment on the road,
for the moment still ahead.

Dear child, tired father, turn
away from your play,
uncoil those worlds and learn
new fascination –
become the day
spinning more than its night
turning hard stars,
more, then, than revolving
stories the eye lets fade
towards sleep, dissolving,
without hesitation
abandon the sky you made
and go down unblinded, go far!

Out of this rotation
do I only seem to wake?
With that sharp consolation
body offers, sunk
in natural give and take,
the starling's agile shadow,
embodied world
ridged on the wintry trunk,
giddily swoops the meadow,
body with shadow whirled.
From them no one can take
the curse, resignation,
that learns surprise no more.

How long the minotaur
stared at his human hands
I need not wonder, for
jeopardy makes him ours,
he almost understands,
almost glimpses our long

174

incursion flare and furl
within his warring hours,
along their turnings his strong
phantoms whirl.

.

BY MUMMELSEE

Down from those bluffs breeding the Ohio
one can take plank stairs, or a rickety incline;
with much the same plunge deepened and turned west,
over Innsbruck the northern rim drops you
along paths or cableway. But Mummelsee
strands you above its bowl without means.
That is a country where the half-confessed
contraction of the tongue, generations now,
has a home waiting for it, activity
festering in the ever-condensing cup
of narrower reality. Inching down,
you sense the pull of huge mass, sequestered.
Only defunct radiance towards a world
spreads from there outward, under the rocks, the waters.
A man told me how, walled in by conifers
he had felt with the draft dragging at him
tempted to pitch in rocks, cones, anything
that came to hand. The impulse itself stopped him
for he remembered a fool who had done it once,
putting legend to the test, and had triggered
a storm, dislodging water spirits smoothly
from the viscous fathoms. Though he didn't move,
nonetheless around him moved the headlong
consequence, thickening the air. Cloud fumed up
clenching, spin-coiled, its first black drops
driving eyes in the water, while offshore
frogs climbed gin-clear eddies in the compression
bubble-pale, becoming girls as they swelled
beneath the explosive membrane.

                              Then, swift chill:
they vaporized, nothing of this was his,
some other mix would measure him for his way,
without sorcery, without its flaring
blandishments. A tight hole in the scrub,
less than the half door on a railway car
when the lower gate has shut and travellers
jam the opening, waving goodbye –
that much opened to him in the steep wood.
He clambered back through it as the last wisps
of tumult soaked into air and water, still
sucking at hearing with a siphon's gurgle.
He worked into the red-trunked palings. A curious
calm possessed him and instinctively
he unsheathed his knife, stropping it on his bootsole.
Slicing into the bark, he found it pliant
and carved a roofline from the town he had left
at the beginning, finding relief in this,
and so started a record of the journey,
continuing out of gratitude. The limbs
lay out in broad sweeps, a primordial page
that he worked fluently. But then he saw
the branch above streamed with script, while below
one with hieroglyphs like a mummy's lintel.
He froze, fearing his irrevocable work,
even though the uncanny narratives
framing his own remained unreadable.
The law of their opacity, enlarging
through the whole forest, yawned a mathematic
ungraspable, unvocalizable. Looking
high among the reaching systems, he saw
phosphorous unroll a tableau, two women
leaning naked towards a figure, the arms
of all three extended for an embrace.
Ribs, hips, shank radiated through the smoky
flesh of each. Death's a bit firmer than theirs,
and he welcoming them, the half alive.
Parallel like yoked mares, the two women
anticipated only pleasure, their eyes
and mouths avid. Below, still rooted, the man
realized that any cry from him
would never reach them, shut off from his plane,

inviolable as the mute legends
cut in the limbs over and under his,
to which he could add neither word nor sign.
His knife floated. The three shapes narrowed that
sealed interval, while nothing in this world
lifted a hand to enjoin their triple clasp,
and he stood shaking for their sistered fates.

SIX STANZAS IN NINE LINES

The way a rope, uncoiling . . .
the way a loop of flax
thrashed and threading, lies over
promising a weave . . .
the way a sunned snake
straightens across the path,
abandoning grass and dust
as fabric to the tensed treadle
of the halted foot. . . . That way.

Way of the announcement as it arrives, real
though only yet the real's herald, love's letters
    in hand between them, the two changing.
Way of the garden row as it sprouts, Strabo's
on his island, secretary of visions
    while sower, stem-binder, pruner-back.
Intercessory glisten of the sweet pea
bobbing under rain, her unsleeping eye
    conversant with him, her sure handler.

I crave the gradual
approximation of measures,
the way the stresses rise
from night's ground and fall
from day's flow and fuse –
Brahms in the fading ballade,
Brahms in the uprising, and
Scarlatti in the resolving
pulse, driven driver, breather.

The way balances though it veers underfoot.
Moon's wobble and the sure seasons' tread, shifting.
    Their reader twangs the rope tight and mounts.
Strabo trued lines in his herbal, sorting simples,
while Charlemagne's sons, big with brotherhood, broke
    across the plots, grabbing wide, hacking.
Orange aura,
                        earth marrying polar air,
spreads for the one who reads late, who looks up through
    drifting ash slumbers of the wide mind.

Thrusting up through root veins,
trafficking among cells
on either side of a fluently
definite membrane, force
fizzes over the real.
I crave the gradual
approximation of measures,
the way a breath pushes past
its beat and is carried, rippled.

Brahms in the salvoes and then Domenico
Scarlatti in the intervening rat-tat,
    beneath them beheld powers not held.
I may achieve a garden but I plant seeds.
Spacing stakes while, spiralling, the vine fastens.
    It is not magic, the quicksilver
bulge of Burgundy as it brims past the rim
and transfuses into the vintner, his hand
    that labored the one now that will laugh.

TIMES PASSING THE BREAKWATER

Intimate address
imperial and addictive
will move to annex experience
it glimpses but hasn't had –
and so, before our beginning, Termia,
before the claimed but unsurveyed
territory of your hair
parted across these decades, their cold neck
sleeving a hot throat and dark speech,
even then, as if you had been there,
my arm swept out in a wide gesture
to net the starched jibs
tacking and crossing –

hand isolated
in the sealed car as that mass smoothly
shot the stone causeway
in its groove of force.

At indigestible speed
Ezekiel converged
with the ballistic pellet, rolled grief word
dropped on his tongue, and swallowed.

Medicine, too, for the contained!
distributed along the urgent
metabolic fuse, into
imploded strophe and dispersed canzone.

Ignorant, what I'd assumed
but not wholly dreamed
was this: possibility as a body
naked, ageless, taking into itself
containment without limit,
curled in on itself unborn
yet with breasts gathered full to the knees
and its hands merged in devout cutwater, hair
pouring forward from the accepting nape:
emblem germinal and credal
with the sun over it unzoned,

179

hills and shores streaming into it
from a lifetime unbracketed –
each station of our going,
boats and their bright rowers hailed
as companions, the stranger
waving back . . .
that much came clear
as it floated off, lifting into view
even as it dissipated.

You had more on your mind:
through noon's bland core you were to stitch lightnings,
bread of Zechariah through his speared tongue,
the word of power like his bomber
planing in for its run.

One day, and one hour
threading the strict eye
of its incalculable instant.
Road by the sea.

*

From a late hearth
one spark, the aimed remnant,
gashes high through the gulf
its hypnotism of space, as desire
would dodge past morning: it has the flight
without the passage.

Neither as one thought
nor as two such, separate,
but as one contradiction
tensing to complete its arc limit,
we were taken up, were held
in one act of attention,
sputtering weld extinguishing first
one flux and then another
in the torch's mute issue,
and how long it bore
or at what frail height it quenched in a surf headlong
I cannot gauge.

                    The crest highway
streams with paired humming tracers,
and closed on itself the eye spins
their homing fire, draining,
until there is only the crew from yesterday's boat
spreading their nets along
the inlet, turning to inspect
cloud where it fumed up, squiggle
on the last high cast of light:
it is they, instinctively, who'll have drawn
some inference. One mind
and the turn seaward, crabs
pulsing through drenched sand.

                              *

Daybreak vapors swift poles past the train's tremor –
slow strobe through wet glass into the stiff skull.
Your terms are not yet those of she who saves,
gentler though terrible, surer,
able to say she'll return
to the light she came from, whereas
your endings extend codas through echoes, leading
down the labyrinth.
                    The signalman
coming off the last shift wades
his tide of returning self,
the numbed powers. What he hid
in the world was his effort,
hid with the unsaid and the relinquished,
his rhythm now their seal. Lodging it there,
he has not lost it.
                    But your manic
scribes bend over its fluid map –
you gag the throated rememberer and inspire
interpreters, as if the savior's glare
flashed falsely over the twelve
as they sat for the first time forming letters –

                              181

to your opposite, then, I turn:
though sleep still drags down
and the wheels' gargle spills me
with every other unready and contained
through the determined curve of fall, this is
one more hour that remains hers –
what has come back to itself from the four quarters
trembles, a needle that past nightfall has held
unveering though it went with me
and with you, her dark sister,
into the clean cold.

JONATHAN

Cancerous sun that uncurls, then
   eddies upon itself,
light that pillages the eyes: is it
   flood or filament?

Foremost in slaughter, Jonathan
   dipped his lance
idly into a stray honeycomb
   and tasted of it.

Bubbles from sandbars in shallows,
   waterbug flopping
over the pondface, his walnut shadow
   detonating in silt –

back, and then back along amber current
   as if I were still intent
by that bridge rail, fluid there within
   my detachment.

From a source, that flow ever newer, and yet
   at the same fixed distance.
And that is a place that I would not
   leave easily,

though the alders, burnished and pooled there
    in a fierce leafiness,
bring me to weep inexplicably
    and without bitterness.

Pressure in the grip thus easing,
    and bronze aim nestled
in a spear's trench, figure within figure,
    I would have rested.

For at every chance he had struck
    head from body,
the same music had welled in him,
    his time repeatedly

returning upon him. Hours, drowsing
    day of the brief lung,
may hear illness, another speech,
    moving towards song

as towards a dire antecedent, and follow
    over the grooved threshold,
one speed, many waters. He tasted of it
    and his eyes were enlightened.

Back, and still farther along the bright margin,
    dissolving until that stream
is neither water nor motion, and one is
    not yet among them.

The lifted forearm of even that man
    may wait upon this, may yet
forget the drone homing, the crow's eye
    poised over wheat.

HELLADE

High meadow: poppy blots
mazily responsory
to our star's impress,
clappers in fire's bell
after swinging, still blurry
in the ear's labyrinth,
while dry shadow trances
the moist floor of air,
weedy, a beetle fencing
with the ant to sever him
and the fragrance of his track.

Ivy twines a column,
girds it to carry it
through close heats burning closer –
has not forgotten rupture
from below, can infuse
fibers of flowing rock
into far architecture
while hanging into dwindling
clamors of fife, drum, yell . . .
rout has tumbled through,
and will, while lattices
cool in the interval:
elixir and alloy
fade white past the ford,
foaming trace of a vessel
that pours further, its rim
a home for broken column
rotting trunk
          and spindle
of the jay's cry, something heard:
ivied, spiralled, embittered.

A final runner's crashings
dim around that rhythm
he runs for, dulled tumult
of his will a winking sea
pressed in its bed. And that
other who fell, extinguished?

Augustine wept over Dido,
the hymn writer had Saint Paul
weeping at Virgil's tomb,
but has the female soul
been widowed by her ashen
husband of foundations?
Through this hot salt, honey
of clarity, the distilled
engendering of bees.

TALLIES

One may have lived much
yet topple plumb into ignorance –
may have mastered or endured such
    as confers dignity
    and cannot be subtracted,
    yet without dignity
    find only sufferance,

    because process reaped
as cleanly as rain-forest acres
get razed for cattle, air bases, and deep
    caves under Amazon
    for the Brazilian bomb,
    or as their burn rolls back
    paths of the trackers.

    At the grave of the unborn
supreme fabulist, whole-blown artificer
of the whole effect, motion untorn,
    no elegist can stand –
    its parcel wavers, slides,
    the name urn-breaker, sender
    of light far, lucifer.

On ziggurat high-rises
wind croons as to terns drilled in their cliff
or sailors swung near a sail's cheek, yet cries
    past likenesses, slides high
    where force interrogates
    thrusts of an anti-civic
    assertion, an as-if.

    A siren's tones
or truck tires overtaking the ear or sluices
through fever or synthesizer moans
    orient it, place it,
    whereas air is testing
    a proposition that lifts
    past its own terms and uses.

    The reaching glory
alive in its own time, not to be set
back or aside, no repository,
    let it be celebrated
    by fires overruling sleep,
    startled gaze blinking open,
    unweeping, irised wet!

    Early traffic
the irritant, a young architect
leaping it, cursing its horrific
    sweep down the Champs Elysée,
    supply one beginning:
    his vision snapped, it wasn't
    the cars he wished wrecked

    but the street itself,
its inability to absorb those powers,
new torrents strong now for the gulf:
    so away with it, off
    with its fungus of the cafés,
    arbor of faces, one's own
    student days, streetcar hours –

          thus Le Corbusier,
thence our block shafts out of blank grass, a park
undreamed of by the kings, the choked highway
          easing through it banked
          under heat shimmer, sun
          a rippled orb, lanes amber
          and diamond towards dark.

          Mold the unit then
stamp replications, cost of materials
dwindling as the scale climbs, as forms of men
          clamber and grow small –
          girderwork, preformed slabs
          slotting from cranes in the dangled
          leap down Mycenae's halls.

          From here, no shift
to a despot's patronage and the worked frieze,
passage over ripples to meadows, the lift
          onto cleared planes of sound,
          glow-edged flesh beyond morning –
          from here leaps aim through raking
          horns past anatomies.

          Deepness inhales, and depth
sighs out its unfathomable device –
no matter: to ride that uncanny breath
          is also to stand at a sealed
          balcony and look out
          on the weather, the eras
          as one mountain, world ice.

          (I was only one man,
I too required the protection of elves,
my birth ordinary, my path no plan,
          and for the bone bundles
          of my ancestors I was
          seeking in crumbling mounds
          for secure shelves.)

The clear light, because Alexander harrowed
the world's floor and had speared his bedmate Kleitos,
did not ripple from his cup. The wine's shallows
in night's tent, in pegged solitariness, though
clear, clean, washed towards a beach fire. From his boat
splashing inshore, he saw one of the lit stones
uncowl a face. It knew him. Led him up knolls,
sand, through scrub, thorn, onto scorified plateau
where a ground plan glowed within the rock pillow.
It was not recognition, yet he felt grow
before him the great edifice he would devote
to the full stretch of the reachable, hero's
and god's grasps interknitting, the peak off-load
of burden into governance. His guide chose
that moment to sweep him high, show their atoll
ringed with pulsating phosphor, then shoot below
to a mica-bright rock set where the porch rode
on the phantasmal structure rearing now whole.

Alexander, raising it, prayed. But it broke
in his face, a spout of bone dust, and time wrote
his term in that blast: one grows only as old
as one's temple. Brain blank, he saw his hand go
familiarly, and yet estranged also,
for the cup. That amnesia, a creosote
caulking the long crack in floorboard, hull, and road,
extends, extends. The desert general goes
in a squat tan Hummer to his triumph, so
the film star buys one, churns cloud wakes of the host.
Analogia entis! But what enrolls
memory in the electron and harsh strobes
through the mind conquering: in sunny dustmotes,
or carbuncles domed over Montsalvat, glow
of night unto itself around the Graal's float
at the peak's tip – these gleams over a cup's hollow
in the nuclear sanctuaries suppose
no acknowledgement: they wait, they impose.

Where does the stream go, where
are people going, and the stripped trees?
For a child's ancient interrogations, tear
    stanchions loose and renew
    the wandering teacher, some
    Dio in tattered linen,
    fire's brain over bony knees.

    Wisdom's river flows
into exile, out to the Dacian tribes
through irrigation ditches that legend throws
    under the rhetor's shovel,
    though to some purpose, glinting
    while sinking, growing acid
    in the soils legend prescribes.

    One foot in front of the other.
From village wells, clear water. Purple sleeves
of memory swirling with Trajan or Bismarck: *Brother!*
    So a world has more than one end.
    The ruling mind spreads arched
    and codified, the mind
    of a Greek is olive leaves.

    Walkers across the spaces
made for them move as shuttles through a loom
trade threads, or shattering sun changes places
    on water's noon piazzas.
    Mostly not seeing each other,
    comets and moons, they stride
    through a galaxy's human room.

    But to pull one tense strand
out of the fabric, rhetor? Tell us therefore
how the lone foot, the uncontrapuntal hand
    climb solo over villas
    terraced beside the sea,
    and over deep arrowheads
    from the tenth millenium's war.

To the grave weightlessness
of Aeneas bearing and leading through pity
the fury of shattered centers, to distress
    made good by replanting one's gods,
    he adds the center's long
    reduction, he stretches speech
    over a world-spanning half city.

How a painter rambling
in his wake might figure him, or disfigure:
over scorched plains a filmy derrick trembling
    into life, ventilated
    with hills and space, the head
    a night flight's metal flashing –
    yet missing his seedy rigor.

Though he means stones to live,
dress him as he is, star minimalist,
cast him as the wind a stone's hollows give
    way to, or as late rain
    tunneling a civic
    rockface while igniting
    mica in forehead and fist.

The choreography
of a plaza, when it unfolds a place,
legs in perpetual recovery
    of falling, mind floating ground,
    actually happens,
    faces willing to look
    at no one, yet wearing face.

Effort at ease, but effort!
What he exhorts them to, what they have listened
grudgingly for, perhaps attentively suffered,
    was what they walked into
    on other business. Stretch
    is what the muscle did
    and grab, but then it glistened.

To teach them crystal is not
fixity but formation in the flow
of event, ingatherings of a knot
　　towards ethical release:
　　this stumps the orator,
　　roars from the assembly
　　swirling in dust below.

Walkers into the weave,
momentarily monumental, living
curtain that rends itself so as to achieve
　　a flow it ignores, show us
　　not motion's decaying heart,
　　but how you slide speechlessly
　　into the ever-giving!

– From there, towers winking
on in the debt-instrumented dusk, staggered
bright bits, brownish purple of the sky sinking,
　　and the squares emptying out . . .
　　there he vanishes, cars
　　idling, exhaust illumined,
　　and the mute faces wagered.

IDES OF FEBRUARY

The flaked racing breath did not say it:
You will taste, one of a host,
the union of this age.
Blue robes hung down our white door.

On the wall Romans tussled
near the pyramid of Cestius,
heater chuffing, easing.
Brown arms piled angles and enigmas,

191

one body both advanced and fled,
one was the arrogant rider.
Blue on great white: ours was patience,
theirs amber, on skin, stone, air.

Danced conflict, half-sorted melee,
one of them king and fallen,
one thrust out of his city.
Snow blotted up the panes.

Each hour carves a circle
through whiteness, and a line
through time's honeyed no-color.
Between them, bodies swirl to birth.

Hours incise each circle, snow filling it,
and each line, once only.
Between, the world's bedded forms
stir unrobed and emerging,

the rider surges away,
contempt lifts him and the king quails,
an elder croaks malediction,
the new exile sees life stretch out,

robes divide white from white,
the towering pine and bed
collect blue, white, and great patience,
bodies tenderness and exile.

Circling groove slowly filling
and line arrowing without bend,
had your geometer set us
at the cut more keenly – yet

two others it was, cloudily
greater, bent on their veering
purposes, who achieved it,
blue tearing from white:

as a captain through days gazing
at butchery misted in cordite
becomes the army, while
at the far end of that arc

an inkbrush master, hour
on hour at his mountain,
the veiled life-giver, becomes
its few soaking lines.

ROMAN ELEGY

Streets under winter rain
at the tempo of violins
scaling the end of their pell-mell overture,
pit sinking to half-light,
stragglers finding seats
as the expected thing
gets ready to take fire
in a glare of paint, palms, curled façades –

where lava cobbles melt
with dung and runoff, and Goethe's
Arcadian wig wilts yellow
in a glass niche, streaming paperweight,
a whore bends down to snatch
banknotes loose in a gust
of the North Wind, and fates
send up their clattering applause
raw heckling and damp cold –

Red managers have followed
their refugees but take superior quarters,
shake hands with the commissars of cash
then slide down runways
lined with blue buds of gas
up, into outer darkness:
though nothing that once spoke for itself
still seems to, there remains

193

this buzzing, this seasoned
anticipation. I crawled
dimly lit galleries
to a crypt where Ugandan dancers
in exile mimed the Return of the Prodigal
and brought one spell of silence
to the labyrinth, echoing

crossing point for power
bypassed and the long crackle
of rubble-filled walls around a suburban bomb –

she has not willed it, but her hand has spread
open through afternoon as a lizard's playground.

And though they didn't inquire,
that pair hand in hand darting
from the squall down there –
though they didn't ask it,
what has that or her other
matinée, her scurry
of sanctity, got to do with
their searing entr'acte?
Whirled in a jangled era's
grasping hunger for signs,
we were not gullible,
yet met them when they fell.
Downpour, drum and soft cannon,
tambourine trailing off,
when again the high footbridge
of Caligula rose shining
against the deluvian and spotlit dark.

Fast through that night they sheltered
and the night of Constantine,
while the blanched eyes of stunned
Philoktetes looked out
from the borrowed eyes of Rome,
a torn spread wing in his fist
hanging along the morning.
And though their balcony
dangled verbena from a smooth earth pot
breathing pale coolness, they slept in the lion's mouth.

194

JARUZELSKI WINTER

It had been a gesture
whose performance you'd have capped
with raw conviction and rude irony:
packing old clothes for shipment
in relief, the realistic
sentimentalist's choice
of one misery from the heap.

Another entire people
put under lock and key
rather than bribe and buy-off
are not being punished, they are being coldly
tested in the cold.
Even if they choose
another martyrdom,
Termia, you and I
by sacrificing warmth
may search fire within ice,
not asking for what is not
given, yet holding to cold fire.

And can we learn? The dwarf
who shadows me resists,
imagining he stems
from peasants who have clustered
around white chapels posted
in stretched fields, a figure
bent now into huddle
with an old pair in their house
perched over a river,
concrete from walls and bridges
ripping past in the torrent.
They have drafted on bond paper
their letter of defiance,
fatal declaration, cemented
with bits from Gracchus Babeuf
aimed at exorcism
of the bullet-headed block-shouldered imitator.
But a snowy blast sucked it
out the window, sailing it

195

into a grove of poplars
still green along the shore
where paper and leaves both flashed
into crisping flame.

   The carton, then, taped shut
over scarf, worn jacket, greeting.
Ash from page and leaves
settled across it, weightless
measure of a madness
heavy with the dear grit
from older sand and lime,
honor, linked hands, the strict wager.
Prudence lies out of sight
curving away, its pull
slower, thicker, its silts
impounding the blood and breath
of patience, a brutal shrug
millenial but not indifferent.
And if you were not here to shudder
at that sometimes wiser
sometimes harder thing,
still your removal lies across it with
the turned-away face of the time,
recoil which shivers into fear squeezing
lower than bedrock now, whole tremors
before the tremendum cancelled,
yes, refusal that prefers
to unfurl that substitute, its own passions,
and lift cold gleams
of fleeing hair over rivers
to capture the sun's ignition
on the flat bends pressed farther,
stilled swirls in the amaranthine
fire of an unstanched flow.

BEGIN'S AUTUMN, AFTER THE LATE MASSACRE, 1982

Oracles of night spilling their catch,
shucked lemons in the Campo mixed at midday
with fishgut under shut booths: one is either
weighing, throwing them out, or being saved by them,
Bruno's ash at the pole of their bright field –
anticipated fruits as pungent crosscurrent
while the cusp of an era digs in, scrapes, drags advent.

Signs of your coming, Termia, cast a salt
lemony, just, prodigal with blood's futures.
But justification is not reconciliation,
nor will the notched wood hanger swinging beside
the pan scale of the fish seller ever span them.
And neither is this momentary Rome
the unaccountable moment men call Rome.
Cloud ragging upward in a silent rifting . . .

remembered . . . thrice remembered and forgotten!
Oracles of day, sentinels of these hours:
the sill cat at drugged dawn, the dog curled
in a bucket-cool stairwell through afternoon,
while in the leavings banking an evening street
a man kicks at a console, angling
for some relic of a signal, nudging loose
screechings and then a faithful listening
in plyed veneers playing back. Trumpetings . . .
unreconciling brasses unless they rise
from seen stones, and those same stones have risen
from towers that lift, evaporate, reform
through a wide arc of day not yet our home,
lift or are lifted, it seems soundlessly.

Or unless the herdsman swung bodily
by his own sheep south of the walls is not
forever the enemy – for they will die together –
of the stubby figure roughly dragged outside,
conspirators with him, agents shoving him
into a van, but not before he blessed them
with a quick stab of foreign speech.

                              The remnant
crouches to find the jewel: a southerner
kneels at a shattered facing block
prying at its focal bronze cricket,
the rot-green escutcheon of sensate life
renewing insensate luck on the caked hearth
of cobbles and the spilth of linked feasts.

Perhaps he knew you were on your way – he plucks
faster, jerks his head up, then hunches closer.

Evening leaves him at it, he too has
his mission. Evening, drawing its hazing
cadence from the unforgiving echo
given us to hear sometimes too sharply.
Over the pall rouging and yellowing Rome
at Rosh Hashanah, sickly sweet, over
the Arch of Titus Legion heaving the Temple's
golden candelabrum high in processional
pillage with lifted horns, there comes the sound
of Gideon's picked hundreds in the fenced compounds
of Lebanon, leveling the defenseless.

Whomever you choose, the hand you take in welcome
will not, in this place, ever be wholly unstained,
here where once more there can be no escape.

IN LAZIO

Saturnian lungs
    of stone pines
breathing up bright cloud,
    and the day's
stone is adrift . . .

a motorcylist
kneeling by his machine
spills oil into dirt
between milestone and plinth,

but there have come offerings
less casual, still filial, black wings
bringing down the Father's
dissociated cries, and wailings
stifled within the Iron Mother's
pledged columns.
                    From her calm
stola Plotia Claudia
reaches out a smoothed arm, towards
day burning past the next shoulder,
form broken off and the procession
weedy, gated in the distance,
past a car junked at gleaming hazard.

The family exacts
its tribute in the staid
eros of stone, its bonded
ranks and its overlapping
ranknesses
                    stylized
to freeze faith, fury, grief,
bravery and breakage in their long line:
even if it's only
the twists and not the ruptures
of continuity,
where are lineages
strong enough for that torque?
From such identities
grouped gazing I have turned
away with a darkened eye
along other roads, but now
I remember: marking out their names
the mason saw already
the red that would carve there.

PASSACAGLIAS

Thrown swallows, called to the delirious
probate of March, declare the unfinishable
resumed and teeming among the stopped towers,
near the plaque for a boy gunned down
at the street's turning, and they shrill their choice
of the entangling covenant, although
each plummet from the topslide of their arcs
obeys a command also.
The call of matter is quieter
than any conscionable inquiry, and longer
than a conscionable care for the way. Termia,
their swoop and hurl alerted me. I stumbled
among their summonses
and then rebounded. You were still ahead.

*

Lighting on him in the throng of strollers
I felt the jolt, your invitation.
He might have just left prison:
shopwindows stopped him, all their things
he watched as if in the next wink they'd move:
umbrella handles (imitation bone),
print kerchiefs, porcelain hounds.
Taped pupa wrappings of the woman drugged
on the church porch, a boy chinning himself
up to a ledge along the baker's alley,
possessed him equally.
He was testing each latch
down the corridor, world without escape.

You invited my half-identity
with a whole error, testing the low hinge
when a door, being rehung, still
twists on one pin and teeters.
He vanished into my fantasy of Michael

200

reborn into a freshened beyond,
his new eyes not yet telling him
that each turn of his gaze sorts fates
not in the old way, but now otherwise.

Your straggler, sent on before!
                                For although
he cannot get it right, still over him
up a crisp flue careening through air's levels
shot a moth bleached and enlarging,
unwrinkled in your fire,
white cell of a vigilance
willing to search high ledges in the flame
though soft, unwieldy:
                                if the sudden
were to show itself as a living
manifestation, this would be its wing,
its flutter, spreading a sisterly
protection, a frail powder
dusting both street and skull –
and if sound were to arrow up with it
clearing our hum, the harmony
would ramify, all trumpet
singleness would fray and the phantasm
fly solid:

                vibrating
strider in mid-stroke
blanching past the known whitenesses
of perishing, past the razored last ridge
of limitation, simply
as kernel of the face
unshown, bivalved seed of the opening hand.

                        *

(Cloudburst: and as I ran
down black lanes aiming for the bridge,
I felt a thing brush my leg
and then keep pace, wolfhound
pivoting with me in the turns.

You might have let him vanish
when I stopped, Termia, but he sat
waiting, a painted drum
strapped to his panting side,
the grey and red of the old Polish cavalry.

Unshivering in that downpour.
And I saw then that you were going to push me
past any chill that confirms your frisson,
past your equivocal election, back
into the ruined game.

Tomorrow when the street
channels its renewed surf,
the moons behind that roil
will send their companioning hounds
whippet-soft and cloud-thin
vaulting ahead, sharp for an unseen target
beyond the elected in his waxed limo
parting the waters with hood ornament
and covey of police, beyond the trailing
bit-players of the interlude,
phagocytes with timed satchel
lending snap to the anonymity
of shadows – past these permanent
rotations of the passing
towards that steel line which their little wheel
seems to have bent around into a stage,
on which they seem to align themselves
and seem to want to pluck
like the deep string of a guitar,
like that one string which the Greek
stretched and fingered, studying –
but forget, never touching.
                              And you were saying,
not how any of this concerned you, but
rather as the wife who sends laughter and look
from her pod of guests to her man, and then
returns to them, their voices keeping him
listening, fighting the near thing to catch
bits of that drift, you were saying
that the odd bond still held.

Your animal, different once more, had come
once more, not quite to remind, not
quite to admonish.

He stayed, then shot as mist through the drenched door
where last week a crone had leaned out
to stone a cat along the gutter,
but it had turned squirrel, pelted
with nuts and her rough intimacies –
skiros, shadow-tail
and ancient domestic
harvesting futures even from these streets.)

*

Bullfinch stoking his truculence,
blackcap his cheekiness: not for us
the ritornelli of divulgence, bland
authenticities of the personal gargle.

Bellied swirls of unclockable
cumulus graze across a calm
neither of us has known in long unsweeps
vaporing the mild furnace of sure days
or in the easing fatedness of rainfall.

If I spoke to my Thou as I do you
she might once more let me catch her
peering unspeaking into a fountain's bowl –
you guard the same attention and refusal –
at washed prawns left there like seeds to feast
on the insubstantial manna
of sunlight from another world.

What sky is to a soldier water is to her –
under the forebrain of the cumulus
savoring the blind bud of its thought,
he meets the overarching and just-born,
knowing as yet none of its dictates. Must
so much death die in me that life might live?

Under the brimming boundary
she locates zones where cities focus, streets
chiselled from house blocks, fluent cuts
that hold off being trued
and go on being quarried, walkers linking
hands like diviners. Bending there, she watches.

BOAT NEAR THE CAPO MISENO

Spur-scattered and burrowing a surge of sand:
   blue and orange down the ride of her,
tilted to hear the smashed breathing of aeons,
   so too the dazed may still live,

a painted fan spun to the dancing floor
   among the blind heels clatter-ribbed
and melting bolts oozing oxide of blood:
   so rummaging love tapers them,

   oh how the adze caressed you,
lightest curve still healing to the hand
   and the mathematical plunge
outward into the Punic element,

   caressed and raftered each city,
and in the Greek horse also it framed up
breathing beams, men itched and sweated inside her,
   outside they chanted hymns,

and now the tarred joinery of the mortises
   lies unburdened,
in the gape and roll of your undoing
   resin remembers the iron.

CAMPAGNA

Wavering blue floor
of a skiff in the field's river
softens a gash of red
down the slant wreck of brick,
marks the air's gatherings
where a language sank and still murmurs.
Columns, tasks, burnt sisterings
of hands torn away, towering
on the lip of sunny dust,
shag of spurting grasses,
mud of the breeding bank.
When I was struck from that tiller
it was in service, the overmastering
pulled me from it
into these alien hours
beyond a downsuck that men
much better have not beaten.
Blue fluency that I'll not
fathom, from that city
I have come back to pray you
never to bear my body
towards your beachings again
unless you set me down
with the other blinking survivors
beside the blooded stone.

'FROM AN ICED BASIN . . .'

From an iced basin at the window, solstice
splashed with spine sheen to a rolling fracture
of the fire entering, bather not there,
auburn Persephone bent rinsing slowly,
corona from the bowl O lucky waker!

full weave, but how could a loom have risen here?
Spindles of steel sorting sun into fibers.
Hers, but the seated one, worn threader
whose sleep was famous, foam washing years from her,
floating the treadle . . . she too was abandoned,
who would have thought these tines could tense and stand?

Wrath feeds on life, ire twists through mastery,
yet masters of life feed wrath without being consumed.
Spears these are, lifted by a sudden rank
down the room, hoarse salute a frame in air,
who wouldn't let them be posted to strike sky,

gather its gold along high edges, then
as one, reverse and plunge that sister of blood
where they stand, planting it to end a thing?
To arrive here their horses came many miles.
This last muster at dawn, who wouldn't watch it!
From calming water day curves up and over.

'HE WHO CALLED BLOOD BUILDER . . .'

He who called blood builder is now memory, sound.
Dear, if we called blood wrecker we'd not lie,
but how thinly we should hear time's curved cutwater,
and never the full song of the falling pine,
that swish the nets make running through swells gone starry.

The steersman heard nothing, and then felt nothing,
toppling through the salt humus of passage.
And when Aeneas taking the tiller gathered
our woody landfall, the turning belt of worlds
spread out sparks of a brotherly burnishing.

206

Memory may work for us as did his mother
Venus, sluicing his wound invisibly,
its hurt going as a flood
                              with which he heard
one life wash over and another rise,
but faster than remembering. He fought again,

and so the other thing may not be refused,
stand with me hearing it: from the bushy hill
the sound of fellings as huge nets hauled dripping,
plasma from slaughter clotting into nebular
founding stones, and smoke breathing screens of columns.

ZURICH, THE STORK INN

Before you had been brought by the forceps beak
of the common tale, before we had been dropped
by the wide-winged forestaller
of questions, the quick question
of being born had been born
many times for the asking, yet still
waiting, Termia, for your mouth
to reframe it, for mine.

   Set down beside the waters
of the Stork Inn, beneath
carousels and outsize
umbrellas, the spill of market Saturday –
leisurely miniature of what will win:
free play of forces setting
its own terms across all the stages . . .
stragglers caught by the throbbing or tinkly tune.
Whereas dark in your throat
gypsies huddled with cased violins
and zithers, cupped aside
from the tribes poured towards Sheol –
not harried this time, it was enough
that they played on your different keyboard.

And from the swung metal
of late summer towers, contradiction
of the anticipated and remembered,
belfries of a now,
camps and vast palaces of a sound
with no one center: from this
the ache to lift eyes wide
and hold them so, for whatever
might spring into beginning
though it fall short, through you, of the power to finish,
and helplessness, under the feathery surge
outward, to know which power may be more terrible.

Those you love you make stand
through a long vigil . . . so now
with the bonged bronze of ten towers concerted
through evening cloudburst
(Saint Alexander's day, though it is neither
his blood nor his forgotten life this fading
Zwinglian clangor seals)
and with snare drums of maskers
climbing towards a dragon
and gallows along a parapet,
I wait for the uptucked wings
of the ungainly bringer
to budge, for his unphrasable gift to cease
welling unpsalmed from afterbirth each instant,
for the prince of the powers of air,
earth, and underearth
to cease withholding homage from the mere seed . . .
thus watching one more hour,
while in the freshly wet
still tightening hemp of the noose
falls a body.

JUNE FUGUE

Down our jagged route,
Termia, you evaded.

Left to me was the plunge
through Capena, horse stairs
threading arches and faces
of the still human, unhidden,
to a ledge's burnt-out shell
with windows gaping onto

a gulf: and there I heaved
your relics, where swallows found them
inalien and steep wind
had long since shrouded the older
offering, three meters
in gold, by-blow of a god.

Channeling the wild powers,
friend of the violent,
Feronia lay masoned
where glass now cascaded
over black goat and straggling
fence line, night rising through them.

Here they put her or lost her,
tucked her in downwind,
Welle was hire bowre
What was hire bowre?
where overhead the crab
pincers its crystalline

alignment shut on your passage,
Hir bowre is of black lilye
seamlessly, although
you live more than the living . . .
her trellis is night rising,
thus in her hand I have thrown them.

209

Their bits are nothing to
the grit from your getaway,
whirling from heels and backturned
mineral glance – and still
they call you *history*,
our secular theologians?

When you climbed advancing
into the fissure, what shut
behind you was the gate
no one forces, although
the rill gurgles its seam,
pressing the cut downward.

Light going down, swallows and swifts throng,
scissoring fields, roofs, then the pine zone
and air's last pastures, grazing higher

always it seems mated, swerve with swerve –
but they do not strive so together
for companionship, they join because

both pursue the same quarry, and one
or the other will sink, roll, take it,
or flex back in torsions of the strike.

They, so much faster and quite other,
what holds them messengering here, down
I almost said, down, among, struggling?

For such balance, such fluidity
mean that the tendons lean steadily
into a resistance, gauging it.

What holds them is what must have cloaked you:
it has streamed us our time all this while,
thrusting the timeless ones next to us

in hovering passage, unfatigued.
Welle was hire dring, what was hire dring?
The chelde water of the welle-spring.

Thirty birds aimed at the unattained
and in thirty turns of their one flight
achieved range and alighted, so led.

Not so the lute player near the door
stretching behind him as a long skein
or gauze all the leafy and clawing

phenomena, all their piled strata
levitant, chiselled out, and flowing,
our world his phantasm, train and veil

for the impossible remarriage.
So she was the figure behind these
as long as I saw her through his eyes –

alma rock-hard by the filmed river
who, for all its years of sound in her,
never did lift her eyes towards it.

Welle was hire dring. Her example
was not yours: her world swept through, leaving
no rumor, and its wind has settled,

and its river has at last socketed
in its curve, so that one is oneself
listening but no longer hearing.

Past a barley field towards the cliff,
fat grasses and the early profit-
taking of dew, unclocked clarity –

sevenight fulle in the mor lay,
so her accountancy was not yours,
sevenightes fulle and a day.

Where night has garnered day
over Capena, tractors
starting up with swallows,
a brown-tunicked stranger stands profiled
on the ledge fishing, snapping line taut,
hauling in a black bass.

211

Where night has turned to water
lucent through the gorge,
he waits with the same joy
I dangled once over a sand bank
looking straight down on three speckle-backs
swinging fixed in the current.

The upward thread dragged by history
mounts through your treacheries towards those
fulfillments your own hand encoded –

the phantasm of your unique bond
radiates from a core blindingness
that takes fire in the eyes of many

but with grace quenches in the bass stream,
shimmering beneath the brown stranger
sevenightes fulle and a day.

Death winged and joy fishing,
winged life and a great fisher
tensing the floated line,
you have laid the drenched weight of your catch
on my heart and played your light tackle
like a stringed instrument.

Mutable lithe wrists,
tendons attuning me,
jerking along my length
as the line shivers and the mouth lifts
wide, unbiting up its wriggling arc –
finding its high, last strength.

And if Feronia were found
that quickly, offering herself
hotly? The fisher climbs
past fine limbs waiting to be parted,
lips, hills, clouds, waiting to be parted,
onto a second ledge

and pulls in his next catch,
past any offering
buried and rising here,
for she has taken more than she gives
or brings back, *black lilye, gold lilye,*
has sealed it with your glance,

the glitter in it a hot
spray like key grinder's dust
snowing from the file –
but again rising to a third ledge
he twangs the line like a bow's, he lands
the tribute, and approves.

My unswerved eyes still smarting
from grit long flowering
in her chamber, the salt
in her galaxies, I would constrain them
into paired wings, aim them below sight,
and prepare to push out.

CENTO BIBLIOTECHE ITALIANE

Filipo Neri collared the gay-blade nobility here, schooling them
in chant and laughter
With a wife like that, and Chiron as fosterer, how not go far?
Intarsia books and lute, perspective lecterns, medallioned cities,
for one man . . .
One shoe off, one shoe on, that's got to be my son Iason
. . . while on hills opposite she strives up the goat path, laggard
sister

Spawned in the sheepfolds of Hermes when that
fleece-gold lamb's back flared
its ruinous wonder through the flocks
of Atreus, breeder of horses

213

Foyer a gauntlet of vellum, overseer the lion-headed hominid of
   time
   What you lug piggy-back may be a wild woman at the river,
      but what steps down is your fate
Newman's hymns drifting over the Notre Dame goal post, practice
   kicks refining loft and spin
      Forethought on sword's tip and shield's ridge, afterthought
         nowhere behind
She looks up, he looks up, their coats on companion hooks, into
   a future
      Snort-fire and the bull's testicle to cool him, then a pebble: the
         demon-army will squabble over it
A memorial film on Mrs Woolf, the five sexes wisping at inter-
   mission
      So oak took to wailing in the kelson: *Wash your hands in the pig*
Stale breath over a stale page: *Stravinsky è con gli ortodossi!*
   obviously
      Hang high the booty, a slow twirl under the thunder shaft, and
         pray hard
Rosettes on Keats' blue last ceiling, through the window waves
   over the gunwale . . .
      Beach that keel in the maw of Earth Trembler, back off softly
. . . in one sound, water in and out of the boat, fountaining
      Now we are seven and again seven: our daddy was a travelling
         man
Looking up from Jackson Knight on Virgil's hot-line to the muse
   – for J.K.
      After she had done everything for you, you could take every-
         thing from her
had tapped into it – I see a friend shovelling worked stone under
   to age it with worm scurries
      Follow the bouncing ball, follow the little fellow behind it,
         follow and fall
The man who savored Bentley's anathemas, at the balcony
   weeping, his wife gone off
      Lullaby-lay, down draco down, lullay-loo-lay
Under oak and glass, Augustinus, sirocco of African mind
      Excellence herself as the matchmaker and maid of honor; what
         then went wrong?
'Ten minutes on the ladder, like a large closet, got the accounts,
   then tea with the Duchesa, and the door'

Magick him away – do the demo, then slice him and ram him home

Elephant in the portal cornice, apse window past the stacks: Malatesta

For neither med school nor law school, yet set aside after getting him through

Hope Not Nor Fear: but make fast that book trellis with wedged mortising

Send the pretty thing a new robe, and put some feeling into it

Van der Weyden's gentleman with an arrow, two red slashes through the grey vane

Send your children to the temple of the wild woman at the river

purchased then lost the same day, left in the locker and poached

Seven and seven ripped from the altar and stoned: let Euripides retell it

Knight of the Golden fleece, pelt as brooch slung from its noosed midriff

Mad Herakles awaits the touch of your red, your black, your golden hand

Gold carcass with hand sleeving the shaft sketch the heart's pyramid

The last interloper, unfixed from the stone bench of hell, packs you off to Italy with your snake primer

Passing beneath the left arm, it has crossed the core and held fast

Like Helen at Karnak, you have a last rendezvous with Akhilleus

There is no extracting it though the gaze drifts far, pooling brown rain

Like Hebe the unstained, and Faust the blasphemer, you lodge in the glad pastures

It cannot be lost, has penetrated and now lies over, the grip easy

He turns away to returning love-boy, she returns to father and recrowns him

Arimathea's ladder at that angle, corpse slung sinking, risen luminescence

—— • ——

The dove flutters contrariwise through the harp of proportions · mineral refraction: bright travellers warped to the loom's frame

—— • ——

One boot in Hades and you're due back there · columns tenoned,
  altitude tasking their footing
  Valtellina and Val Camonica · walls in the House of Aietes
One page, gusting sorrow and wide night · louvre those
  clerestories over the Corso
  Hands aloft in prayer, sun aloft · arms forked and fire also
  reaching
Inter pres · two ceilings from two lives, the equation breaks there
  Larches rain on the stone map, doodling it gold-orange ·
  Etruscan then Latin
Your lady's poison but your name is medicine · over the lintel,
  twined serpents
  Fields, roofs, wagons, ox teams, recorder of deeds · decimals
  saved us
Stuccoed headstones dug from the garden, our door · *Inter alia*
  The sickle moon on Falera's low stone, eroded · humidify the
  Physics
The zodiac cupola's jungle rot · light reddening in the hair of
  fleeing Berenice
  Swordsmen facing off on raked raceways for ice · lettered
  lintels, numbered stalls
Monops, monoglot, monosandalos · plenitude in a point
  Strike high fire's dangling rays, and a hand greets you · buttered
  thumbs on Bread's vellum
Hair shining down his rube's back · at the coat check, gleaming
  baldness
  Water in the moon's saucer, aligned with sister stones on
  sunrise · stretch and rise
Sun's home and dim hall of invisibles · that white head cradles
  half our catalog
  Five knives and eight parallels new under the sun, berry stalks
  and stag · focus floats and so gathers
Escort from the hel of Helios, that girl-Odysseus, his fire in her
  veins · gild the bronze Psyche
  Magnified I frays, the groove's ridge stutters · *typus*
Vellum yellowing insensibly · scissor rocks nipping the last dove
  Plant a tree, raise a child, write on stone · water, bark, rag, hide,
  acid, gold leaf, berry juice
Lectern pews for praying shoulders and impenitent knees ·
  Herakles at the oar bench
  Knives laddering the rockface · her wedding prelude a clatter
  of unsheathings

She will empower you outward but not to delight · marmoreal
skirt swirl
Orfeo accompanied by drawn swords · plough sword stone-
word, verses epos script
The central steps ripple, flankers holding fast · Orfeo tipping up
the hatch cover
Lump of earth my milkmaid · 'You clasp me? For your
children's children I am home.'
Converted church, stacks brimming, time's catamaran · keel laid
by Athene Argó
Solar sisterly stares, Kirkē and Medeia, murders emerging ·
candelabra in both corners
'Well, buried another pope. Let's get some coffee!' · Deathbed at
rest in the archives
Miming the moon's curt circle, troughs for blood · margin
gutter margin
Rustle of ledgers and poplar tips · Orfeo to Apollo: Crystalline
passage, please
Even before mucky Chthonia went sun-bathing, Aion was
mixing and matching
Dry stench of bindings, Phineas' food · Apennine thermals, Rietian
breezes
Quartz veins through the image · chevroned angle of reflection
Dragon vomit and death's vanquisher · herb-smoked scroll
unrolling
The Son down from the cross leaves the cross · corpus down
from the shelf leaves the long house
On both seas active, the isthmus sleep · sun cresting on PLATON
every January
Codex a cave uncoiling · stone cerebellum labyrinth, death as
seen by the sandal
Portage through twelve nights for three women · time's keel is
lettered but the sea's eyes blink at nothing
Kirkē's Italian hearth scorches off homicide · uncial obits bound
in pig-skin
The Son of Man led the Round Dance · whirl of the twelve above
caves burgeoning with amethyst
The walls whirlpools of gas, within, blindness · equinoxes a
fever chart
Spirit's fierce ring but only while forming · nape columning up
out of salt sheens · or resolving back to the standard and
twi-handed

Flint's channel · quill's wake · subacid superiridescence
Swing your partner · round she goes · cross-indexed raftered
    ribbed
  Ich bin Kristall · the boat's strict rib your skull's hammer · angles
    solid content variable
left right · above below · on back · leaving homing
  Roseate ·dodecahedral · smaller than carbon's ring · in and out
    of time

sections, LITTLE FRIEZE

[2]

  Looting fury and torches:
  sheeny cuirasses hovered
    in the smashed portal,
five rays fanning in as the flat steel of swords.
  They stood sweating among timber shreds
  Looking in along the probes of that steel,
  walls high around me, terror unswallowed.
    But then with muffled drone,

For one thousand years, for another thousand years,
  the spread of a crown claimed that glare and upheld it,
    broad silver in the tired house of blood,
    flared prongs in the glad seat of blood,
  Through one thousand years, through another thousand years,
  and the fading chink of stonecutters, and the dwindling tread
    of women bearing them water.

[3]

Huge light, calm pool, and a great dawn shears evil,
a sky lens, as one mind, lasering it –
but overfull, shattered, salt Isaiah or Ezra.
So the raised voice went awry, the wind took it.

Now from Potomac to the old land: the Pershings –
new angel gave not the hardened but the mobile.
In one contracted room curls her prone form
while space, wingless, extends the vast lily.

Below, circuit and angle propagate
in fragments of wheel rim and axletree
while night skims overhead with their iron pattern,
black quadriga tugged by foam-lipped breathers.

The sleeper, still real, dear, ephemeral,
neither withdraws from the messenger nor draws near,
while the city, not yet returned to the dust
drifting down on it, floats beneath the reins.

[5]

Let the high grass caress
saving errors with the wind's hand
and keep the lines of transmission
open.
        But is it easy
to man the lines when the operators
have taken to spoofing the notion
of getting anything straight,
and dismantle the switchboard, and
issue bulletins about
the filmy nature of testimony?

The antique bomber rumbles.
A bowl on the table trembles.
Sun is a pool on the rug.

What do I look for now
in the long push of river,
coldly living head
anchored like a salmon's
sculling within that power,
anchored over shadow
    rippling its bed
and fluid sun of an hour,

219

net that takes
gradual gleaming hold
bending, and shakes out fraying gold.
What do I swim for now
in the pouring length of river?

Cries weave out in common
from the hawk-shrouding tree.

[6]

As with a spark blown upward,
dangerous, sudden, clear:
a city swung below,
Ephesus, its far bay
and a yard where silver burned,
smith hammering the Graal
still early in the day,
bell sound, shiny crack
threading cores of suns
packed humming on a wire
curved close enough to touch –
then silence in the colonnades
when Apollonius turned
halting in his speech,
stared and stabbed at the air:
Strike at the tyrant, strike!
Domitian dying in Rome,
god there and here, the dreaded
inadequate god of two aeons,
submitting on the small
anvil of a man's reach.

   This in one roar
over the world away,
this from estranging height,
our demos frightened or blind
or both under faint cloud,
while the half memory
of some cold, clinging fight
sank to a darkening floor.

220

[7]

Warmth at the long window
out of the blue split wide:

a man planted his cane
into cobbles, peering right,
the wine seller flapped
faded yellow tarpaulin
free of dust, a girl
jeered at four men playing
soccer by their shops,
a red-skirted woman ran out,
her mouth clamped across pain,
a crone lifted her finger
toweringly along the sunlit
ruin of her face.

Facet of the stone, flashing,
that seems to give life to me,
yet this is only half
the grid, and the jeweller cleaves it
open with a dark stroke.

THREE LITTLE ODES

Auguring come the phantasies of a boy
who though becoming no builder knows transepts
red as the underearth of Pharaoh's temples
furrowed from sandstone, the sea's crumbly amber.

Under the fate-winker, high, hugely fallow,
the blueprint of our seed has lodged in halls
judgingly neutral, where an effigy
plows up sleep with man's hands under man's head.

Explanation goes on through the long watches,
soaks warmth from the mute fires. But already
when they were children murder thrice renamed
silted their air to stone, blotting the patent.

Bryhtnoth at Maldon let cold sea harriers
unimpeded achieve the dirt causeway
being a fair man, fatally he let them.
Loyalty, estuary fog, men's cries.

*

I gathered my childhood songs
far from my birthplace, in eroded Carthage,
  tenements burying the moist
bulk of uncarved tribunals, mossy blocks
    dripping rough Caesar's rust,

    where I heard again the crumple
of the rotted beech back of me on a hillside,
  when the crash made me cry *Domine!*
Not quickly do men cherish their walls and rooms,
    and travellers take their way.

  To be alive now as the
custodian of momentary escape
  is to dawdle after the first measure
among pediments edited by sharp grasses
    nodding towards the shore.

  When the present bells out to a bowl,
a shell of oxides, enamels, airy forest,
  then the month called nine falls eleven,
and throws down its shields along the steep path,
    and lives wherever driven.

  To be alive when the tether
of order has yoked the sun and severed it
  with a stroke heavier than the legions,
and the oak of Subiaco stands vaporized
    by a thought, the unknown imagines

  but the flesh will drive to know,
will ready itself to harbor, and not hold off,
  nor chant the fallen trunk upright,
nor call the swallows back from their long homecoming
    to the fire swinging from sight.

*

Not one of the tragedians
drew the knife through Iphigenia's neck.
None of them was able to haul that far
   her slight body. On the altar
a meteoric deer bled mountain blood
   when men dared look.

   And the imponderable
weight of her betrayed promise they hurled
delicately to the outer limits.
   The young bride dwells in black Tauris.
The separated lamb grazes grey rock tufts.
   It is far, the world.

Far while flowing through, its orbit
arrowing up within diamond freshets,
pouring with animal tact through bloodrush voices.
   And so I shall set out for the straits.
The rumorous stages, the sting of the Black Sea beaches
   will not outreach it,

   the shore will unlimber, jamming close –
the last approach, guessing her gown's salt fleck
from that long thunder, quickly over –
   and the first touches will mass, meet,
the frail, granular, shuddering green rock,
the grey, greatening, ponderous, fragile wave,
   fuse in the shock.

TURNS NEAR VINCIGLIATA

When April
gusts through mold-marked cypresses
lending tough sprays to flame shapes
along lanes girdling Monte Cerceri
and a flag iris ripped from the wall top
splashes a nova
over night-shining curves of road at midday,
it has begun to be far;

when paving stones
mound through returning rains
not so much as cameos
or ambers through the flash-stasis-flash
of a carver's lamp under the centuries' wet chisel,
nor as the hermit crab's hump
through tilted sand runneling silver
after the wave-suck, his canker
the clamp of a back-tugging aeon,
nor even the multiplying
curves of blank wakings, not quite stone not quite eyes
neither a street nor a face,
then the span has stretched far enough
to take the measure of more than trudged-out aimings
and to pull them all, as water
over paving stones, tight and straight;

when rooflines lock
into their habitable puzzle
or genially crazed plate from the ridge,
singular angles nestled and absorbed,
it will begin to be far yet still
condensed around the renewably
outworn, winking on as air darkens –

even bridge piers
on the far rim will collaborate,
letting ungraphable
convergences poise the cone
of remnant fire on its arches
and two dolls flat along the span
to bear a towering figure, neither future
nor evening's vast figment, its wide arms
not to fall until what has passed for life
has been swept by its updraft
into its imponderable stand:
not all those weddings we have forced
with Death the Drummer, our
demanded certainties, but itself it offers
in the fires it kindles and veils,
blesses, it seems, the pair there,
though whether they give human place

to its height and pressure is obscure,
they lay there because for them
there could be no other crossing.

Not for them the climbing glitter of our near shore:
we shall be known as the ones
over whom a flood of the unlasting
swirled its picturings of phantom
abidings and bright cheats.

For them, seeing has been changed: the readable,
replicated in a bland light, grows arcane
while under sun's weight the encrypted temple
raises its profile on a near wall.

The soul does not need many images – the needed
impress bites and takes hold
with sounds maybe of speech
maybe of demoniacal or divine
flutings to be disentangled,
or as hands have sometimes etched it, the winged sayer
not blatant but muttering to her
through a wall blind and mortal:
if lucky, a sound
fringed like a philatelist's window
with the gentians of mint issues,
cored with the shifting glossiness
of phenomena over frail perforations,
all of it to slip towards whisper
and be far enough, the valley past
uncandled flames at the road's bend
fathom green and then lighter
under the clouds' passing.

ANIMULA

Hotel window, and lakeshore
mists throwing lamplight back,
yellow of landing lanterns,
into the room until
a boatman snuffs them out.

And this immensity
expanding through the black
O little one, this thing
in pang to begin to live,
swung by its feet like a bawling
Petrarch, what use will you
make of it?
              When the shine
of the high hours goes, a man
may seem to give steel to his years,
hands welded to the wide sill,
yet gapes like a child before
the dark auras
                     flaring –
may seem to have come
to a new footing, watching
couples from the boats
trail after children at the lit landing,
yet stands there under the spell
of the hint, the requirement
of our hard second entrance, its keenness
lifting the snail-wet umbilical
sheen of far inaugurals,
no longer far from this shore.

BEFORE A JOURNEY

Laying down small branches as a kindling bed
for the lopped giants. Piling them into thatch.

Their bark rivering the palm with a cow's tongue,
their weave roping childhood muscles over shoulders.

Crossbracing the topmost ones with fatigue's blessing:
though no meat roasts here, there is procedure in this

older than the last ice, its curtain through this valley.
And the hour stands over against us in grey robes, Abram

with reaching rod: *These cattle and sheep I scatter,*
herds of smoke will remind me of who I am.

Beginning the burning with deliberateness
and no voice, with steadiness, seeing whatever greatens

among the feeding tongues, knowing I have stayed
to labor for them to the end,
                                                    when I might have

pictured more completely, adequately,
ungovernable dangers and so cremated this present,

might have tumbled with others from the suburbs
after the prophecy, sermon, mass baptisms, tremors,

and the vermilion cloud dusting Constantinople,
streets unechoing at midday, the Emperor

and his bishop camping in the fields. Last branches
pour their forms out boring down into blackening gold.

BORDER

Swiss bunkers on the Rhine,
weeds bearding concrete that bears
plank marks from the forms
to shade trout fingerlings
nibbling in shallows, leaping

and we have found the leafy
Roman watchtower base,
four vanished stories, and crashing
through have startled hawk wings
widening out over the motionless
fieldmouse

       There is incalculable
speed in the floating thing self-contained,
weight hanging in empowered
patterns that have not yet unfolded,
which even those who have lived out their fates
have feared
         so is it a hope
that may go farther,

            hope for
  life of the path
that goes out, that looks up
  and is not crushed –
down that path farther
  or the wheat track
a German farm girl had made
over there, Swiss widow now,
made every time she hid
her friend at night, a swimmer
either side would have shot.

KAYAK ISLAND

From their shore into the curled race
   they push off, battling foam –
   slim prows finding aim
   while helmets spin and shine.

Bright primaries, fibered resin,
   aluminum, impact plastic,
   with timing in the trellised
   nerves, the inward tree.

Bobbing in line, hovering where
   rip eddies buoy them,
   together they wait out
   the rhythm, alone in the rush.

Each cycle one or another goes down,
   righting in a slow pour –
   we push out but go also
   into, into and under.

And then back – the risen spume swooshing
   around one buried tone,
   men and women recircling
   through their insistent image,

working it deeper on crumpling silk,
   restamping it in melting
   silver, in forming pewter,
   founding, establishing.

Yet where we clung once was a ledge
   rimming the tideslip, breached
   curb to the suave returning
   surge, the great opponent.

Where we came who remain scattered
   though watching, was a place
   where brown kelp sometimes lost
   their holdfasts, and went out.

Blunt margin of a binding law
   whose teeth whiten and drain –
   blunter than fear at being
   called out of the known.

To have been led out is to leave
   each other to that leading,
   where periwinkles smashed
   from their rock crevices

will make their way on a piled swell
   to native height, and grip,
   come back from their diffuse
   endless captivity.

And we are cut off, we begin
   to go forth secretly
   out of confusion, many
   are those who must go forth.

Somewhere already they are leaving,
   their feet sound in the small places,
   the ear hearing them loves
   that going and waits long,

waits long through the attentive pause
   whose gatherings are farewells,
   whose psalmist is a raw
   scattering of crows.

The last fleck in the lifting flock
   maintains two intervals
   tenuous and electric
   with earth and with his kind.

EVENING CONCERT

A swollen pink hand shakes with palsy
but the trio sweep it into their current
where it lives, master of the meter,
mute interpreter of water.

As in the tales there are two of us
yet everyone else is at hand also,
transparent to us without our looking,
murder with love in the lull before pizzicatti.

The violist steadies, and brotherhood
spreads from him, his companions nod to it,
for these are the kin privileged by twelve deaths
under moons no man has inventoried.

The one who feared his own will to heroism
but came to a martyrdom new under that name,
newly hidden from our sight, stops
his bow at the steep end of that phrase,

so that the scribe, Entangled Figures Master,
who insinuates Job through a vine arbor,
can cut through it all with one stroke, and where
history stammered a listener now leans forward.

Polimnia in the steely gauze of Cassandra
disshevels herself in a whirl, my heel-sharp
Polimnia who then tucks one finely
clenched hand under her studious chin.

Even in the last cadence, spotlit,
a tripod of pine burning by the doorway,
night planted near it in striped pantaloons
and those who came to hear entering in.

END OF JULY

Of longing, Termia, the sharp specifics know
no end, and down its progress the sharp days
lose no edge, the hours
crumbling streambeds to strand
the source deeper in summer. Orchard ladders
lean into the moist sheen of dark globes.

Near Baden under swallows, one
belltower cut through vineyards, banners out,
when the wish fixed me, rash
as blind archery, to lift
one clean impulse streaking out of the ruck
even if it landed wide of your touch
while quarter-hour strokes
through worn maroon face rings rounded
on their gold mark.

   Slow tones, swelling
things to a lightness – but if
that shivered me, it wasn't from forgetting
how separateness the cold angel converts us
to our fixities,
nor from denying she turns
each of us in her fire
like hickory seasoned for a torch,
nor from ceasing to share in her trade
of thrust, chill, thrust, the injustices
giving and taking justice in good time,
no one shouts the recognition,
it will not cry out in us,
yet they rang out, bronze
minutes, the bronze years,
with blunt frayed rope those changes
threading the spin of one swallow
who still climbed slabs of vapor thickening
over vine and crest, then
targeted down through harvest,
his poverty with ours
uncancelled yet his riches
plunging, sounding there

while bolted counterweights
thudding inside their dry tower argued
you could not hear, and claimed no one could tell you
how they made medley, before the orisons
of Roman candles and rocket wails
broke from streets below:
Unification Eve.

FANTASIA ON A THEME FROM DON GIOVANNI
A Jocose Apocalypse in One Movement

Bring the strings up from nothing,
   violins from the sands,
from stone powders for the justicing
avenger who promises a fire
that will set all right and cure the heart.

Sets fire and holds it and wields
   his rapier of care,
blade of ages a quick floodlight welds
to hot feeling ever returning,
high motto of Don Ottavio!

A knight's pledge to the besieged
   soiled soul of the world,
the betrayed spirit in silks and edged
golden nothingness without which things
sink to lead, ooze to the final mud –

pledge sealed by snorted or yelled
   refusals, espousals
of *No!* by the ranks and rich, one guild,
revolutionary quandary
when at last headed off or bought off . . .

we've waited for you, sir, have
    longed for you with dull pang,
though each heave of our animal love
trails the rakehell Don through his pell-mell
descent and pillage and abandonment,

trails him, anticipates him –
    our master sniffs the air
and we take the contagion, the drum
guiding us at wrist and heel, ruckus
of blood repetitively wedded

to glad eternals of mood
    gladly delegated,
happily feathered in haphazard
changes of role, though we'll see it all
inscribed, oh yes, we'll chart each sad bed.

Brahms stayed away and Shaw stayed
    farther away, rather
than watch the radical thrust downplayed
to the jovially curial,
its low triplet of protest turned cute.

The relaxed second cellist
    with her small part, alert
to the stage, smiles up at a new tryst –
and yet her role is not marginal
if she lays down her bow and gazes.

Two musics from life's two books –
    marrow of the mired bone
whistled forth into astral statics
by the mouth of rain, then man's long tune
whose constants get woven as one dance

for the three orders, gentry
    and pass-thee-by middle class
and pipe-shrill stompers from the country,
woven as hum for the Don's ballroom
enthrallment of a pledged peasant girl. . . .

But the force of a dark farce
    pressing real darkness
from a whole order into one man's cries
leaves out our armies, our furnaces,
summarizes no red horizons.

From the Sea of Marmara
    one stone inscription
cuts lines far into a tomorrow
Mister Zarathustra told Mister Nietzsche
to watch for, tap-tapping at his door:

Oracle of the Sybil:
    when Dionysos
shall have dined to his satisfaction,
then blood and fire and dust will be poured
together. So then, good luck to you!

while the Church had its stones curse
    badness with harsh goodness:
VIRTUE FEARS NOTHING OF ITS OWN FORCE.
Can you step past these, knight, can you hope
to innovate for love? Though it's late

for love wholly to remove
    its supercharge of rage,
there is time for the steeled voice to move
iron law in its own heart, and draw
more than hurrahs for tessituras.

Idolize you though we will,
    give you the stride of a god
as you approach, like pylons in file
across our hills under great cables,
you must remain human or go down.

No difficulty
                there! You
    will most likely carol
coming revenge while making soft-shoe
shuffles to the rear and a side-door –
our cynicism, your realism.

(But the unknown makes a suspension,
while the known confirms it: our version
can go only through the end of the first act, leaping
where the stone father has not been, and go on hoping.)

The second cellist, her hand
   resting across the strings,
mutes no smile, she will not understand
anything not amorous, and not
hopeful in the end. And she's no fool.

Those furnaces, those armies
   out of paintings, came out
of an eye so far within it sees
from a high cliff, to the lowest shelf
of fiery dust, through the still-wet past,

to its last zone, the open,
   the unblinking, the wink's
density of now
                  infusing then . . .
where
         the first ones – the pair at last
meeting – under clear bells stand mating.

A kiss on the shore of space,
   curl of the wave turning,
green-windowed comber rinsed clean of mass,
of forest slash-burned, of shafts deepened
under ramming arc-lamps . . . yet no dream.

Kiss no kiss will inherit,
   earth given unto earth . . .
water loves the low places, spirit
has gone there, and we into desert
no more to damn the red earth that is Adam.

(Goodbye Leporello, Zerlina,
Donna Elvira, Donna Anna,
swift interchange of faces, Masetto and the Don,
motion out and away, Norma, Margaret, Tam Lin.)

Sundays, German villagers
    gather on knolls and hills
by the Autobahns, to watch the cars –
old and young lovers as spectators
of all those others, the bright rivers

slicing in close pass-pass, phased
    procession, recession,
lulling and agitating the gaze,
a vast circulation without rest
not quite festival or spectacle.

This is no city, this place
    between cities, the sheen
of glass and metal and a swift face –
this is a step out from that, a leap
past the walls and gated terminals.

The Don led his parade down,
    to be sure – absorber
of essence into his heaviness
the way a stone sinks into snowbanks
with the sun's weight, hurrying black heart.

Through Dresden, skies of London,
    through flares of the long fire
at Alexandria, eyes undone
by the fall into their space may pull
evening from evening, going

out of focus in the deep hearth.
    Yet a glow may show through
the altering floor of the betrayed earth
the way wheels take form in the ice walls
of a cleared mind at its blue demand,

shine as the ground's own vision
    of itself to itself,
plain thing that will be a hard doctrine.
And so shining, like the steel-bit line
of the engraver, it may give her

a seed picture, no summa,
    and desolation may
rest as the plane of return's rumor
trustworthily, not for unearthly
restorations, their cloud salvations,

but as rudimentary grid,
    spokes of the wheel awake
in a first motion, an unhurried
leaving, with the woman and the man
tracking coolness through the heart's distress –

winding to their city, bound
    for the edge of all edges
at the rim of western fire, the wound
of all light held by its towers and healed
by the many
    beginning to speed there
        over land and sea,
    beginning.

STANZAS FROM THE BRIDGE

Darkening the dome
of Peter and the castle
of the smiting archangel,
swifts in churning billows
    finish October,
revolving without sound
through the eve of All Hallows
    over Tiber.

I number my own dead,
but while these clouds wheel
I feel a change of scale,
dilation in the breath
    and time's working –

238

more than a thousand, they
will not scatter to death
   without larking.

Suspended, blankly lifted,
I watch them weave confusion
layer on layer towards precision –
the near ones fast and black,
   the high ones slower   .
and grey on the hypnotized
dome of the open. They tack
   and dive a full hour.

A man with radio
pressed to his ear stares up,
a widow in black cape
buying tomorrow's flowers
   squints, holds the view,
and coming home from the flics
through bankside sycamores
   lovers look, too.

Who among us has seen
the thing? who alive
has numbered the beast that will give
its sequence to our days,
   what our days saw?
These don't tremble while tossing
and shuffling the fierce maze
   of the hidden law.

Gladly, now, they're embodied,
the tiny and terrible
cohesions of the small
levels, the burning bonds
   airy in things –
silently they are bodies
pouring out along glands,
   bone hollows, wings.

Men and women alone
who sometimes become seers

of terror the Alone shares
feel only brief terror when
    giving it greeting –
feel that unspeakable touching
go through and then on like spun
    galaxies meeting.

Hours beside a candle
before the cooling dream
had consigned hours to time,
that was a time for learning
    the way these play –
flecks of soot swimming hotly
to the sipping wick, then turning
    in bursts away . . .

if I'd looked up from that
and at that moment become
what I now am watching them,
it is the pale flame in power
    I'd see overhead,
swimming unreadably
above them, this tall hour
    of the living and dead.

RHAPSODY FOR THE GATEKEEPERS

Alas that was an encampment where I had bivouaced too often
    before reporting for the first time.

So that warders required no password and the barrack-allée of
    winter poplars whistled up my intent.

Numbed and skittering from me: piety. Through flickering
    documents strewing my discontinuity: piety.

This was no whirling fatigue of a strict passage followed by its
  clear fields, but a Suebian stone rolled shut behind me in
  the embrace of blank acreage.

The expulsive sword of flame bent back on itself at portals where
  branch tips nuzzled spurs along wire, perverse similars.

In beerhall windows masks wobbled on, blue fur sheathing icy
  tusks, and through their heedless warmth I smelled boys'
  hair, defenseless.

Vessels calming in coves, landing parties foraging upcanyon, had
  dwindled to naive predestinations, trellises down June
  avenues, in a crystal lattice whose interlock was all our sky.

Ranked poplars sentineled a ducal quiet while snow squalls in
  reverse tremolos indulged the sentiment of time.

Filleted, dispersed guardians, did you swirl past me towards the
  child straying on the soccer field, did you gust over punished
  olive and juiced green and the jell beneath them swarming
  like choked elegy?

On the cinerarium of unrequitable ash, white had melted but
  clung to ground and wall.

Cranes spindled over fresh housing while my wrist spun reflex-
  ively, this and that evanescence where bared necks, buckling
  once, had granted to the ongoing a precious narrowness.

And over these the tent pegged for a man's measure, sheetsteel of
  sentinels withdrawn into the longer watches: thus to tend or
  be tended, where the difference fractions into aftermath.

RIPOSTE

    No, don't ask us for
the heart as heart stood once,
don't expect . . .
                but I've heard
the bells of Cerveteri,
bells of Tarquinia, and
Fool, I said, *be quiet*,
neither dominion, prison,
nor single breaking of chains,
thus populous, these are
the bronze thymus of courage
and resignation, long
interfering intervals –
no pope or Krupp to melt
their pulse, unchangeable –
while the folds of those tiles,
squares, tufted fields
roll out unharvestable,
irreparable, forage and wall
of seeming's harsh rumors,
of a held sound that hangs
out from us and colors
and claims the sometimes still
intolerable throb of body.

WEATHER OVER THE LAKE

Bowl that lifts roof and path into one round,
road and roof brimming the bowl with living, dying:
morning's wide breath relinks patterns on water.

Lights in the factory at sun-up, hull lashed to hull at midday.
From strictest quantum simmer and along foamy rock
probers lean out, finding the next ford in the river.

242

A shuttering of light from behind, grey going grape blue.
Though I went on working, the hair on my neck frayed
like cable in the museum, flax from the Stone Age.

The creamy paint I layed on that man's house, which tarp
kept off his cute little Max Ernst bronze, had been mixed
to resist dawn shadows, noon shimmers, and now this.

Black sheering up while the powerful say, *We lack power*,
roofblow from a black root blooming icily, flashing.
But even Alexander poured the one full helmet into dust –

for a shout can break forth in which any cry wakes
to limits, and the drums be uncased in acknowledgment.
Though it reach our tongues, it will be spilled, every drop.

'SIETE VOI QUI, SER BRUNETTO?'

Not the Polish physicist
asking for help with busses, he
a new trusty tugging on his long leash,
but a Palestinian
who swung against me from a hand strap
downhill past the leaning
tower where tales fix Nero
during the fire, blurring whole eras, crooning –
out of all those
identities jostled on their way through,
nameless, this is one I have tried to name
when the face even of a master ebbed
across the interrogated dark and this one
hung there, like its own star, over no ground.

The Tiber synagogue, thudding
helicopters tilting away from it,
had just been bombed. Better a bus than the street . . .

The squares past midnight, tame
as the moon, lull with their amplitude:
when I swung out to scan the slab of high chalk
inscribing those from the neighborhood swept up
in the last massacre, a car shot in
whipping the inches behind me. Fading radio . . .

But it will arrive, the longed-for
vanishing-point prick through,
far from the tracked place
or haunted wall, will finally quiver out
from a past crushed till it must turn future and
twist living through some inconceivable knot.

That spring after the quake which levelled Acre
a traveller to Nazareth
equally hard-hit went into the church
eyes full of ruin, and he heard
preludes, swelling chorales, and then he saw
the organist leave: a ten-year-old Arab boy.
Will it be such a fine inversion next time,
would it be scorable, even – the dispersals
incalculable and the penetration
of a jewelled theme to the chance ear from thrusts
of air, of tremor. . . . Face in the dark that stays.

LIVY

When the Leader's orders came down –
    Blow up Paris –
the general cleared his desk
but left each bridge, every stained
roost for Abelard's pigeons.
And so they patrol cornices,
gurgle, strut, it is they
who change the guard over that courtyard
where a boy frowns at dust
ploughed and mazed by hunkered, persevering
Archimedes with stick –

244

thus the geometer, the sighted man
    not yet effaced.
It is still a mortal's
privilege to encircle
with hickory or linden
fingertip, deciduous point of the mind,
young feet exploding through that dust, those patterns
when the short sword, when the tank track
fueled by Marcellus comes driving,
the consul over Siracusa
at halt as he looks out from
the love of cities through tears
manly to preserve her.
Spelling each other down
the watches, astronomers
listen to the night.
And that year the sea caught fire.

DEAREST, INFERNAL GRANITE
  – Akhmatova, 'To My City'

I guess, from report, conscience's effect
carried like coppers on the tongue, paid in full
for lexica carried milk-like in the smashable
pitcher, vessel of clay, singer, I mutter,
but learning how to hear in that name a sounding.

Depths, I say, dreaming the lead dragged through silt.
Mist drifts through lamp cones in the parking lot
flat on market slab walls, shiny on the cars.
No fisherman splashed loose this muck, no bowsman
exploded it with his line. But these are our shallows.

Here swim now the lights and the half-lights
of the expanded world, spectacle for its god
which to gaze on brings blindness, which to steer
among gives slowly a counter-sense of homing.
Towards the condensed world. Through the ever-converging.

SEVENTEEN YEARS AFTER THE TET OFFENSIVE

Not the wasp's cycle, but the cicada's.
Jellied fire afar then and rage near,
the form we had sought in furnaces as our ward
repouring, beaker to beaker, a corrupting flame –
this as backflare to dinner among candles,
guardian lindens, mullioned seals over twilight,
where the host, healer
in wineflushed age, bellowed,
Not men, but viruses
each year withstand onslaughts
and come back stronger, more inventive –

in the long line of change
they are the winners, mere crystals!
Candles in line, and seasons,
as metal somewhere below shifted its melt,
crusts rupturing red-gold
and boiling through the vessel lances of air
still climbed among the flown
ladders and tried arbors of pattern.

REPORT FROM MENDRISIO STATION

Candy wrapper blown
        in the freight's wake

No longer to be gulls, twisting
after this thrown bit or that
while the crimes harden

The platform at Foligno
another July gave a blind
veteran, medals sagging
his lapel, lifted
onto the blackened local –

here one does not stand speechless
in a circle of yatterers,

246

one simply stands speechless
for a long waiting follows the fixative
gaze of the sun withdrawn
into hazes veiling hill rims,
a long heaviness invades curve, angle
which has not yet become gift of ground
        not yet wheel, rose,
bronze disc or the shut lids' blood

for those, those revolve here
where clattering through shiny
points the donkey switcher trips
empties and a brakeman
leaning an orange vest
out from them drops
snatching a clip-on red lantern
from what had been the end

CAUSERIE

Exiting rue Bonaparte I might, for a wink, deceive myself
as if trailing Theseus up from the stone bench of hell.
But no, from the outermost province, distended acreage
of an idea's plantation, I traipse with light baggage,
yet even so I was here before ranked floodlights
were set drifting past these embankments on scows,
their green bow lamps turning the muddy wash fauviste.
Faces ranged on twin decks, galley rowers
suddenly unchained, dazed as the smutted Louvre
flares up with the phosphorous of their passing.

If the real would yield to broadside scrutiny, illumined.
If loudspeakers amidships could amplify the hidden name.
If palaces given over to the many might truly receive them.
Ramparts of the detestable and cornices of the desirable
shine out and recede, rhythms of the strange.

From outermost centrality sped on the backwash
of an increasing acceleration.

Seining fish from broad lakes, inching down factory
smokestacks with troubleshooter's radio and brain,
combing threads of microcircuitry, my blood
regulates no maintenance of elided *de*
nor ancestors forced into the manor garden
to take their meals while sentinels of the new order
saw that they dined plainly and not to excess.

The long lane debouches onto wide frontage, winter sky,
journalism, thin chapters flapping in river wind.

Aging, Jefferson wheezed beneath the plaster
hardening into his life mask and so was not heard
in those rooms he had designed for his children, jolly
confections of classicism and styles quite contrary.
With him, the only such rooms. But beyond his cry.

If posters did not float the vanished, Dali's starved
Elephant of Space prick-eared and stilted on spindles, burdened
with the obelisk of Poliphilo and Bernini.
If Bonaparte had not penetrated to the core
of the pyramid then returned blanched, resisting.
If the masonic eye gleaming from tomb's tip on the dollar
were Sarastro's, flute handler and president of hope,
initiation master of marriage, gowned in corpuscular red.

For the pulses of a sure artery, into the capillaries
of a future, not the severing of a vessel.

My aim was not to feel again the squared granite
shouldering this flow and scan cold revetments
dividing it under bridges cleared by wily kings,
as if I might arch back and retrieve thread bedded
in the labyrinth and return with a dripping trophy,
returning so as to look past the hooded gaze
of fur-capped Franklin, instrumental man. Nor was it
to emerge into sky vaulting the spans, here
the last monarch, thereby effacing cycles
and foregoing the trial. Here again but at harder speed
mortal gates swing back on the deep whiteness
of the underworld, inviting anew the lunge that could
carry me crashing soundlessly through its vapor wall.

RIDDLE OF PEACE

From the bright tip
of his bill,
his bony little
lip all yellow,
he sang it,
the little bird:
through eleven
centuries and more,
bald cleric
looking up
from copy work,
and out of the future
breaking open
over stone
chilly in the sheen
of the beach,
he spoke
one note of it
above the grey loch
from the cover
of a heaped branch
all yellow:
a blackbird.

And from a wing
white and far down
in March scrub,
unheard though singing,
self-thrown
over the rooftree
of Francis, cool cave,
a wing quick to see
from the blown knob
of Subasio,
a small bird:
from the burn
of that white falling
a breath
of the same telling,
while the climb beneath

249

that torn air
was also a climb down
to the sea at night,
the sea hard at noon;
from the slight
passage of the bone-
colored bird: a dove.

sections, FRIEZE FROM THE GARDENS OF COPENHAGEN

Towards a train for the city, a wrong turn.
Ships, drizzle, islands
and the blank Strandvej, and a high wall –
rising there white heads
over white breasts, karyatids,
and the hot jump of a band pumping Swing and Blues,
tuba at the end of a sweeping drive,
hospital staff, and a conclave
of diabetics under umbrellas: they had wanted
and gotten their serenade.
Nurses told me where the station was.
And this was Dagmar's house, Queen of the Russias.
House of the widowed empress when
she wandered home again. Low scud
and laughing brass dripping where they stood
and telephone through the lab window floating
in a stainless steel
cradle for beakers, were the fairy tale.
I found the train, and walled faces,
and walls that merchants had laid on the cold sea plain.

Then schoolchildren questioning:
Why does Mr Muir say
'stretched him on a rock'?
Is 'him' this crazy man?
Rain had veered to sun.
Sun also estranges
the holdout raging through sewers clubbing rats,
thinking he drove back Ajax slayer of cattle.
Rats skipping across the scurfy hills,

250

'scurfy' is 'skurvet'. Dragged
into stony day by robbers.
What is a 'smooth sward wrinkled'?
'Sward' is your 'gronswaer',
and that green spread is our garden,
dollops of peace puffing the cloud screen. *'Him'*
is the old man himself, his fury like Priam's
but he lies there without a name, resisting
until the thugs have killed him,
the figures writhed for them now,
wrestling, the young readers
forming those lines cleanly.
So this is how you will tell them?
Perhaps they already know,
although their fathers only
pretend to tell them. Ask, then.
And from their tongues a curled clang
Under Troy's riven roots,
'riven' we have too in our language,
another resonant room
in the city long since leaning
and holding into sea wind,
Where is the treasure? one girl tittered while
green sun smoothed out the blue
of sturdy delay, blue time overhead . . .
but *riven* is where they take us,
those of the seeing tongue:
fractured ground, and raw heat
crisping the blown branches,
divinatory hazel
hanging over its lip,
and holy mulberry
singed by ire of the updraft.
                              Blue overhead,
but held also in eyes searching eyes for
the color that listens and is still life,
over, under, sheen beneath treasures.

3

For those who were never in it, luxury of the god's eye,
as Neptune's at Marseilles screening it from his green floor,
    each hull a pod, its petals
fanning sunlight, slow oars,
    each pod a solar rose
        self-igniting, tar flaring,
bodies a pollen drift weighted with armor, trailing
        the slow mass of the reflux.

And because only a handful heard Homeros;
and *Faust* was read chiefly for its hi-jinks;
and because Melville moldered, came Vietnam . . .
one wakening or another for those who were never in it.
        But we are in it, alright.

Sunflash seen from a freighter, humming black flower, floating
big chopper, petals flashing,
    petals fanning the air.
Probably it was ours
    or if British, a Lynx
        with Seaspray screens, Decca panels
equipping the Argentine over South Atlantic,
flower of the fascist pampas drifting in sea wind,
and the god's ear listening through a U.S. Creditor
passing those officers,
    The last two on that trip
tight-lipped Frenchies
    our own Flying Nuns. . . .

And for those who were never in it, view down onto spread waters,
numb participation not to be avoided,
    we are in it, alright,
        it has never stopped,
cold blast of the door draft, splayed limbs
    as the forms fall, a rippled
tearing around the human
        fact diminishing.

6
The one whom I met? Take him for one among others.

Two boys had lagged behind their school tour,
had taken the wrong fork,
and evening was reddening snowfields
on the peaks, so I doubled back
and took the other road, and saw no one
down six turns of it,
                        when he stood there.

He had seen me first, for he watched
to be sure that I watched him
set down the blue wheelbarrow
to which he had lashed two posts
freshly barked: *By God this is hard work,*
and wiped his face with his apron.
Jawohl, hard, and then stumblingly,
with gestures: *Have you dug the postholes?*
Yes by God, and that was the worst part,
water coming in through the marl.
Makes this part seem
                        even harder, Yessis Gott.
Days unfenced towards evening,
one field and one path,
and if you had gone looking for him there
would he have come? This is the gentian's hour,
the outcrop's vapor, stone set aside
in unmarked allotment.
Have you seen two boys? and I signaled direction
then pointed to his posts: *the size of these.*

If you heard, even if you overheard,
their speech is not yours, their speaking
is to no one.
                No, Yessis Gott,
but if I had you may be sure, Mein Herrn,
I would not be carrying their little brothers here
all by myself, and touched the peak of his cap
and went towards the dusky crown of that turn
and over it, before the pair of them
jiggled back, yattering in the distance.

253

7

One could stand on a sea cliff before the house
long since mortared there, and know himself one
by fronting all he had ever called the sea
with all that his nerve had raftered as his own.

So that place stays. But if even heroism
alters because the torque of it, twisting
out of a spiral, pressing from it whole,
is a blind blue thing turning in the chasm

that is sea, and is space, and is a new house
shaken, all intermingled, and with him there is
no similar, and no tomb loaming
his novel landfall there, what is our case?

We would not stay with him, even though
we'd cherish him no less. Nor would we look
back along the high bending courses.
Nor scale down the cliff. But we would not go,

for there is a mouse burrowing in that field,
wintering in the stone cellar, listening
to the sea bash and scour and to the man
in his sleep moan and in his prayer weld,

this persistent, most moderate brother
who will make the necessary accommodations,
hearing tunnels meet and the grains ticking.
He, mouse, go-between now, ambassador.

10

Past smugly boobed sphinxes
at the Dane king's hunting lodge,
herds of well-to-do deer.

Kestrel and kittiwake
mingling in a sea air,

an eight-point buck stripping fuzz
from his rack on a 'phone pole,

and down from the lodge sea lanes
past twelve acres of grass,

and deer rarely shying,
strollers with liquid eyes

in pairs and clan linkages,
cyclists abstracted, fauns –

this place is as good as any,
beeches in low spreading clumps

and shadowy stands, to begin
the accounting again.
                For here

the lull, the lay of parenthesis
in sweeping but struck phrasing,

is a calm too assiduously
preserved to remain restful,

passed over by too many wings.
This is the lagoon.

Then a lizard peering up:
Attendez, this is not quite the place

you may think it is! And I nodded
in deference to his seniority.

Nothing personal, you understand,
but deposits should not be left

uninsured, the management has become
notorious for its fudging.

It would have been an affront,
asking him how he came there,

or inquiring into his ancestry.
He sensed my tact and ventured,

255

Betrayer, and destroyer,
and now you're turning the knife

on yourself? They will live.
But differently, differently.

There is much humor in this,
as I'm sure you have confessed,

much that is ridiculous,
irreplaceable! His eyes glistened.

Pouring through forms, a peace
that would not end though they would

made the cloud-swish of wheat-spill,
of a scythe's way-making

or voices dimly clamorous,
pushing a little group

out through a gap in the dirt
under his breathing feet –

so peace was going to be set down
in the windy book yet for good –

a widow sickling her lord's field
up and down one long day

in order to free her son, and
finishing, she fell down,

my intact lizard grinning
as he reclaimed the acre,

its colors wheat, sweat, and sunset
under the blade's hard breathing –

hush, little Four Legs, don't you tease,
you have led me far enough –

and where I stood was stubble
on the berm of a raised path,

where I swayed was cleared ground.
Peace will try many forms,

Abram and knife and ram
and she who was each of them,

fabled but untallied
where the doe arcs and slides.

Space, the dying stag, browses
in the wood of Charlottenlund.

Grace in spotted flesh
darting and the wide light

that returns, leather tuck
of his mouth not yet anticipating

its red froth, and over him
breathing's blue lull

harboring the greatest
fundamental, expectancy . . .

a pruned and changeless zone
ruthlessly to be changed.

Kestrel and kittiwake
planing in from the sea.

11
That which does not pass but returns to peer in
     from the top corners of earth's hand-painted page,
little moons looking down curiously, little suns
     looking down blandly and benevolently, for these, too,
there is laughter, inaudible but presumably full, a long chorus.
     Was the laborious hand innocent after all?

How did he manage it, this durable cross-section
in the colors of berries, a breviary of muds?
He discovered something. What is it? Behind the gold leaf
it stares and winks, behind the stains also.
As if waiting for a response. Though what can one do?
A man's lifetime tripled, clacks the stammerer, that equals
a stag,
three stags give an ouzel, then three of those an eagle,
mounting to salmon and finally the yew tree drinking three
gulps
of bright dust to span earth's age on the rimmed octavo.
Merriment ripples at the corners of fire's mouth.
And the fair daughters of fire, hair cascading their treasuries,
nymphs outliving ten ember birds, choke with pitiless delight.
The one to whom they consistently attend in the great garden,
the one they relish most, is a climber with donkey.
Undulant pebble nudged up the crest by heat shimmer.
With him a boy, slaughtering knife, and kindling.
Do? Even the being of the wood is unintelligible
to the strictest simplicity: at the fuzzed edges
of imagined weavings, drift your growth, fibers,
and unlock, unfold into the full amplitudes
of your reach, and to your unclaimed auras go.
A dense thicket, bees resuscitating the hive,
bundles loughing against ribs and blown flesh sacking.
From the plain below, the crystalline rowdiness
of a wind band starting up, bass drum pacing them,
lighter than pulsebeat, the clarinet rippling upward.
The rest of the strenuously recommended procedure?
Huge bodies dragged across puddled lines of altitude
and beached at the appointed minim by more than volition.
Dimension thrust and cinched through the pack strap's eye.
Feelings framed in the throat's pit, only there, in that gristly flower.
Reason coming in, as it must from its ardent nature,
on wings with an exigent, an already created ram,
dear reason in the dress which it gallantly adopts
out of passion, the partisanship of creatures,
parliamentary gallantry in a moment without rules.
This one is sober, cry the high ones, he's no mere belly,
he has done it, has really lifted himself to the first step
and is going to follow through! Then more laughter,
whose attitude is not open to scrutiny and whose

unsearchable quaver does not yield to long study
    as the knife is taken out and used: thou dost not.
As the fire is kindled and the wood makes rendering: thou art not.
    At which the climb may invade calf and thigh, memory with
        forecast,
anticipated descent stinging the chest like woodsmoke
    at work in the persevering eyes: so he has accomplished
this thing about which the stone is speechless, crackling wood also,
    over which the soaring chorus also flies speechless,
done it like a man up there on a mountain in Copenhagen,
    over the gardens and sea. And the aeons of light were still.

ARS POETICA

By silvery increment, by mineral touch of the remorseless,
the irregular stone takes shape, though it derives shape
from the ruled lattice, denuded hegemenous crystal.

The bitterness of salt is a taste waiting to be changed,
waiting with the power to change every other savor,
dissolving under patience of the rains only,

like the rich man's regatta fading down evening beneath
the outflowing half of breath, towards the pulse's cusp,
and masts creeping beneath their spar candles.

ROUND

Belled ink and umber, shouldering
needles and humus, pleated
flesh earlier than ours
gilly near deadfall after rain:
inverted flasks and cool fire
licking down from Pluto
tongueing them with solving
showers near sunset in March's underworld.

      Whence this clearing
opening through mind,
         fume of cut grasses, wet stone,
granular manure of seedtimes
abud in the shadowy inane?

Opening with the persistence
of an aging Samurai
who thrusts off a welter of coverlets
shared out by his rook-and-rust-haired
companion sleeping through dawn
in the drug of her youth. No one
to see him reach for his sword
without looking and calibrate
dripped rhythms from the eaves.
As out there on the grey
silk of advent, its *plisses*
sliding, so here in the day.
Looking into the sidefall
coil in her neck, he knows
that his long dalliance
has woven no ornament
but sought the basis, yet also
that his death, circling towards him
from the forest, probing mists
across the chalkline into
opportunity,
would prefer him like this, trying
to get to the bottom of it,
sword hand hanging, gaze in the auburn pool,
still trying to get to the bottom of it.

That is not his way,
anymore than the unexplained
vanishing of the demented
boxer Kleomedes
in whirls of fists and blood,
into the fading cult
of heroes. Greater images
there are, but are not here.
Past the end, honor or dishonor,
the thing he was will be swept
into incalculable
enlargement, keenly hard:
therein the mature assignation.
He swings towards the converging
adversary, adjusting
the quotient of welcome,
exacting from it the testimony:
thus was it to have rendered
account in those mucked years.
Swings away, name and face
rounding to the zeroes
of the bookie, but we say:
      he achieved
in the reign neither of Akragas
nor of Finn Broadhand
but of Wen-jo Ice Eye
scanter of food to widows,
and to that degree the luster
      was the more his own.
Behind four pines on the ridge
the fireball bulges, darkening
less, melting its solder
to the crest, seeking
no basis nor avoiding
an application, but proceeding, proceeding,
as the rust inkcap at his knees,
whole in his hands, lifts with them.

Why has he spun and fallen
in the perpetual flurry?
fighter, yet unprotected.
Crouched thighs listen, studying

the afterburst: yes, how?
Time winding in the fern thicket:
shrill of the last oriole
as dewfall shrinks the heart,
then from the peaty floor
of hunger, with lunge
skyward through the stiff swale,
those drumming wings. The sound
enlarges the cicadas
months gone, their legendary
test of our conversation
compacted to this single
stroke through our parrying –
big wing and huge flutter
to assay our persistence
in asking and listening,
clatter and the thing's gone
into low hum abiding.

A messenger starts from the point
ordinately hidden:
this is no new-fangled song.
Ascending spirals he draws
copper fine as the rinse
of flame, paring alembics,
blown snow withers
through the skier's cheek, he has
regained the aperture,
his speed is the egg's,
                      the pouring
ridgeline soaks evenly
into his glasses, and the sound
pits and drills their black slopes
drenched with the heaviness
that he sheds now, going
    out of the mountain.

How begin? fret the sceptics
over again: it all
comes again, hugest wheel. . . .
But have they yet descended
to the hobo frying his catch

nightly under steel spans?
offering brew as tart
as might the disinherited
could they gather and pour it,
tins over spidery fire
clink this inaugural,
their delegate hunches down
stirring, no mutterer
nor shifty waster, he swirls
the layers of their hours,
in fellowship he offers
their endura: take, drink.

Neither pearl weigher stave shaper
humped track finder nor squint
genealogist of forms
the genie springs from the point
hidden in, so as to manifest it:
this is an old-fashioned song.
Ascending
        the horn's bell
                he draws
copper fine as the whoosh
of flame, paring that spiral,
for in his eye's nook a wind
feathers from summits, a wing
trails vapor and the beast
spins forth, slipstreaming wet fur,
a flank wound licked to silver
unfurling its pulse, or riders
moving into the luster
of their steel, polished mist of armor,
passages sunken in metal –
nor does it stop there, children
link hands, centrifugal
days bulge out fired colors,
the beast would reach after but his
talons rebound from that nova,
and their cherishing him begins then.
Cruelly begins, as blown snow withers
through the skier's cheek, he has
regained the aperture,

his speed is the egg's closure,
the ridgeline soaks evenly
into his glasses, and the sound
    blears from their curves
drenched with the heaviness
that he sheds now, becoming
    that mountain.
This is the ring of hours,
a same and different metal:
touch it, the tone tapers.
Across it through afternoon
fat flakes drift
into the open mouth of this realm,
one million melting, ten
welding and holding. As when
a man with a boast on his heart,
or a cursing, or the prayer
that tatters into argument,
lets it out: flakes of it
swinging down the gulf
and stitching the tongue with cold
repeatedly: no drink,
but over the dark months
a matted reservoir
contoured to every curve.

Ring of hours that hums
with planetary subflux,
interswirling streams
through magma, their churnings
brighting all that dark
and steadier than the drone
of cicadas. Stymie or
still them and there could be
no gambit for Mr Franklin
trotting off, interest fetched
by a twister over dry fields
growing from spurts of dust:
They say that a shot, fired through
a water-spout, will break it! – and canters
into the skirts of that turbulence
thrashing it with his whip, eminently

and passionately curious;
not heedless, nor meaning
wholly to straddle that fracas
from which his horse shies, none the less he
reopens the game: three miles downwind
and leaves still settling, what is it
that has come into separation?
He will wait upon it.
As under, so above. And as
from tins over spidery fire
with a suckling's persistence
assessing eyes gauge you
training flame to twin points,
sharp for no prizes hunted
with the clan that dreams by day
and is not satisfied, so also
from the twin lobes of day
a genie springs facing
two ways, you face which way?
Soon after, it quitted the road
and took into the woods, growing
every moment larger and stronger,
raising instead of dust the dry leaves
with which the ground was thick covered,
and making a great noise with them
and the branches, bending
some tall trees round in a circle
swiftly and very surprisingly,
though the progressive motion
of the whirl was not so swift
but that a man on foot
might have kept pace with it.

      Stone with chisels lifted
from working, steel
      ringing from stone!
Towers converse across
      the intervals,
ages of the ant rotate
      through each passing eye,
but friend, how stands the hour?
And where is my similar?

Heron leaving the pond
whitely sheeted, and banner
taken in from the staff
fly in the breast of one
lying in muddy green
with his gear slackened near him.
With the world, for the world,
trackless in exchanges
    not of the world.
Mild days invading winter,
warm days and mild low cloud
bathe the sleep of the hunter.
So his ribs sweeten
with the unseasonal clemencies
of a false August.
But he has lined out ahead,
not fallen back. His rust flowers
from the crowning treachery of worn gold.
Cities beneath cloud-surge
break into patchy view
through that domed breathing.
The ordeal from which he rests
has not yet concluded.
Do not touch him! but follow,
for he set out in this way
when the tribe mixed its ecstasies
and blundered through the circle.
In him the city lifts
a hillock of roofs, long falls
of vine greening an alley,
an unsuspected mountain
spiraling its spine
to the heart's blackened hidings
streaming in a mild rain:
follow saith its deep veil, here you shall
never be alone.

PARABLE WITH BROKEN FRAME

An old architect at a littered worktable
   sits through morning, eyes fixed on ocean,
intent through evening at the study window,
   motionless though his hand rebuilds years.

Down razory defiles to the rockledge landing
   stands of flittergold awash in wind,
and through soft lolling labia of the waves
   tiny boats coming in, setting out.

Priest and corpsedresser begin the climb to his house,
   their empty craft nibbles at spindrift.
A bridegroom and his man steer for the islands,
   plinky music unrolls with their wake.

A last stone has been set in place, final tile,
   the bride folds her face in streaming hands,
the black duo mounts to the door and goes in.
   All of these I have been, none holds me.

POSTHOUSE

Hearing gone rain plink into a cistern from the roofcorner,
amplified down a swift tunnel enlarging yet clarified –
long after a thatch-haired groom stabled and fed my horse
and I have climbed to my room and lie awake, not
exhausted from my mission this time, simply alert
as never quite before, with acuity not quite
personal for the night horizon through leafage,
rustling of the morning star that had been evening's star,
and the fading dialogue, dialectic, diaboli:
Now I know what my sins are. – You do not know what your sins are.
Plink of the remainder from what had dissolvingly
leaned across the province, slate gables, and the messenger
I then was, and had there opened a corridor
down which disinterestedly I might find passage.

267

And what I would have heard was the itineraries
of another man's travels, and that man was myself.

Seeing two or three lines of a parchment letter
slightly magnified, boundaries disengaging
furry luminous shadows from their support –
not the pauses of stagecraft, nor the gleams of spurious
admiration lifting them, but the planes
parallel and plural among them filling out,
with the nothing about which they can declare nothing
fountaining while they tremble into or past question.
All the while my veined hand pressed them in place
on veined oak planking, blood to sap humming like the sail
that tugged at rope in my grip as the chopped harbor
widened around the jetty's hook and tension
in the sheet slackened momentarily, then
firmed for the last stretch.
                                    And what the ink disengaged
as a squiggle of known headland from scudding grey
was another man's unknown terms, and those were my own.

Sniffing dawn's hollyhocks as they brush the sill,
wet speartips dipping a little in cool drifts
from unseen brightenings that glint the grooved wood,
paint gulleying glacial cracks under the same wet.
The eye of the body is not always blind. Sniffing
the eyeless soul spurting in turns along stalks
I had not seen from the dusky door, had often
overlooked, but met now and greeted. Loosening
were a knot's interferences. I could say
that I stood at that window and saw rain in the wheelruts
both mud and silver, for that would have been the finding.
But I had found the flower. Straw-flecked courtyard set
on stacked settlements, stalks vaulting then withering along
uncoiling longitudes, turmoils of succession.
Fiber of mixed evils and boons a seed for the savior
who spilled along one just as phallus and the other as god,
spores of good expanding incalculably if not nipped by
bunglings fouler than mire. And through me that rope, passing.

WHITE DEER RUNNING

Baucis and Philemon, having forgiven their killer Faust
and been resurrected to this life, to reenter their rest,
have come south and bought a stone house in the Morvan.
Undulating woodlots, hamlets beyond Autun.
Windows west only, into the long evenings
at midsummer, butterflies wavering in throngs
while rooms hold off heat with deep walls and embrasures.
Serendipity and sublimity are peasant sisters
waiting behind trees for farmers to find them, scuffle
with a pod of wild boar, and extend a barn from the wall.
Sublime and serendipitous, their last possession
for a renewed aging, lindens cooling each description.
The forest is named *Socrate,* a leader of the Resistance
dialectical in his disappearances,
and the barn wall was used for executions, by which side
there are varying reports. This too is to be had
in the idyll of ownership, a filmy disturbance
across the tabletop's oak grain, brown generations,
apples mounded in a plain crock, clear wines
draping colors over board and fruit, all this the senses
manufacturing from drift and ripple of syllables
before anything can be verified, yet the sheen falls
across an excellence of properties in trust
to no single appetite, in a place where sheen seems made fast.
   Narrow, the gate into our garden. A black sucking,
and waters crash, but you must not cry out or cling.
And then you are there, and you may come back if you choose
and report, though boasting is indecent, there are other ways.
Space there is not really different nor the sun,
but attachment is not what holds you, all that has gone.
            But that is
no possession: left listening and seeing, I was.
Apples, glass with ruddy window in its belly, the ruse
of solidity calling across the spoken was and is.
A low forest in Burgundy, woodlots in Massachusetts,
the last field before that drop where the river cuts.
   Against the clearing's edge
   at evening, already sliding
   among the indistinct
   stems of December trees,

white deer running.
It was perhaps an hour
over the page, Arjuna's
refusal and the protracted
gleams of his charioteer.
When I looked out the window,
ranked birches turned in wind
silver through shadow, over
white deer standing.

THONON-LES-BAINS, UPPER TERRACE

With amnesiacs, she explained, her means was speech: to lever
    them back
by bending the throat's moan, suddenly memorious.

If a story may be halted while the life flows, it follows:
life is no story. Might we recall, then, what it is?

Below, a steamer preserved from the pre-First-War haven
nudged the landing's tongue. From its belly, a moist hoot.

A city gardener drenched rosebud clods with a hose.
To wait there above Leman halted by a layover
dearly companioned and, meeting this other, to let
afternoon's vast cup exhale vaporous fire
was to tap a vintage I had forgotten planting.

As a tyke in rubble streets, she had been dragged with sisters
by their starved mother in front of a tank. The precious *I*
is the pointedness of untold momenta. It stopped.

The cipher *God* was not so strange to the ancients, but then
the ancients had not become quite so strange to themselves.

Deft with camera, she squints and rewinds, that some of it
might be netted and hauled, and behind, gathered waters
stilled in their moving by the abyssal eye of good.

And if
      it is not a stretch of carpet thudded out on looms,
if it is not plotted, what is it like, then, existence?

(Unplotted answers will abandon aim, it seems,
without abandoning their course through awareness.)

Like a sound rising steadily through wearied alertness.
So do you choose to receive from that low hum of the chorus,
its unison at the frequency of an archer's breastbone,
or a keel pressing into the cold surge, riding level,
from it do you choose the arrow that shows two points
only so as to prong the eyes of evil, one unswerving thrust
carried by this sound that attains, that does not end,
subtlest of the creators? – But assent, like the air, already breathes.

IN A RAILWAY COMPARTMENT NEAR GLARUS

If it were solely three Croatian workers
talking of war in Croatia
who made me shut my eyes,
even to their city on the sea
Assisi-like, smoking,
where a stair tread
though grooved smooth leads to no exit;

if them alone, I wouldn't have shuddered
at the impulse to grow dark,
sporadic but twisting from the core,
then at its raw opposite,
Henry lunging down passageways
cursing his sons and Eleanore, Harry
craving some blessèd door, a young queen
hot between aging sheets, or a crack shearing
through the stone roof to grant him different issue
out over rivers, flocks, forests,
cunny's gate or bird's beak for blood's ire –

shivered at all of it and longed
to turn it into a turning, only thus
to see nothing though it all be there,
blink all gates blind though the wall rear up.

Then it came, swinging from the side, a tunnel.
Rumbling tons aimed us
with a steward two carriages ahead
tilting a tinkling tray of drinks
and bent flawlessly, entering –

and through that sleeving dark I groped
armless, like torsoes in the Book of the Dead
(twisting from the seed but not towards darkness),
for the skull's ridge, its pale fissure,
ladders rotted or thrown down,
beginning to remember the steadied river
overhead, radiantly fast.

NEVER YOU, IN THOSE SHIPS, NOR TO THOSE TOWERS . . .

The means may seem to have slipped your grasp, distractingly
        splendid.
As if you came to Vézelay and heard behind doors
massed choirs already into their requiem. In dry grass
huddles clustered near an angle that released
a trickle of soprano, trombone, and contrapunto
while over the roof in deepening blue drifted Jupiter.
The gangway was being pulled up: such the illusion.
When singers left with families to cars down the long hill,
their vast plea finished, stragglers inside mooned at lit stone.

But what in you can awaken, to bear and not look away,
neither to cry for intervention nor to intervene,
may have no rendezvous on the choired ridges of July.
The ranged faces, cleared, recousined, may be no more your means
than a black lake you happen to come on at midsummer,

waves shoving inshore from the relentless passage
of boats in hundreds, running lights and mast lamps gliding
from some festival for the city, that means densely its own end,
engines humming, wealth pulsing one way down the dark.

Time is the boy downshore sorting gleams among pebbles,
and time is the girl sidling up wide steps to the narthex.
His eyes part the sheens of strata over endragoned nuclei,
hers penetrate pillared gate and avenue to the prepared
table of making and unmaking. And time marries time
though they will be separated, time and again, by the blade of fire
and our pity for their pain, sung in choruses, will have been
        misplaced.
What they met in each other was more than themselves, and it
        passed
through them to meet itself, so that lustres drenching the beach
withdrew with the wave, and footsteps trickled down stone.

AND FRESH CUTTINGS FROM LIKE THINGS

May it be that one morning given to me in this garden
the pack and walking stick, the boot with taped inner heel,
will carry foot only, bread and four-color map, and go with me
unburdened of agitation to the edge of Flussturheim.

There, not the copper beech surging from cobbles, that plume
burnishing the black root's force while thrusting sun away,
not that but its double will fill the air there, silver-pale, exhaling
the rustle of the latch in the door-catch to the beyond.

And I shall not startle, for near that trunk rises
the gurgle of the fountain of recollection, in Flussturheim.
Surge and relieving source. And I shall drink there before
coming to the low parapet belting town from river.

May it be that the haze will burn off, and the confluence
shine through beneath the notch, with its ford where
one king was slashed while crossing, and the murderer
became another king, but only the toppled man hero.

For it will be there, under potato gardens, tilted vines,
by the toll bridge open now to free passage, that heroes
will have set out for the crossing, leaving the moon foliage
of passion's copper, and entered into a plane of the far garden.

Below on the stone span, in blooded homespun, a girl
hooded alone at mid-arch, market basket on the rail
quite empty, her inscrutable gaze filling with the same green
that I might be conning and the identical hill line, but altered

by their having berthed long in her, refinding their way down
her stem of quiet, along meilinated quick to the remakings
within rootlets that surpass undoings and the suck downward,
force that rivers reversion but makes of return a tower.

She will not be waiting there for one of the heroes.
Nor will they pass there, processionally relinquished,
not in Flussturheim, where they have ridden out already
and left the years channeled and tapering towards rapids,

years that were, and that are, years in eye and in heart
going down – and she will close one over the other, and go out
on a fire-cut path of seeing, as its live tendril, past moored
flat-bottoms square at prow and stern aslosh with gold-pale leaves,

and the azure-backed kingfisher bursting from shoreline shrubs,
along her own corridor, through the harshly oncoming, oh my girl.

KIRSCHDIEB

Sooty rogue of the middle air
  shunning the curlew's bog
  and shag-delighting spume

came down on the cherry branch
that angled up to my window

and he asked, *Do you recognize me?*
  I answered, *I have hardly known myself.*
He asked, *And the wild Celtic Fathers?*
  I said, *You are not Him, but I hear the rills of home.*
He asked, *Has Merlin eluded?*
  I said, *The trunk still sways.*
Unblinking, he asked, *Will the eye see itself seeing?*
  I said, *Bending, the wing points,*
and then I asked, *What has shrouded my thought?*
  He said, *Love will tendril even through hell,*

then stripped every ripeness
  off the glistening knuckled twigs,
deleting what I was nurturing
  those summer days, whose evenings –
    but how did I see this
  unless through your climbing eyes –
  whose evenings ruddied the peaks.

from
SELVA MORALE
(1995)

TOWARDS NAPLES

Stutter of a blown lampshade, no,
my bed is the day train, I wake to poles
raking the moist glass,

pelting limit and law, then peasants
down the rows of their green patches
standing to unbend,

and a motto from the centuries
of carved stone on the mind's mirror,
Not Somehow, but Triumphantly –

no weight or separateness erased,
not the humiliated, they at their unthronged gate
of truth, yet I'm allowed

to pass through labor I shall never make
my own, with my sight to its piled crest,
and the world open.

'SING AND SING ME AGAIN'

Sing and sing me again
sang law silently to the cantor:
hand's eye and ear's heart thereby
smoothing the mind's clamor,

and when mind vaulted forth
in body, windowed on primal fire,
stone groining stone grew leafage
to bear blood's root through air

and revolve animal
variety through the full spectrum,
haunch, tusk, and cock brightening
where the beyond stained them

carnelian, sapphire,
rose shadowing caverned amethyst,
viridian source pulsing
into arc-welded west.

Spirit seeks stony night,
body sweats spirit in that high cave,
yet that too is a burning, and
gave as one law for love

an outset at hazard
aiming at one long-hazarded end,
nor ever held us, these best
images of the hand,

and gave the form of one like
Man, and with it the linked hymn,
Who are you, then, and whose child?
and *I am*, and, *I am*,

for the temple is pressed
from us, diamonded in the mire,
archeus terrae forced out
under extreme pressure

into ease of being,
and unforeseen, unforeseeable
this gist of earth that is ours
though it become single, whole.

TO AN UNKNOWN POET

Watching firelight leapers
at Lupercal, studying the limbs
of Africans, a boy
felt the thud and whinny of his calling
when he saw that the arm's melody
phrased pain, and that the planting
and uprooting of the foot, too, grew pain.
Prattle of embassies
                    and decay downward
were evidence for others,
his sense of it felt simpler:
language had gone out with ox teams, keels,
chisels across the lintels of grafted gods,
while something less had come back.
Mortared a world while the lime in it drifted sand
and the sand whispered of foreshores, of time,
not quite in one moment, or from one place.
All this on a glistening
Nubian twisting for Severus
under the Fool's weaving chant.

THE WELL OF SAINT REGISSE

Soundless waterfall, cave-in,
and from emptiness the infused nova
as sense burns more flatly, and window
gives onto window in receding series –
even in the center, extinguishings
whose turbulence, carried, is a working also.

But Andersen's father, permeable to each wind
and fleeing that sorrow in his father before him
carried his boy at the first sign afflicted
out to the dispossessing spring to leave him
through the night on Saint John's Eve, a cold year.

Cinched into leggings and mittens with hemp drawstrings
and canvas from a wrecked fishing smack,
he was set down in the strict, abused place.

There was, in their case, extenuation,
huddled towards a cure before drenched April,
consigned neither honeysuckle nor lily,
with belief even before hope, before cloud
had towered and dissolved through June of the ruins.

Tempest came with breastplate clangwheeling
through his chilled dream of armor, and the mad girl
scrumpled unseen near his feet broke away in a cascade
of labials, leaving him sprocketed to after-flashes,
unable to lay hands on a shield, leaving him
through years growing tenuously glad
for other lightnings, those that retain passage.
As if yanked upright he tore from that ground
oddly surefooted, agile through pitch downpour, on his back
the fame and fate of shattered armor for his countless sons.

ARCHEUS TERRAE

rear ruth as the seat, rear her ureaus, cart cheer there
char the rat's tree, sear the cause, hate the rest
he, she errs, thee erreth, eaters at the heart
earth, aster, tar, hut, star are hers
use, re-use tears, her rarest chart
star's heat teases the archer's reach
thus true care, the scar, rehurts, reheats us
ear sure at the hatch, seer at such heat as
rush sheer arches thru the scare – thereat, the rue, the hurt:
rust ate these earths at the heart's rate
at us, teacher, the art tears: steer us
each search reaches the hearts there

RAINA

Lulled on the placid silk
of an upside-down heaven
ringed by Austrian peaks,
she let the boat drift
and the big paint-flaking oars
slip out through the notched oarlocks.
Her little cousin prattled.

Cattle in the high reaches moaned.
Purpling stillness listened.
Bolting downslope, their bells
faint as those in chapel,
the herd rolled for the bridge.

She flailed with cupped hands, ordering
the little one to sing
and bail with a picnic spoon.
Farmers in market dorries
pumped on poles and wedged
into the hewn oak arches
of the unshakable span.

Cloud bellied and broke
into bright jags above
matronly hips and cellos
swaying the railing, prows
nosing under, the bolted
lacework of the trusses
soggily giving way.

She chanted to herself
then spoke it to the empty
landing, *I didn't steal
the boat, I didn't steal it.*
Creamy froth over chocolate
worked in the matchstick narrows
a hypnotized dispersal
of heads, humps, apples.

She yoked the tie-up
around a brass clew, watching
its crown swell in the sun
just then returning, bead
bulging on the lettuce
in a drenched collander.
Vast urgency gathered
in her throat, helpless

responsibility,
and though that easing wash
of home light has come down
many times since, even
past the fence of the Camp
where they took her father
and then took them, too, all

those black tunics crammed in,
mouths repetitive
their foulness towards her boyish,
though even there it fell
on her skin with the same
laundry freshness, never
has it quite assured her
of the real things of earth.

LAKESIDE

interlude. Under turreted walls
cognac ripples the legend
adrift among banners:
how they caught a buffoon
and drubbed him to the cathedral,
pummeling his backside
along with his unrepentant conviction,
which he bellowed as they dragged him off,

284

that he had found the passage, the rhyme
that would unlock the entire epic, yes,
the *clavis apocalypticus*, though just then
he had forgotten it. Through the portal
he goes, a flash sucks him
into the pit . . .

(Opposite, a doctor from Sicily:
four countries and two camps, over his drink.
I met him in my last weeks of detention,
a fellow surgeon, you see,
our gentle captor. He had billeted
in our villa, I could ask him
how much of it was left when they went.
Now they were really losing, so I pressed him
on this and that, and he plucked out
the little Marcus Aurelius bound in calfskin
that went with him in his kit.
He must have read it on our verandah.
In Latin. Paul and Barnabas,
healing the sick in Lystra,
were taken for Zeus and Hermes,
Zeus the taller, Hermes the one who could talk.
The castle behind us hoarded
the relics of Sikorski's legion,
those stranded diehards.
                              A butterfly
lit on his shoulder. He
recognized it – of course –
teasing it with smoke from his cigarette.
Conditions change, and he with them,
deepening to blue when he meets the turn,
le grand Mars changeant.)

. . . while over the rise, vanishing
downslope among boulders
goes a boy with his loud crew before
any disasters, and before our religion
chose history, and one story, over
the variously angled gleam
of wisdom, the varying presence
of the sayings – into an air

that braces him and shakes me, a wind
that fed him his hint of being
and with that his own chance
without his knowing it:
down, into raw April wet.

WEAVING AT FELSENEGG
Adliswil, Kanton Zürich

Shee-oop, shee-oop-fup, from
skeet shooters down the gorge.
And on the trail, beneath
the crumpled letterhead
of a heavy-machinery firm,
vocem? bene mihi
venit in mentem . . . One rock
names this comb of the ridge
simply, but then a piece
of litter from the wind
brings the condensations
of power, energy,
self-improvement and self-
escape into the high
puzzle of this place.
Not Paul's voice, not the haunted
consoler and monitor
thrown by a voice and then,
schooled like a child by soothing
Ananias, told
what to do. Though Breughel
set it in mountains, not that,
not here. Some manager
at Latin, parsing half-heard
transcendentals, while
under him in the shops
or out on the rebuilt street
the worst work is carried
by sons of Attaturk,

or in the sorting rooms
by daughters of Anita
Garibaldi – revolver
and sword laid away, nation
and empire, alphabet,
sweated unity,
to sweat again. And both
are yoked into the same
harness, villagers
humming courtship songs
while the other at his screen
toys with print-out. What
the southerner sings is love
pulling against his brave
extension of himself
to win advantage while
nearly betraying himself.
So love sings of love wounded.
But hobbyist Latin sings
something incalculable
questioning the voice
it claims it is glad to hear,
but cannot rise from silence
to listen, for it owns no
quiet, and so cannot
enter silence again.
And now both, a gray file
off the train before dawn
entering between sacks
of cane sugar and pipes
for milk and cocoa, with
one man at a keyboard
suspended in a windowless
cube with a calendar,
both of them humming scores
that will not stop.
                          To climb
over this is never
to see above it all –
so easy! – but instead
to hear things from down there
still bustling in a quiet

resting on the all-seen.
Memory of each
wordless heaviness
lends anchor on the heights,
drag is a safeguard
when thermals shift up defiles
for the young planing out
on bright sails and frames,
for this is one more time
of unmoorings, of loose
shiftings in a wide sway,
while gusts from the roof-thick valley
lift a roaming hunger
for voice, unspokenly great –
out of our inner sky
in ancient crispings lodged
at random: we are not
ourselves or our own masters
thus, in disquiet seeking
disquieting relief.
And what comes of it will not
simply rephrase the annual
din in Alexandria
raised for the Maiden and the
newfangled god of time,
but may speak for hungers
cracked open with the rights
broken and the rights wakened
furor universalis
made keener by our wars,
rising with a sound of waters
simply and terribly
believed.
Against which this name
Cliff Corner hangs itself
out in air: corner-stone . . .
not as a skateboarder,
twisting from the hip,
hangs high into his turn,
or the airliner whining
to full scream leans back half-
ecstatically in takeoff,

but rather as the climber,
opponent of the dreamer,
gains the grubby terraces
of his sweat, balancing
one life against what deep
disturbances in the core
have shouldered to some ledge
of possibility,
here and no further; where
the grain of mineral
change in the torrential
swirl of the air's changes
poses a crystal limit
for itself, while drawing from us
some one inalienable name.

TWO LEUKÉS

Slippage of moored banks
and going of greased cables,
a garden sliding down
to the salt edge of sight,
compact original
of many deaths, one speck
to ease gull and eider,
sheer falls of that island.

This I may tell and tell over.
But the black jut of more
than unfulfilment, shouldered
up from sunken cores,
only the phosphorus
of tribute heaving there
establishes, thrown broken
before that unswaying place.

THE DREAM OF ARTHUR

Beyond sentiment,
what term do we multiply
in the endless argument?
A spiked seedling, or is it metal,
steely in sweats of the moon,
sprouts once more in the pathless
thicket of affairs, blind
as bracken hemming crofts
saved from the Clearances. Stone barns
huddle through mists on Barra.

Stern usurping stem . . .
and there is no strength in these hands
to root it out, though once
in a spun night there came
a force like great speech thrusting
out, down my arms, and I was set
before the thing, silver trunk
cold from within. I hacked at it,
it toppled darkly, but I, too,
stilled then, fell dark in that place.

Tangle of balked speech
and the stunned life that clings
after the crime – do these
give rise to that only? Threadbare,
the tale of dispossession
works to a filament
that disappears, the weave
from there going inward, to be locked
away, or to break out
in a last ravel of forlorn flame.

Legendary Britto,
hunting, unwittingly
murdered his father. Driven
from Rome, from the wide shelter
of his grandfather's name – Aeneas
who had fled once also – and cursed
by strangers as the killer, too,

of a man killed by Aeneas,
he found those northern islands
unstained by vengeance.

And Layamon, a priest
sifting wrong against wrong
in his poem, drifting
towards sleep over
heaps of the abrupt
fantastic histories,
came to that battle in which Arthur
slays Lucius, the emperor
of Rome, and to the dream
that kept Arthur from Rome:

for he would have moved on it
had he not seen himself
sitting astride the roof
of a great hall, his nephew Gawain
before him, but his son and nephew
Modred hewing the hall's pillars
with a huge axe, and Queen
Guenevere pulling at the roof.
He fell, his right arm shattered,
but with his left he struck

Modred's head to the floor,
butchered his queen, and scattered
his own people. It was then a lion,
gripping him at the waist,
bore him to the sea,
and he remembered watching
waves being driven on.
Their rush whelmed him from the hot mouth,
and at last a fish fetched him inshore
to the long fever of the land.

Salt film over skin.
Baneful broadsword sliding
to its scabbard while thought,
circling, smoothes its tumult,
spreads the vast page. Gimlet

291

star of morning and first sleep.
Romans on the hill
where their first spade turned up
a severed head, laid down
the Capitoline. The page dries.

The story has been worked over
but it wants composition,
the same things get left out.
Or rather are they tended
by a care so regardless
of its sealed heat and pressure
that we may look for the charred thing
to crumple, and a glory
to spatter out, the tongue
        spilling embers?

So then the black ash tree
bronzes, that burly sprangle
flinging outward and down,
fountaining the hid aspect.
From itself, staying, it has wrung
more of itself. In its own story
immured, consistent, it has burnt
past vigor and beyond
that final hold, the bright
mirage of restoration.

GOAD OF THE LAST CHAPTER

Could not locate the hour, nor return –
as if leaving a night bar newborn
I spun on updrafts like some bittern

who has forgotten his marsh and scrub hut.
But my dead friend I could not forget
though only his back showed, for he taught

or rather shamed me to read story
in brute new wrong and not look away,
falconer's eye down through the bird's eye.

Shame not splendor the sure teacher! Hard
following, to find his face gathered
to a blur, and that I caught no word.

How long he had stood by that water
only water knew, on a bay where
port cities, armlets of strung amber,

ventured linkings along their own light.
For greeting he pointed to the wet
pilings, swung his feet over, and sat

with legs blurring in the black riffle,
his calm inviting me towards that cool
abundance, wings whirring its wide lull.

I still tried to form his face, failing,
while his shin swung like patience, bleeding
white in water, timing the shore's long

whisper. Always he takes me this far,
until sunk spurs yield in the offshore
terrors he slew without shield-mirror,

hair snaking with a pulse that offers
no handhold for its fluency, clear
as eely weed under flood waters.

It seemed then that he would turn to say
how he found honey, how I might see
bees hive black sun in each far city,

wine of the small worker, rare basswood's –
but you did not say how that hunt goes,
you looked away, my troubler, as glass

bends in water along a new course,
or light burying in stone shatters
to overplus, before sight prepares.

SAINT THOMAS, STRASBOURG, LATE AUGUST
with motifs from Thomas Vaughan

Weep, eagle and leopard
of Austria and Flanders, bend, British lion,
but not for the death of this man.

The Marechal descends
where an obelisk latinizes
as an elephant plants its feet in the ages,
calm after bombardment

Thou art the First Matter
in whose body is heat and rain
which notwithstanding are hidden from the wicked.
Water and wine, gold and silver.

They have salted the console by Silbermann
into a side aisle, for Mozart
animated its black keys
Not so very many at my recitals
hearing him manipulate trompette and voix humaine
But consider, O man, what God
bestows upon thee by this means
prestidigitator past death's
final bar, eagle of cadences,
limits the white Marechal
stoutly declines to conquer
Torture the eagle till she weeps
and the Lion be weak and bleed to death.
These tears and blood incorporated
are the treasure of this earth.
Weary Herakles stands weaponed near
the small door ajar
heading not out into fields of Lorraine
that develop northward and through orchard labor
and swells of sunflowers burnt
staccato at their hearts
through chain-link yellows

'AS STEAM ON FOREST TRACK . . .'

As steam on forest track in sun after rain
as stain in a horn's bell from the spread fingers
a passing face may print the permanent eye,
      passing, one face.

Going, yet through its integrals of power
factoring forms that grip it, girl by freight car
after the war in Poland, golden hair,
      sun after rain.

Passing while permanent: hand on door grip,
feet bare under the black coat, grave regard
mutably ancient, eight-year-old hair burning,
      fluidly ancient,

as steam on forest track in sun after rain
Bruckner in the hammer, Schumann in wind,
woman in patched coat with her as they vanished
      Bruckner the hammer

and smithied the wrist's arc when a woman's hand
lifts the horn's bell, steady the rodded sun
through bright curls over that track, in fires we set
      our feet on that path.

BOOK OF LIFE

It rested on no shelf – had never been there, and so
the search began with a rerouting into
boundlessness. Turning away from a river's
slow bank and the avenues end-on, to face
into cloud avalanches, memory of forests,
I harvested the streaming of everything seen.

Turnips, onions anchoring the piled colors,
pears in angled bins, behind them aproned breasts
leaning out into the clink and staccato of exchange.
It was not there, though I chose voluminously and paid
what one does under those awnings and the wings of scavengers.

Feasted. And then sought the cool alleyways,
and disciplines with all of their interleavings,
interstices, gutters reamed and drained, seams caulked.
Foraged until warm, blurry, my legs dragging
clotted pollen from trellised planets back to the hive.

That was the first rhythm in the sarabande.
Whose long central passage opened onto parquetries
of real wax, genuine oak, the swarming fire-grain
resolving. Partners interchanging to shape the one,
and interludes widening, cold-rolling the substrate
into sands shelving onto the roar of space. I pulled
back into eddying sweat and powder, pomade,

their swirls surging over the floor to ram high
through arbors at the temples, from the indeterminately
memorious, vaulted matter of the heart.
A scarf it was, existence, that fell over my throat.
Web-soft yet inseparable, a harness woven
from seed-piths, tourniquet of seasons.
Then my hands found it, open at the last page:

He was born in a small city . . .

FIREFRAME

    Eyes kicking open
but the crash gone, and sight fed
    out among tungsten
unblown bodies of white seed –

    was it one burst, then?
rifle that has bequeathed space
    this one-bladed thin
scissoring of high grass

and has already
cleared away into creases,
    into powdery
deposits groining the leaves.

    Now for the last time,
perhaps, I have been set here,
    into one more home
so to bend, break, and enter,

    though it is enough
once, and forever this once
    to breathe, burn cleanly
down the arc of severance.

    In that wink before
the hunter glints through downfield,
    to be that first scatter
of rain bunched in dust and held,

    one more stone rounded
on its own grains into free
    compact, abraded
into empty lucidity,

    a world returning
the look that is bent towards it
    and which, slow borning,
is the least hinge that holds it,

    coiled swarm lifting
from a dead hive in pale noise
    where that comb, melting,
offers up fresh crevices.

    One more summer
the roof glides against cloud as
    first wasps finer
than hearing poke at the eaves.

EARLY SUMMER EVENING, KANTON ZÜRICH

Calming through stilling air,
sails hover down-Lake.
A heron, far enough
to coast on the lifting brim
of light, makes his patrol.
Roses tuft the scrim
of arbors, orchards tough
with years bud plum and pear,
    while the peaks take
their mass farther now, whole.

This is the bastion, this
the angle nothing breached
when light went and the wall
was not enough to balance
outer with inner dark,
and the stray bomber sank
slowly, trailing the swarm,
to meadow fire and silence.
    This is the hall
through which the archaic arc
of the sun narrowly reached
one cave above the abyss,
to bear skulls in a rank
within, high over harm.

Rome in Jerusalem
smashed temple, tribe, tree, wall,
when the wall of Pardes opened
for one rabbi.
            So he went
through that gate and returned.
He would not say what happened.
Whatever he may have learned,
whatever from the All
to the little came through him
bled out in a Roman tent.

The gulf of deepening haze,
the line of mountains, gleams
of house lights down the shore
gather out on the edge
of terminal awareness,
framing the corridor
to sleep with human bareness
and blurring stone, a ledge
drawn out, a gate that seems
the guardian of days.

KESA* FOR THE BUDDHIST PRIEST MYŌE KOBEN, KANTON ZÜRICH

Sorrow for the people of this district.
I dreamed that I trailed a narrow ledge of rock,
a folding screen, I and the Lady of Itono
clambering, grasping in the same places.

> Wing of the heron, sail
> a scrim hinged and swinging
> lunge and crash of the octaned
> metal and last ammunition

Terror and happiness in traversal, and we
stepped out onto a seabeach. There I stripped
dived in and bathed, while Lady Zenyū
hung my robes on a bough heavy with peaches.

> Pear orchards blooded plum
> legionaries hacking
> Akiba entered the strait gate
> illusionless, and tasted

* A mantle of appliquéd squares from silk, gilded paper, and compound satin.

I pulled down a hand-shaped fruit, deeply fuzzed,
ate it, and seeing Yatsarō far off
sent bunches of it to him, its combed-out hair
shaved even at the ends, white and long.

> Awareness at its end,
> cave ledge housing the ledge
> of the eye's cave in great bear,
> bleached bone waiting for sun

There have been times I wanted to write letters
to my cherry tree for news of this world
under the gate at Takao, but who will tell me
why I crossed this once to fair Zenyū?

> Akiba returned
> tranced on the low stone,
> disciples waiting, but once more
> enmeshed he could not speak.

Myōe interrupted his discourse
and ordered me to run to the washroom
and go to the big bucket. It was a bee
spinning slowly, sinking. I scooped it out.

> Sails down-lake leaning
> over a lost son of Śākyamuni
> greeting returning figures
> of the Law in waters of no return

> Bastions deep mass frail scrim
> pastorals sheathing our hells
and I have been unable to tell you more than
how to begin the path, you now straying.

TOBELWACHT

Into hidden symmetries of the known
the unknown floods and withdraws, side to side
over stained, disregarded walls the blown
foliage shadows of fresh solar tides . . .

into the flared cups of cranes' eyes Arcturus
funnels orientation now, distilling
beady burning points, *rex quondam futurus*
no more brimming there with the age spilling,

and so not into the brown skulls of chiefs
tilted upward to the Milk Ring by beaver
near Yangtze, Yenisei or pine fiefs
of Lithuania and Maine, nor into slivered

finger bones of the prince inheritors
bubbled through reeds by the spawn lifting them,
but into streaming mind of the guardian shores
fire trickles, to aim the wings' beating hum.

Tenses and eases those rippled sentinels.
Who stood on one leg, dropped their gripped stones, woke.
Who rose, responded. Yes, in the luminous hells
of the closed infinite, for them light broke.

So seems it in time. So I mutter: is, was!
Crack my tooth, wisdom, but let its gap whistle.
Because they stir and turn, lifting, because
they follow, time is the thrust flooding their rustle

and their chant, which told Hesiod's peasants
when to stop working, and sent Christ's visionaries
back to their deaths; a sound sweet across distance,
although from Troy, fateful yet sweet, it carries.

Far thud of time, a soft plucking of strings
one intimation, or the heartbeat sleeping
in a dear hand – steadily a crane sings
what we, the whole race, have thrust beyond keeping.

Our force lines! Along which slip borderers
melting through mesquite down the gullies, drawn
by want, pushed by terror, out beneath roars
of helicopters swinging their searchlights on,

into which lean, at the bows, the firm, the queasy
backs for German ditches, what Athens learned
with Split to keep on sending through Brindisi,
where dying Virgil ordered
                              his poem burned . . .

a long indraft shaping the dust, a turbine
blurring into its own field, thicker than light,
provoking, in that spread iris, the urban
glow on its trembling pain, something like sight.

Glory – not only an archaic matter –
denial – not some strictly inward measure –
twisted with each other down through the shattered
breastbone of Turnus, honor's anger's closure . . .

black silence: sealing of imperium
Virgil framed that but did he also sense
in gold inertia inaugurals of some
unstoppable implacable intense

violence against time? fevered blindness
thudding thudding towards a seeing-through
through glory and denial, through harsh kindness
even, beyond the species, out, past blue. . . .

The forms of life thinning beneath onslaught,
the life in light narrowing under weight,
give to radiance one chance, and give to thought
one radiance: becoming small before the great

demand and limit of this manifold,
sheathing each weapon, shrinking into space
above the crown of the head and learning the cold
speech of the wind before we entered this place.

Which kindled
           the fever in him. Which advances
through the fire in his book to the fuel in our scenes –
shiploads of horses for the mud of France
harried by the first German submarines,

Orwell in Spain reciting *Felix Randall*
in the trenches, farrier at his forge,
the Little Prince hovering, lonely spindle
of farewell, with his beasts at the planet's verge . . .

and more, but do we feel them? Like the faces
ranged inside us, instantaneous
in their release, yet from the law's deep places,
she he newborn dead simultaneous

penetrating thinking anguish or sweat
beside the river under a branch the stilled
profiles, and the swift stranger's grin, not yet
finished these fires and their channels, not fulfilled.

Gaze of the crane or heron, the whole round
its field, from shore aeons up through black new –
crowds in the retina swept by aura then crowned
by the full surge from an exploding view

of the haze-haloed aqua unlidded eye
sliding beneath . . . for as one whole it lives,
and has them climbing to follow that, or try,
follow and yet spin free with the force that gives.

Surer than fury, steadier than passion,
calibrated to the errancies
of co-original fires in flight, this ration
of fire's scorched heaviness, visible breath, and ease,

this spinning recombining web of force
our home, holds those fliers fast with her gaze,
dot generations fluttering on course,
her linkage to them whirling through what is

yet steadying to a wheel, as great year's arc
in a hand feminine and fierce, some tall
fir in the Tobel stilling its terror and dark
alien soothings, that and some heron's call

across the plash of shallows where she hunted
under the falls an hour, spear thrashing soon
devouring, then calm and, while the slanted
sun levered its heaviness upward, was gone.

KESA FOR MYŌE KOBEN, TOBELWACHT

> If I'd been born in India
> I never would have studied
> but trekked to the five great shrines
> of Tathāgata, sweet practice.

Fluttering on course they thrust deeper
act into law, law act. Under the fall splash vanish.

> If the mind can descend
> to fire then it burns without
> being consumed, it sees
> fire where it is: everywhere.

Dozing at the hearth, he rose: *Light the lamp!*
and sent his man to shoo a hawk from a sparrow.

> There can be no rush
> into luminosity,
> the evils you have lived
> will rise up, or quick pride.

Solar tides that never withdraw, lunar
swells that never subside: pierce these and rest.

The crane at rest is flying
on his quick stem of balance,
the flying crane rests not
no cloud his daydream, to the end.

Not yet finished these fires, the view exploding
wake sleep wake to that bright and battering sandal.

My bucket of sugar lost? Two came in the dream.
Torch the poem of imperium, gain worlds.

SPRING-THROUGH-FALL EPISTLE TO HAKUIN

Hands balance doughnuts
over throwaway coffee,
   not your two-edged sword.

Winter hanging on –
over my steering wheel slides
   the truck's big shadow.

Moon above snow squall,
heart smudged with cloud but seeing:
   shifters eye to eye.

The door latch clacks up,
sun lifts one sparrow. Will one
   voice reach me today?

The need for heroes
spells grief for an age. Nameless
   loneliness of old pots.

Vacant stool, ice hole,
and wind tuning the taut lake
   as white dusk deepens.

Speech trails in tatters,
letter shapes decay, because
Justice wears gashes.

Armored privacy
regards it, garrisoned
property sees it, not.

From Ike through earth-death,
fall of empires, plague, the same
fast cars and slow towns.

Dust hath closed the eye
of the International
Monetary Fund.

Their steed propped at rest,
they groom each other, the black
leathery bikers.

Two crows skim carcass
in the fast lane. The Ballads!
in our swift desert.

Write for the sixth grade!
(Trainers in large firms.) Harrowed
March fields shine in rain.

And endless airstrip
under our prisons on wheels,
the paint lines worn faint.

Fresh celery tips
of the willows: no grief
remains this morning.

At ease in fresh grass,
plastic and robin's-egg blue,
a gleaming Luger.

Slide, slew, slurry
of mangled speech: tug of all those
things they will *not* say.

Lincoln spoke Blackstone,
Shakespeare, Hooker, and a wily
horse trader's hum.

In your Japan, our
young sitting Zazen amid
our debris and noise.

Engine block in sun
on sawhorses in a drive,
freed, gleaming, at rest.

The warbler plops down
with the snap of a battery
in a Seiko.

I have watched
fir needles take the shine; I have seen
fir needles weeping.

Forgiveness: shadows
withdrawing into birch stems
as the light stands up.

In night's cold expanse
the hot heart accelerates,
brakes, dims its high-beams.

When the bird that chirps
and the bird that hears sail from
one branch, be the sky –

when the bird hearing
and the bird tweeting land on
one branch, be the tree.

Chekhov's manor house
fifty years later: blank rooms,
turds of prisoners.

Sand grains insistent
in the eye's pool, gurgling spring
glittering cosmos.

'WADDING THE YEAR'S LEAVES ...'

Wadding the year's leaves into bags, unbuilding
ground of its swirled colors – blood, silk, hours –
I stood in the cold air's

cleansing tower, the steep lean of its stone
emptiness, there finding myself empty,
yet feeling the lone tree

dried to dross by Rome's summers overhead
where I'd bent smudging a page with arch, column . . .
a drone in the dead hum

of idle making, as Allessandro Sette
frantic refashioner of the hive
toyed with the weighty give

of avenues, domes in delirium, yet wondered
whether Achilles' beard was blond or dark . . .
Had found my own blurred work

insufficient to salve my worst errors
yet saved it, caulking the memorial
plinth with it, merest wall

before dust's ocean braving dust's fiery current
dry spume and twisting pillar, braving nothing
less than their torrent hung

over all my roofs, through all my streets, pity
no part of it and papal or Greek glory
blown clear, the blown city free

finally of its own roar. Cool time stands
silent in its tower. In morning's cool
shudderless vault stands whole.

WELDER

Though the streets fed
into the loggias of Tuscany,
they funneled air that was Isaac's,
slicing beneath tentflaps, sauced with the shifting
    and raw silts of the fords.

Night dusted gold on the coverlet's
plain border, with illegible notes in ink.
Morning, a storefront card game, *La Vie*, twenty-four
landscapes to be recombined: plumed
Zouaves, hoop skirts, pines, hoop skirts, carriages.
But life is not . . . lift is not simply life.

The distance to the last well, named *Rehoboth*
or *Room*, stays unsettled until the wellhead
has been left undefiled and the belled herds
    go uncut by marauders.

Think of it: at a new fire on old ground
old because final, that man extracts the deck
and spreads his span of combinations.
    Neither is that wholly restful.

Rebecca!
        Molten pewter around the piers
poured through reflected gawkers, one rusty duck
floated across a man's chest. – May the air
be at least that fine in our place of mirrors,
bridging the aorta, rubbed at lifelong.

Down a last street I glimpsed him: in the black
gap of a garage, a lean mechanic
lighting up his first smoke with cupped hands
and praying eyes, welding tanks set by
at casual distance in that greasy quarry,
benzene from his anointed floor already
    cutting into the morning.

I STRUCK THE NAME 'PROVIDER', ASSESSMENT ELUDING ME

Though an outsider, I saw a towering chair
carved from great trees and burning cloth, and a whore
climb to it in perverse glory, whom
a raw voice, an endless cadence, commanded

to sit there, and I understood nothing.
Then shuddering Hosea bent, being ordered
to hold and kiss her. And he, he obeyed,
the long payment beginning, as some say.

Explanations, the raised hand has framed them,
the bowed neck hunts them, the storied tongue
rehearses. But the excluded hug pillars
in the stone shadows, the dumb trail in homage.

I saw the face of Laura Livingston
in Golders Green, saw the Bishop's tall sister
as her young self in Berlin, stepping lightly
in Golders Green Road the iron rescuer.

Yet Israel who brought children out was trailed
by Messerschmidts until no flotsam showed
on the wide bay, and his oak spindle throne
was moved to another Berlin house in London.

Alien sister, was that whom Joseph clasped
in the deep harbor? But they say wizened Jacob
greeted him saying, *The great things you have done,
even they are our lesser work* . . . and the heart fleeing

passes beyond, as the ghost plume of fire
beyond the children in wastes poured leading, over
those who fell away and those who held fast
and those transfixed in some unforeseeable chair.

CONDUCTUS ARGILLUS

For which of my sins am I suddenly mindful of Tiberius,
though it is early morning and the tormented emperor
cohabits uneasily with the renewal of day's chances?

Great abilities guttering in driven sensuality,
large aptitudes unmet by completion, and his one happiness,
Vipsania, stripped from him: which rancor of that self-islanded
self-brutalizer darkening over the world's summit
works through the soil of millenia to thrust up here?
To him we owe the first and last attempt, his eye on Judea,
to have the Senate proclaim Jesus a collateral god.
I would be shriven by salty laughter, and blessed
by the good hand within myself, but neither yet lifts,
I would pronounce the exorcism of Greek syllables – *phantasm* –
but know that such judging, shunned, would come back as
          knocking.
Was it that the second Augustus did not grant embassy
to the abscess in himself? That he exiled it? The rasping
blackbird does not repudiate her bituminous allure
to monks looking up from the page inscribed *universum*,
nor the setting star deny its isotopes of viridium and lead.
For all his jaded strigilations of mood, his
carnal researches, paddlings in grottoes and groins,
it might be that Tiberius never learned who he was,
starving his grandsons, whipping Germanicus' widow because
other elements obstinately would not serve.

311

The backhoe starting up bows its toothed maw to pavement,
its lean arms green as shamrock and the tubular mantis,
nubby incisors press into hot tarmac as the contraption rears,
sidestepping in a slow arc, and the operator peers at forepads
resettling with the fastidiousness of a ballerina,
himself a beefy man but his aim equally fastidious.
Between bunched wiring and callouses, the beginnings of gnosis.
Then the bucket, lifting again, swings in to address raw earth.

CONDUCTUS LUPUS

From my eye's corner at an intersection while
the car idled at a stoplight in the small hours:

A woman tall in the reach of advertisement
herself stands axial to several intersections,
behind her stone and glass, glass and steel, the spread
of that crossing the scale of a small stadium
cleared except for her, a form bent slightly forward,
attitude variously readable, but in any case made
a stalking horse for good clothes. She herself,
exposed, seems paralyzed with the need for protection
not knowing where to find it in that place.

Luxus, luxus et lupus, though the shine of its tooth
has been transmuted, so that a momentary grid impales her
in this hard web of conjunctions, space and angle, flat noon
of the camera and flat glare of dissipated night.

From the other end of seeing it is these obdurate
surfaces breaking to slide like foam, less even than
the ruined chambers of Mary Stuart, seeing which Mendelssohn
knew that he had the beginnings of his third symphony –
only her form-shadow indexes a presence
immortal in the embodiment that must soon go,

immortal to the degree that it can concentrate
and solidify its for-now single chance,
to that degree deathless behind the reproducible
invitation to want her for what she cannot keep.

Spark of the undying held incognito in a bare place,
as I myself might be glimpsed waiting at that light.

CONDUCTUS ALBINUS

And they came to Jericho. And as he was leaving Jericho . . .
At Bellelay, monastery beside low hills, where
now the unstable are billeted in the name of that
harboring bed, the klinē, creaking level bearer.
To arrive at Bellelay on a day of misted overcast,
approaching from the southwest, is to take in a park
of unbounded extent, the firs not confined to stands
and seldom herded into groves, strollers absent, discrepancy
already inserting its white tongue. A park without gates
towards an abbey which bolts its chancel because the offices
are not sung, though bells keep the hours. *Lead me
not into temptation. Let me behold Your Face
without terrible suffering. Take refuge from God in God.*

At Palermo, outdoing Paris, the seven-galleried
cavern of the Teatro Massimo, which cradled Caruso.
The floor, dotted with red armchairs, some tipped over,
the backstage webbed and geared like a microbe ready to pulse
with mitosis whirring the replication of mirages,
face each other suspended. Below, a singing master with mixed
chorus of children, glasses sliding down his bookkeeper's nose,
holds them to simplicities, the hardest things to carry
from ear to throat
                    without spilling. To enter the garden, hard.
Presence may be invited and rehearsed but it is
also consistently withheld: heart's whetstone.
This place prepares a home for that proposition,
carrier for the uncarried, bridgehead into blank.

313

When it comes, do not expect the languages to hold it.
Scarab whispering to Pharaoh, Sokrates discoursing
to the younger Plato, Jesus hinting to his few.
When it comes, you will not require curtains lifting
over house lights coming up. You will not even be
its witness. It witnesses you, and does not judge.
Firs in mist are their sentinels, the choristers chase unison,
their singing master stretching in their small hearts
the ventricle of distance, slopes framing the path down,
sheltering ridge, the rooflines crossing. Ave, Belovèd.

ALL SOULS

    I am here and am not . . .
standing lurch of bodies,
strange, intimate, clutch
sliding, we are cargo
brought to a stop over Tiber,
rain wavers down the glass,
our breath fogs the near side.

Beyond the island smoke
of the hospital, the bridge
called Broken arching dusk
when the word *Wait* invaded,
arching rain also,

came from far but of course
closer than my skin –
voice or face will change
but there is no garish tremor
in some false mystery
unless we thrust it past
the actual place marker,
this time a woman's brow
jammed close, grainily
moist at stellar distance

with a day's weariness.
Stellar weariest
of the last rank of them
posted here among
the outmost rank of us –
we need not say it. Our names
would startle them as well:
sister, cousin . . . it is our bone
in the lost or anticipated
hills and syntaxes,
articulations still
standing, not home from work.

Past the Greek bell tower
island of poured wheat
and lazar house, my piled
ranges ghost their weight.

The favored one, that legend
winched from the pit, who watched
his father's hills near Hebron
slide past on the left . . . he did not
fly to them and go back.

Around me my strange brothers
and sisters, and we can't move.
What was that name the boy
gave to himself while going
down to the ever-flooded
peneplain of death?
                              Usarsiph.
Usarsiph in the feast.

FICINO'S REST

A clear day, distilled from years. Trench the hill,
sleeve its cave with seaweed and hay on snug stones.
Then mound with me, reseed, fertilize the till.
And thrust deep the Greek-Italic wines.
Below, a weedy ever-growing ricorso.

The ditch between care for the ancestors
and restless rootings-deeper every night
by torn floating images of strangers,
deepens anyway. Fate digs it deeper than sight.
Sturdy ricorsi, I curse thee, though I see.

Fear tendrils its sides, the tribe in us tenses.
Backward along it some would lead us. Day
as the air's drink, from the vintages, to senses
of a future we forgot to hope for or pray.
Returning rewinding mind, though you burn you grow blind.

The hidden world sees each worst, each forgetting.
Hidden sunlight behind the sun, unformed.
Rape and the mass grave rise in it without setting,
but hidden, hidden, the core that shines unharmed,
unreturning core round the hidden turn.

Him I am, yet myself, cried Antigone,
cried and lamented. Him you must cover over
or return, me you shall have till he's free!
Hailing light, vine is the stake's twisting lover,
mercy's recourse the course of the spiral there.

They watched Da Vinci spread out banners, lances,
color chords of the mêlée, his attack
on the Great Hall of the Council, one hand's advances,
only to see the high wall soak them back,
as a brain siphoning down its dream, returning.

The narrowing horizon of the idea
of homecoming explodes upon impact
of coming home, or you have not been there,
traveller, it goes with you as the fact
of breathing goes with a salmon leaping, entering.

I cede the meager magic of my art,
break here my staff, thrust it for budding rod
in the earth's cellular heavens and hells. My heart
I take back to Milano, with the sod
of my body. What returns is not spirit.

I must journey suddenly through aeons,
span the cosmos with micrometer.
One house I must leave for another, distance
a change not a going. And for this incur
the price, risking return, to venture the priceless.

VIGIL OF PARMENIDES

The one character 'barrier' hides the deed.
    – Master Shūhō celebrating his pupil Kanzan

Self-stranded, in a raw strength
not untested but contained, cornered,
he held himself at the poised heat
of that whitening hour when wind stirs,
when it licks at his high ledge, laying tribute
to the mute opening with a mild motion,
sighing itself through seeds and sweet herbs.

For then, as a thirst joined at thought
of slaking by slow pourings of sleek water,
his mutterings, having met night's monotone
with sunderings overheard, strains hoarded
in rock by the range's rigid syllogism,
could ease, and his eyes then close over,
and the weird gutturals weave down as waters

to their last source, spun through soundings
of his ears' own inward coils.
For the work of undoing was a dark one,
and, though intermittent, ongoing
in its fetterings. The fierce legend folds him
in that openness of the all and one,
unfreighted, fixed blankly in the feral cold.

317

FROM KATSCHENSTRICK OVER EINSIEDELN

Jetliner smudges, pink balloon in the notch,
monastery slopes shadowy with liquid manure.

Paracelsus strode out of this hamlet
with an overlong sword, laudunum pills in its hilt
inscribed chemically to Venus
and so to nature in exile.

A sower of discord bent
on reducing turbulence in the body
and inducing calm of mind, not from day's fires
but the lightning of Saturn diabolus.

Red ants waver over stones.

He invoked as one thing and cried high
the *lumen naturae*
as if its strobic flashes did not embrace
each deranging darkness.

Car tops huddled in a wheatfield,
toy planes flashing in dogfights,
their yammering whine insect-clear.

Theophrastus Bombast von Hohenheim,
come in, we read you, we read you,
you have been cleared for landing,
disease brings one to essence,
strips the essential to
quintessence, turns one home.

In a swift mêlée of pastels and primaries
shussers slice down from a drift's lip,
man and dog trail hip-deep to their barn.

Let obedience, with the half-stripped and accelerating
last chapter, under branches blown bare,
be what desire dodges: the Iliaster, longevity,

and then turn shape of a restful limit under
the long storm of unendingness, a calm square
opal, silver, and bled promissory of gold,

soothing vapor across the adamant
and waver of toothed pines
deep in the eyes' furry thickets –

and so lifting when they lift, but weighed
as ghosts, a nerved emanation

gone from where the heart grounds its outpost,
Saturn's flash but not devilish, past dirt, crystal
and up through blue a template still electric
so out into the dome of royal, going.

PASSAGE TO THE ISLANDS
in memoriam John Mattern

The making of this saint was a model affair.
In Ireland he left no bond unviolated.
And once he reached Iona there was
no turning back.
                   – from a lecture on Columba

Yellow stones and brown, white-brown and bone-yellow
        in the swash of the shallows
dropping to greens intimating safety,
        vision's liquor tapering
to darker drink but not lost, the wake settling
to an unbraided dispatch of cold annealings,
        of released levies,

after which the knee-grooved cell with its register
        of the week's intercessions:
For Joanne committed last Tuesday, and her two boys
        For William, out of work
For the soul of Jane Irene Watson, stillborn
        For Jill and Robert Watson

319

The prince stands close at hand, the Friend,
    slabs of his identity
lean or resist in cloud-roll from the straits,
his advance guard having made reconnaisance
    and taken up vigilance

    eroded yet ground-set,
sheltering also Emerson *The country stinks of suicide* –
    what here comes in on all sides
goes forth redoubled and without commentary,

    outcomes tiding to beginnings!
Sheltering also my attempt to release
    that peak sunk in the hidden,
that one center of the hidden for my finding.

    Set close to the jabbering land
yet inviolate, barely lifted clear, incomparable:
    pride of the prince translated
here for replanting, preachings here struck dumb
    within the dense focus – let
    the accessible bury the accessible
and comparisons will take care of themselves.

    Sorrow, there is a river,
great path beneath your adamantine path,
    tugging it like a midwife
then breaking on these shores in its own birth.

    And joy, there is a blackbird
who will navigate its way to this washed margin
    and waking you in the morning
even you had not imagined, will have you speak.

FOR RADOVAN LORKOVIĆ

Widened, floating, a singer's face discloses
known earth as unknown ground, as space –
while the bow arm, yearningly reaching, yearningly closes.
Finished, the part, unfound the place.

O provers, in full flow, that way is not end,
that goal, past doing, goes past the art –
rivers bearing more than yourselves, descend
to cloud crystal at last, rock's heart.

But simply, first, for us the simpler, be
that master teacher carrying
back to Croatia his truckload of fiddles, free
his actual reach, his varying

means, yes, his reclaimed island convent, wake it
with water sounds: past roars of mortars
carry his light load of attunement, take it
to those bare rooms, lead memory's daughters.

But then, with them there and studying, let come
past Europe's final intensities,
past even such effort meeting the surf's drum,
an end past effort, hence past ease.

Have you found your way, friend, to that island?
Those who go there speak no longer.
Behind their tilting, carving bows they stand,
behind strong sound, seeking the stronger.

A lone driver at night, his free arm bobbing
to the tape's beat, or a fevered child
spun heavily through red darkness throbbing,
converge there. Lone, uncovered, wild.

And Rudiger Nehberg with them, blown on the swells,
radio mast shattered, breath stressed
through a Christmas harmonica to shark skulls.
The *Yanomami* mattered, death less.

He with pedal and sail west to Brazil
stepped aside as soon as splashing
inshore, an illustration, briefly shrill
for the mute hurt ones, moon surf crashing.

The first priority is the last reward.
Shell-torn roads, an eroded shore
fall between, though sandpipers spill their hoard
of hungry keenings, goading the more.

Lone-wild, first-last, though frugally prepared . . .
intestinal drag and keening, then
last flight as tremulous as first passage, dared
as the bow lifts while leaning in.

You have not spoken puzzles to us, law
of our being, nor have you blinded us,
but seldom can we hear beyond the draw
of sound, or see what reminded us.

And thus have you sent them, those who go all-out?
who gather learners anyway,
to finger, listen, retune? Across the shout
for safety, to begin to play?

'OPPOSED TO THE DRIFT OF THINGS . . .'

Opposed to the drift of things, carroming streambed tumble,
no single way of standing or swerving can win out,
but even so, one morning, from knots at the margins,
that morning a flaw of wind will choose the expectant,
and sight will turn in them, lifting out over harbors.

Will take them like an embrace, that unanimity,
inane to the prudent. The slips will have fallen slimed,
refuse lacing them with a necklace pruned by gulls.
Yet the first to move will edge past rusted bollards to scan
that tremulous boundary for the returning grain racers.

322

Bulkheads pressed by wheat from the pampas, with
five masts or seven, holding up the pale cleavers
of the lateen rig, they will gain size and lean in,
the *Potosi* and her grimed sisters, keels of marque in registries
that melted with the glaciers and their stranded hotels.

At jetty's brow a scarred one will hunch over, having seen.
From his coat he will extract a slim bowl of stone,
white thimble for his divinatory weed,
and finger its smoothness, searching for the reamed transit
that would accept a stem, probing though not finding.

And back of the jetty, dropped there from omnivorous fire,
a monster bell whitened where flame-ripple sagged it,
pressing into its crown of grasses. *Festa colo,*
begins the embossed stream circling its high throat.
I call the living, I mourn the dead, I quell the lightning.

TWO ROOMS

In a block the swarm, in the flowing the firm, both
meeting at a threshold. But to find the trail?
     In this first room the light
though held by new glass and wood
penetrates to gray paving,
a stronghold's base. Iron loops pin one wall.
A queen has her men lift a floor slab, over stairs.
Filthy, into that hall, slowly out of that rift,
prisoners enter space
under her rings. Churls at their rail
gawk into the saving
gap in time. Yet down that room your sight
travels as far as theirs
without quite reaching, for the clemency being given,
the justice cured, the hardened
faces shining wet under that woman's touch

stay as no haven,
momentarily pardoned,
recorded as such-and-such.
Eroding, this room is one truth.

In the next room the light
though flat on the next wood and glass
breaks in as the sun at four,
honey with a shake
of pollen hanging through,
igniting branching curve
and pillar: some lord's chapel. This burns through arch
and stairs where a plain couple
sit chatting, turned away. Since they stay at hand
yet let things happen, they mark no ordinary door.
Employees of this house, they work also elsewhere.
All one would have to do
to get there would be to cross;
leaving the gray half dark
is all, it seems, it would take.
But into that chamber sight has traveled along some swerve;
at ease, still it would search,
at home, it does not understand:
the place outpaces loss,
he'll reach, but already she's there.

And the antiquity
torqueing into the image,
withdrawing it momently,
already is pilgrimage,
motion in steadiness at the brief portal here.
Passage along its range works as both a near
and far possibility: ours but like someone's legend.
It would be like achieving the lip of the entry porch
at the Apadana, into ruined Persepolis.
Spanning a century, Ker Porter and Colonel Sykes
rode their horses up the double flight of broad stairs.
Like that, then: your stallion taking the wide risers
with a flick of spur, coming to a stand under first stars
before the spread sentinelling of dark gray pillars.

MONOLOGUE OF THE MAGDALENE

I am not myself, I am my sisters,
yet not utterly, I am their unbound hair
in hands which, resettling it not after love
but recognition, not after tented
tastings and feedings, but after gazing
to the garden's end bringing
lightnings, lifted and were gone.

Thus, though she only
set kasha and the wine,
and then stood with back turned in the pantry
while the two men grew quiet
as the third one, the hooded stranger, gathered
them and time and blood's beat
                              and her also
into his low speaking, I took her
chill hand, stroked her hot cheek
while she held as a bell does its own deafened
expanding center.

And so with others at the window near dawn
in a palace, and by the gusty
bridge rail over a barge's wake.
So too they needed
me, having been me.

It was because they hung there that they
went on, because they guttered that they flared.
So that in my heart I can see, sleeping
to pain and the past, waking
to that something more, escaping yet always here,
which gathers at last to the mist
which is the heart:
from unstill waves,
from tugged silk of the waters,
mounts the moon.

READING LATE AT NIGHT IN JANUARY

Over a stone wall, the man leading,
he, come vigorously already from among
the dead, vaulting it easily and going
toward the high room of the stone barn or broch,
windowless dark surging with loam breath, strengthening,
streaming out – this in the account before me;
the far wall of that room already different,
then his finger crumpling it, he vanishing
towards air, grass, and the white disc, spring's convoy,
and this still in the account before me,
but what I saw was a brightness platinum
and actual, which began before his touch
folded the barrier away, was over me
before its fabric broke removing him,
and raised within the crossing a rune outline
    cycling near headlands,
her nature freed of some one thing and entering
some other, in the candid sheernesses
of Baltic morning, her curve concentrated
within the unpeopled scene, a first savannah
for her going so; and I could not breathe,
she gliding free of me though now I had found her
steadily borne on. For at the touch of his finger
no longer bodied there had gone up around her
what alone now and now concentrated
    she was entering, gliding.

BALCONY

Dipped in ultraviolet,
a single thigh of crystal
gleams with two armatures,
that two-handed river its revealer.

Adonai flaring on Sinai,
and the river-born man shocked back
so height dangles hotly
downward, and clay clambers
to meet it on the summits, and clears,

as tungsten quivers inside
a globe's eviscerated shimmer,
twin coils and fire's shores
framing low flames and higher.

The genius of the abyss
hungers for the heights,
his famishment exhales
their morgana, their tremulous hills,

and Sophia who will live
through every wavering
is amorous for him,
his smoldering her organum,

fire jet her fountain,
fountain's fluid topknot
his cooling loosening,
wine's power to pour out a thing

inhabiting them both
and having them both circle
into and under,
wherever there is, so ever.

Behind them, tiny pair
facing out on a balcony
leaning like children, river
coursing narrower where their gaze goes,

to where they will never reach
nor ever need to, they
warming the stone with their middles,
while suns roll and armies cloud the farms

and cities wink out, slide,
and woodlots reclaim
the shifting edge of river,
for the tempering is long, and a strong mover

establishes them there,
stated reinstated
along that balustrade,
vibration the generations have made

quivering out solid
could you watch them standing,
could you stand with them through
the long annealing, going where they are falling.

They are going where the thigh
fell gold in the red mouth
of the mountain, they are going
also where fire wheeled a man high and flowing

while another snatched at the thread
of his passing, they are going
where those two filaments
singe our sight blind or into trance,

ultraviolet
flooding, and crystal gleaming
with two armatures –
but the pair, the linked watchers,

though they knew did not look
into that furnace, and though
they had warmed themselves there
did not turn to it. With each other
they took their turn watching by the river.

sections, FOR WIND INSTRUMENTS
Farai chansoneta nueva
Ans que vent ni gel ni plueva
– Guillaume IX of Acquitaine

God's joy moves
from moon to rising moon:
the ordinary orb
sucking size from horizons,
then hardening slowly away,
shrinking to regency,

a long red pointer slanting
down to one queenly lid,
one discreet hand like a latch
across her lips: so much

to see and to say, to govern
unsayingly, dear fortune!

What enters the eye with blood
should leave the mouth with silence.

*

Waking at Le Querciole:
hole burning through fabric
over a double plume
of steam beside the mine,
and slow cockcrow
probing haze down valley –
that much closer, the invisible
calling the visible to its calling
through the veil, before
belief can take it in:
already it must be
the Chapter of Coming Forth by Day.
And your voice shaking me
with my own name from the next room,
from a bed where through night no one lay
to wait for flame to eat through,
for the upholding pillars

329

of vapor, for the slow cockcrow
at Le Querciole.

*

Like rain before it falls,
like dust before it lifts
spinning, core fires of life
gather at the next
turn of a life, the next
undoing of the accomplished –
remember God's joy, too,
in your happiness.

Have I remembered it
too well? The bright figure
posted in dust past the platform at Foligno
admonished without speaking,
and back of her, like faint
arabics on the thin
pages of a red numeral wall calendar
swam a file of her sisters.

She did not require, there
over powdering dirt
in the day's faithful strobe,
that such an awe be either
embraced or cancelled. Neither
X nor Y, she did not move me to stoop
for the little briefcase key
rusting in spirits
of air between the tracks.

There are times when its silence
wells up steadily inside
its creatures, brimmingly
to a climax, even when
staring into their faces
we have known them not.

TO ARTEMIS

After the broad blade has sung through, swung off, there stand
hearts, archipelagoes, forested shores
etched into promise by mist, anchorages
for the unerring dives of swallows: bear me there.

For the bronze beetle bursts verdigris and chirrs,
bores with Egyptian massiness through my vespers,
threading them with gaieties of the ageless.
And giving out he's in the mire by morning.

Tell me, does wheat still rod down tandem lightnings,
breastplates hung on the beach mirror towns at evening,
candles that fell with a waxy crack flare mended?
For what are a year and a day in such a cause?

Having rubbed the vanadium of the clocks
clean of their numerations, having passed
a century of lictors and felt my loins
pass heavenward through my feet, I shall not ask

about flocks buoying shut wings among
berceuses of rocking power, your blinding reward.
A closing scarab gleams, the sarcophagus
of his own sea where dolphins sun and sink.

MERLIN

As if while in a garden
he felt its nourisher
        conjuring columns,

as if millenial mass
had sprouted from her hand
        and bore his breathing,

331

for neither beginning, ending,
hope nor fear warred in him,
    he'd crossed their circle

without foreseeing that –
as if these things had happened
    all in a garden

as pith climbs in the stem,
as rubble the faced wall,
    drinking up midday

to drive the last leaf bud
high through the heavy column –
    fresh death uncoiling –

she, butterfly hallower of bitter weight.

ANTI-RAMEAU

Le maître pumped his baton, powdered and perouked,
    lifting sonorities.
For *le roi*, god and mortal pursued their affair through
    candelabra forestries.

Passing thence from the perfumed interior
    into evening, the mind
cooled and cued could find that transit out of one
    cinema into the other.

Thence to the real effort, or its anticipations:
    the orchestra dispersed,
the premier willer and disposer will have sent home
    his courtiers, nothing forced

or anxious in that revolution, so much of the score
        behind it, cadencing
with liquidation, each finger of intrigue
        back in account books, chancing

rule of its own and submission to the rules
        of the scattered ordinary,
tyrannies of weather and then weather's blessings.
        Sinking in, staying it, weary.

So that all tasks may funnel at last into
        spirit's tasking, nor is it
found at some furrow's end only to be counterposed
        with plumage mute in storage.

So that avian intensities rise, volley, thin out,
        river shoulders slip shores,
and undressing within itself air casts off
        laces and stays, sheers

away through the white sliding appearances,
        and who shall say where they went,
who notate their arrivals and recombinations
        and be dubbed *cher maître*, exultant?

Down the air's risers steps Lady Four-Wings
        to rest on a twig tip
among fuses of the water lily poised to spread,
        her blue fuselage up

and quivering for take-off, which the king shall witness
        because he has abdicated,
unbuilding the throne I AM so as to enter
        blossomings where she glided.

FOR MY DAUGHTER

Late into that spring
when straggling snow blanketed
the garden in the next plot,
flagstone shapes melted

upward through the sift,
homely, where the first builder
had set them, dark through the yard.
Place, thus, the marker.

What a father gives
is never any one house,
nor was this roof of ours framed
with regard for us,

yet an emerging
ceremony bids: set down
in the place thus provided
each odd talisman.

Calm and heavy as
light within a room's binding,
reflected as if sourceless
and never-ending,

occasion, whose sure
havoc you will not escape
within your own walls, allows
also such worship.

No blasphemy! for
from your own life life will rise
contained, free, newly marking
the ordained phrases.

So the vine, planted,
sent tendrils around the searched
center, where your finger traced
holds and the sun touched,

rife from its burst pod
of flame, timing great slowness.
Fathered thus, the anonymous
shadings of that good.

IN ZION

The narrows-canyon
afternoon a high ribbon

Warnings posted
for storm floods
so we listened
family
over water roar
for thunder

Close, rippled walls
and for each step on flown rocks
gave all of
focus, balance

to earn
light that deep in the earth
purpled walls, strength
and cold in the streamed bones

and so found
the strenuous, gleamingly
strict and swift path

Cries of the three we were
going there

X AND SON

Beyond one ancestor bundled on a Boston stoop
comes the drop-off into the bound-out, without blessing,

into the Midlands of the eighteen-forties, where already
many could not be seen who were there, very many.

The spell-binder had to rise, know which roof to lift, which room
to peer into, while cupping the frail warmth inside,

and then choose type, name, and huddled posture
for my one lodger stiffly alert in pre-dawn darkness,

compulsive ideation tied to the weaver's bench, irruptive imagery
unrelated to it, and their agonistic articulations,

to supply knowledge of a new kind even though it derived
from musical laws venerable as the irrationals,

serving up aery stones for the bread of ignorance.
Quickly full then quite empty, however hungry.

From scholarship I grasp one crumb and chew it:
the working poor reached out to the high shelf for food,

Mrs Gaskell's novels, and Percy Shelley, Lord Byron,
as determinedly as they lugged soft coal in tin scuttles.

Let the strident effeminacy of *Alastor* lie on his table,
bituminous carbon infiltrating it from the sill.

Let them converge, but ignite no wavery completions
of the imponderable story: how coal entered the city,

from which mines, how far their shafts sweated the long seam,
when weight fused it there, and the leaves fell, under what suns.

REICHENAU AFTERNOON

Here, hither, henceforth
                    the island's low arch
insinuates as would a self-easing breastbone
while the boat's diesels splutter.

A phrase in the broken, hieratic
rhythms of the beyond. Henceforth?
Where Strabo cleared weeds and hoed herbs
cataloguing them, ranging them in hexameters.

Spared, it may be, from awkward visions.
Speared like straight seed into plain labor
including his futile letters
to the brother kings.

Come, enter in with ass, oxen, the sudden
Kings and their gifts.
                    Under that memory
runs the deaf river, shifts in the bloody shores,
rearrangements of unsheltered ground.
But I am the island, lifted out for how long
O Lord to hold into flows
reddened or sunned, and to breathe your starry
eclipses equally with the days
of your standing. I am island
and worker beneath its arches
and digger, shy of your wrath,
hoer to not go astray.

SKETCH AROUND A MEMORIAL
in memoriam Robert Bowser

Summer, etched into summer
thickly, with cricket's burrin,
intercellular buzz
mounting to hypnotism
then holding: green sings this,
earth stemmy, earth of seas,

full-voiced saturation
flooding the range of fragile
mortal lights, absorptive.
And my eye's light, confronting
this hum and suction, spills
as lightning through the wave.

By unfixed spirit brought up
short, I wait in one yard
impatient to live through
the afternoon, its topple
of river cloud miles west,
and every roof in view –

through and through, then slam shut,
driving steeple and ridgepole,
in the air's tremor loose,
crazily looser, further
into what we are not,
wagering their whole use.

The Meeting House precedes me –
lightning arrestor, brass
tip of the Yankee pledge
to heaven, fuses suns
within its vanishing point,
and slopes the grave slate's edge.

Light precedes me, tidal –
flecks borne along the foam,
sun mottled on the yard
at sinking angles, these

338

blot into being while
falling forever forward.

To have done once with all
perspective, in one flash
of the transumptive –
a wren's ascending fall
already savoring
recovery from its dive –

and then let space rush in
as when it first grappled
to flesh, in joint arrival
on the crisp, given branch:
one perch, one balancing,
sealing that interval.

From the town green, band music
drifts over, thump and trumpets
intact, miniature,
waking the sick perhaps,
gathering a loose knot
of watchers for an hour.

Fix your gaze on the crannied
wall around you and blur
not the infinities
fronting there, but rather
the unconvincing disclosures,
slide across their frieze –

sedimental debris
back of which futures boil
too fast, entablatures
rearing up the crags
of the written, rearing back
from the black sweep of erasures.

If we're the ones beyond
the islands – if we're those
within seas, yet breathing –
then the tales we try

to recall twist impatiently
over fire drowned, ghost pot seething,

urging, gurgling in us
rather than bubbling high
and greater to who we might be.
One I know tries to rise:
cut off near the Meuse,
a captain of artillery

found the enemy bathing
and held them with his pistol
for hours, his trick of hope
being to slouch with them
sweating in the same skin.
Theirs was no formal group.

His stumble, he discovered,
was a non-random walk
to the uneasy center
of tableau, breaking clear
into tense patience, a plunge
into flow always entered –

theirs was the labyrinthine
chance, beneath the will
for taking, to yield power –
forget what they had learned
and wait past retrieval:
cloud in river, then river.

Too much of what I have learned
would have me hold them there
until waiting ends
in deliverance, dusk
a wide prelude shaking
with the gust vision sends,

waiting caught up in change
that does not perish, body
otherwise than it is,
sight itself the life

in what it sees, fusion
of *to be* with *it was* –

which cannot catch the living
river's breathing slide
of what has not been changed
still moving through itself,
captor and captives in it
caught as the moment arranged . . .

no, it must live while not staying.
So if for one of them
dizzied, fire seem to rush
through colors in puddled bronze
pooling around his wretched
legs in the muck, crushed

chromes bending through his low
fever, skin tempering,
if it mount whole through surf
of the earth's heaviness
to put on more than light
reflected, more than rough

prophecy wearied out
and time's renewable terror,
may that illusion break
surface, a colossus
wobbling up through sweeps
of the illusionless
and breathable, awake.

CAUSERIE, LATE ADVENT 1993

Through fate's downbeat, a birthday,
Beethoven's jingoistic
medley for Wellington's victory
gets dealt as a wild card through
wake-up broadcasts of Mozart's
Tafelmusik, when the source
of a tract on muscular
geoeconomics turns
out to be the writer of state-
funded recipes for *coups d'état*.
Not meaning, this is a time's weather.
Flaws of wind! Yet through music's misuse
one learns to attend to the timing.
And to each timely frisson.
Like the tough makers themselves, these are
not held to set strings and fingerings.
Not really welcome, the evidence
that some take up subjects, harmonize
feelings not routinely given: that
emotion is not given
but brushed back, against the grain.

Yes, comfort will be given!
But not always by way of
the choirmaster, not even
the athletic voice trainer
I heard one cold noon in Sainte Eustache
tugging from his young reader:
*ConFORte-toi, conFORte-toi, mon
PEUUUple!* Enduring, the echoes,
persistent the wiry man,
above the massed huddle of those chairs.

Depth of feeling stands forth from
thought the plow, brightened by endurance.

Massing as a cleansed anger,
the curbed slosh of longing, mist
breakers feeding the pines' mountain.

Praised be the outburst, thanks be
to the psalm's clear cadencer,
but lend allegory to
the bashing of an enemy's babe
against the rocks, let not my right hand
in the choir with voice twisted!

Brother Jew, sister lapsed and
renovated Protestant,
together in one tinware
communalism, its clatter raised
against Ishmael, can this
be right homecoming's romance?
in the last raw province of
heavyweight Assyria,
to roll over with the question
that hugs each sleeper, *How to pay less?*
The republic's middle thus
evades its renewed extremes,
sealed cells gleam down the fast lane,
static crackles through the receiver
like twigs beneath the heel of
Cooper's Pathfinder, or teen pistols
in the playground homicides.

These are angry syllabics
for a pang that seeks measure
in a world whose exiles scratch
asylum from one more nook
or savannah of the bind.
But that bind, psalmist, binds thee:
harsh emotion flowering
carries in bud the pip's point
of evil within oneself –
so one must hold out for, one's
children require, emotion not
simply resurgent from fine outrage:
one has the right, even, to demand
the unexpected, but from oneself.

Do you hear it start, psalmist, *Dienet*
dem Höchsten mit herrlichen Chören?
Dactyls, those clangers clustered
near first mother's birth clamor
when she brought forth the new balancer,
to shelter her cries. Angry
syllabics turned thus, in thanks
to the German immigrant
housewife, wherever she may now be,
whom the police of Redwood City
lugged to a black van from gates
of the napalm shipping point.
Alone behind barbed wire fencing
the manager sported a red tie
with a pistol-shaped clip.
She wore a long print dress that caught
under the shiny shoes of the cops.
I did not speak up back there
in Germany, but I am
not going to make the same
mistake again. Yanking hard,
tearing her dress, they pulled her
away from the microphone.

STARS OVER EVIL DWELLINGS

What do you see in the billion pointed?
Lenses lend them haloes.
What do you glean from their winkings?
The glass eye trims them to crosses.

I look until I see through.
Then come poster-paint splotches,
Davidic overlayed triangles,
where a chubby hand attempts
first unions of up and down.
Chevron of blue shadow
penetrated wetly

344

by one of verdure, or
dried blood's doubled triad.
Threeness, thing that will be,
that must be, regardless.
I watch, seeing through fire
until the earth is cross-haired
and sightings prick out crude rays
faint on the field of the will
but still enlarging. Condensers.

It was said they swung over,
now they retreat, growing redder.
Will we never again
crane our heads out through
a cracked roof into the clear?

Spun clear! until momentum
like sugars in whirled milk
achieves the crystal, though
on glass of the partition
it is the toddler's wide brush.
Wheel spreading to a sponge,
green pressed out of it
still vital. These novas
burst all the while we balance
incompatible weights,
two here, two there, harsh four,
and climb out onto the fulcrum
tottering yet steady.
Balance them and burn
with as much of the broad world
painted inside as we manage,
for no one enters here
who has not squared the circle
and brought his wooden triangle,
colors, and bowl of water.

They've said the worthy went there,
into that light, that hardness.
'Into' fades to a tale,
the spread-out spectrum says so?

When you have peered down a well
at winter starshine, that
telescope holds up fiery
water to flowing fire.
There, on that film, they are
deep in the tale already.
When, in a face, you have gazed
past recognitions . . . well, did it
start with you? and can you
see to the end of it?
Not over and done with, those
phosphors always coming
down so as to press in.
Seen from an airplane, sun
annealing the Aegean
pierces a harbor's mouth
past the dolphin monument
into – well, what? You count
five seawalls on the haven
and drift off, sliding among
glossy pages giving
five sides to the house of power,
quintessence of the no-face
that armored innocence . . .

Starred were the souls of the great ones,
enstarred not ensnared: stored
radiant guide and guard . . .

. . . or you slide out and away:
godlike you gaze on cities.
Pentangle scratched in dirt
yokes in the little houses
again, while pyramids
fused from laser beacons
sway, separate, recombine.
Elektra searches the face
of Orestes, but stirs
no recognition. It was
necessary murder,
and murder to end murder,
yet it leaves these house much
as they were, as they are . . .

346

. . . for stars were fate, our fuzzy
here and now clear there:
isn't that what they made out
January nights
beyond the need for sleep?

. . . while over a Mantuan
ash seedling the georgic splicer
bends to his cuttings while
around him civil wars
orbit, star readers squint
and scribble, recalculate
egoisms against
slave revolts and blank
nationalisms coming.
Knife, tar, linen bind in:
what had been metaphor
twists animate, his lines
accept the graft, scorched furrow
and sword, timed stratagem
and fallback: these save the farmer.
Saturnus' loamy field,
furrow of old Mars, planters!
These fiber the denser sphere,
up through a spinal tree,
while cranially overhead
evil has branched, a spectral
shade spreads high over houses.
He labors therefore the up-down
stem of the actual
rooted and flowering
in both realms, and the stars
seen are in both realms fire.
Stars over evil dwellings
in them both while one knife
hacks at growth, works on, in.

I have been refactored by the equation
    coming forth by day
across that shoaled fulcrum called waking,
    through the equalizer, time.

Osiris has been planted strangely midmost, mastlike
    through the sequence of toothed hours,
though nearing the solar cornice those hang simultaneous
    in a suck backwards.

Double draft, the torqued wind of figuration,
    any one of your currents
may seem to span and spin the others – architecture
    as the air's light husk lofted.

Hair streaming in your corridor, and eyes
    sanded by Isis, Maria,
steadiers of sucklings towards a source, am I
    thus reassembled, reaimed?

Meanings thrust means. Threads of living driven but then
    taken, take fate farther.
O toothed frame of the weaver, braid them on out, each
    sealane, each arrow's track!

(A stewardess bent whispering, hovering ice
    orchestrating a glass,
Ireland white-rimmed, then Brittany, then, bleaching my pillowed
    skull, Homer's foamed skerries.)

A loom nestles rolling bowrace in its webs,
    cradles the thrown waters
where a beater thuds out birth, where the weave tightens
    and deepens, each rammed pattern.

Only the healed leper saw white blossom break
    from the rhythm of that hand
lifted in benediction and rabbinic
    release which brought a sword also.

Only the block drum mallet could have set the beat
        to which I pulled, counting cries
of the white fliers around Christ's brother leaning to
        day's rise with tufted reed.

Dismembered stander, night swept you back from the foredeck
        to lift through the weight of the tree
bearing our rigging, its hemp and tar, its contrary pulls
        and creakings, over the threshold.

But swept here I felt only the opaque scandal
        of immunity, our prow passing
while busses with German plates, returning weary
        workers' families to Tuzla,

spilled them among shellbursts in the same sunlight
        through which a bride enters
and the newborn squalls and shy hands, touching
        each other, rekindle and take.

Passage indeed, but how your multiples bewilder –
        under the white-gold shinings
of your maniple, there is the oars' heavy enlistment
        through the foam's treadle,

and compassion threaded from the unflinching,
        and care from enduring, this
the anchored warp gating the crystal, this
        the fabric of the stone.

TREE OF LIFE

Daily, and daily, ramifying from high roots, inverted torso
    not earth's, not air's,

nor indistinct, yet sliding past the full round
    of sight's fingers,

platinum and focal in the gray plain smoothing
    from a creased shore,

scrubby arrow down through a life's strangeness,
    and from here to there

a stone's throw, although I shall have to pay
    my penny for the chance,

and hang my birdbag, my muddy coat and snares there
    and all my sweet gear

and withdraw my hand from the shrubby encavatures,
    warm immemorialities

of earth's cunny where on the surest urgings I strove
    for awhile to nest it,

and drop the mossy entablatures, hoarded porous photos
    and summer lightnings

to pluck from tempered leafage that food I studied
    to pay for, more than recompense

yet less than visible even at this distance.
    Go on, pay up, go over.

SURA OF THE DIG NEAR SAINT DENIS
with verses from Sun'ullah Gaïbi

Pavement lay in rubble on clay mounds between bazaar and cathedral.

Abbot Suger's honeycomb for the dynasties long since ravaged, bones tossed into a field, though the nakedness of ruthless men beside their stripped queens, caved cheeks and sutured wounds rendered, gleams from raised effigies left unscathed by the revolutionaries. Such the prestige of this sanctum that the Butcher of Wagram had himself crowned there.

Huggered mounds for the heaved bones long since reopened and tamped shut, wedded fragments reroofed in calcined anonymity. Shall there be detection and a sorting, will the sifter articulate them at reveille? *The soul can study only soul, take as your companion your soul only, and if you have come to wisdom there is no God but God which has become yourself.*

Work in the street's wound was careful, superintendent rechecking alignments of grid strings. Leaning on sawhorse barriers, Algerian and Moroccan men slouch towards the unhidden, children darting in tag and mutual harry, steam from braziers among patterned rugs hung from braced poles.

The apparent efficient cause: one language for army, bureaucracy, and the bishop's men, uniformitarian from pyramid to wadi; yet shaken intact from the vast tree these whole graftings. Beneath medieval pavements the Roman base. From sawhorses and tents the still unviolated chorus redisposed, fragrant, commercial, burrowing, ululant, encaved and wandering, filial, *illallāh.*

You went by, you did not catch fire and become light. How could you vanquish the portal? Buckets poured over shards in mesh trays, studious splashings. *Amor cleans filthy doubt, the dirty dog sniffs after the world looking like a seeker, the unrinsed cannot gather.*

Regal obsequy or imperial funeral, the order of procession meticulous but in its sequence enumerating no findings, gathering no aura. Whereas Heinrich Böll was granted the honor of his request: a gypsy band led off his Last Post.

Retaking Strasbourg, recovering from cathedral cellar there the Grünewald altarpiece pricked with wounds, and liberating Colmar its homeplace, fabulist and filthy Colonel Berger, shepherd corsair Malraux, in whom one priest said he first encountered the *miles* of faith.

Stillness of the world before the first moss pavings, before the empire weave of trees, before tread and wave surge of the saurians: it nestles at the center of gardened labyrinths in carpets fingered by kerchiefed women. Stillness now of the Merovingians: by them expected, by children ignored, though working like an itch in the superintendent.

That stillness between the gypsy band and the eulogies.

All of these infolded into one desert stillness at dawn, into the nakedness not of stone but of unhiddenness, into fragrance not of turned earth but of the companion, when those who made camp the night before detected, from traces in the dirt, from scuffled pebbles and leavings, that only one day before, in the light which they shared across one span of travel and travail, that fire of sequence, certain others had broken camp there: the caravan of the Belovèd.

PARAGRAPHS FOR A MANSION

As castles go, it wasn't much of one.
There it swung beside the stained coach window
on the commute that curved me past its hill
And straggle of pilgrim poplars not followed.
Single teetering pebble of shucked power
rolled to a crest, abandoned, secure at last.

Yet now opens. Every existence protects,
and from itself will shield, the corridor
at the end of which a barred door . . . but not so
where veiling shrubs part on a still pool
and past it the unimagined courtyard.

Opens, or gathers? I felt sliding off
all those cloaks that have me address myself
in turn and turn about and, with their swirl,
invoke others . . . air that grazed your cheek
as the shawl brushes intimate commotions
while settling: the lover was he, she,
and yet far more. Filled with justice, the air's
circulations: your core will not be denied.

This is the place the years left, that even
sisters at their hours under the bell
left beneath leaves . . . but a wind lifted and lived
through them and their frail gravity, more so
as I leaned into its thrust, quick, harder . . .

quick there too for the rumpled white sleeper
bars of the moon buoying him while paired
whisperers bent above him: *Found your city!*
his pale ledge Carthage's, Liège's, New York's,
indifferent to a sprawl of dead sheep, a bull
crouching parched, cab driver training a flashlight
on their tangle, slimed bed of the Hudson
across to the Palisades, hazed hump of Elba.
One lamb's jet hoof dangled at rest a pen's nib
in the unblotted ink of shadows from which
a herm Jefferson coveted for his foyer
spindled the chill *Dragged Herein Sweet Soul*
axial to a boy tugging the breast
of his slack mother, father bent to push him
gently away, cupped hand masking stench.
This place the dreaming man began in fact.
And so he had to leave it as fact. Stirring,
seeming to look,
                    he slumped lower, slept.

For good was the summer's fruit. Why ever the strewn
menage, dogs at corpses, and the scorched
granular earth, who did this? Clarity
is a strange chill from stranger passion, curbed
by an arcade pillaring out of weedbeds,
seared limit. Lightning, here, is the long sun.
Door here I have brought with me, swinging

at the touch of the Belovèd far in, towards
garden grown growing, who has worked here long
and waits everywhere unseen. If it were not
to be found so, then how was I, the stubborn
looker-away, with it so? Give your hand
to the door, the wind rising will take you
in and over, give your all to the hand
feeding all to flames of the kindled eye
whose garden is fire doubled, its roots reaching
with hingepin thrust and water's swung sound.

Could look no more. Turned away. Yes, human
perhaps, but this was not all that was wanted.
As the orange bud on a stick of incense crowns
for a long wink, in self-surmounting flutter,
then pours transforming through an upward chute
rolling in at the edges, flattening,
then rippling across its low arch with the ribs
that carry a subway's tunnel or trilobites'
little backs on a fossil's bulge – so the turn
of mind, what is easily called mind
but not so easily caught, rages glories
vanishes reappears burrows bogs down
while aiming, as a whole and in potential,
to empty out. Aiming if aimed, pointed –
though into warming air the aroma aims.
Tenaciously trailing scent, the ant tugs back
and forth the crumb of the soul: oscillations
out of a sand pit through sweet grassy knives.
Birth caul, weed-lettered stone, into bright cloud.

Thus rose of dust enfolding its bright sister.
Entering their tightest clutch, eased by scent
which did not fade, I came to a square at noon
I seemed to know, but all had gone in to eat.
The gurgling fountain near its heart had sixteen
gleaming see-through skeletal seams unmortared.
Drawn up steps to a seeming church, I opened
on bareness and, high in the apse, carbuncle
turning, was it aperture or point? diamond
in steady piercings. And in something like time
I stood though it too wavered, itself pulled

by something other. Fear with it, and joy
like the aurora on oil-filmed water
bent, easing its coils. All that was prelude.
Community through time which those walls channeled
worked to the taste, honey dark, of solved bond.
Then, cries of children chasing hoops, their sticks
thwacking curbs and the spinning round. Melting
splash at the brimming bevel of wet stone
brought me old brightness. I cupped deep and drank.
Weary. But thirst to its taproot sank changed.
Empty. But over, under, a great cistern.
Thus that chapter, mine because of my limits,
trickled off. Bereft I was not. Beheld
was I neither. Barcarole, berceuse,
what is that tune for the swimmer as she creases
morning's harbor for her waiting skiff?
Head in and out, she would catch only half
then it, fading to the condensing shore,
would yield to cold swoosh, and the sun's track melt her.

TRIPLE FRIEZE

      Inattention is a strong lye
and forgetfulness also a fine etcher,
      firm through doggy latitudes of the body,

      but I must see out
what burns through from the base, phosphorus
      climbing the given mountain:
a man seated as if groined with his ground,
incorruptible in the flesh following
      warfare, like air at evening.

      Wind riffled his page
      but his gaze was not severed,
      lathered harness furrowing
      the atom's churning back.

355

Nothing cuts him away
from his purged whites, those
orgiastic billows,
far branches bend and gleam.

To one side morning, and the axe rings
on springy iron of root knees, high strokes
laying hatchwork over the cliffside trunk:
      one must see and hear drivenness
across some valley before one can assess it –
      how that man can chop wood!

Shine eats at the seated towerer,
      rain bronzing then dissolving
      his stilled spin,
acid ripple like a felled skyscraper's blast
      or the brick campanile in Venice,
head into waist, the levels puffing out dust –
here was both codex and great codifier,
      how shall I watch this out,
the woodsman growing brighter as he quickens.

The accursed blessèd who do not look away,
allowed to retrace under the Bear their route
outward past warm windows and the guard dogs,
      recovering boundaries,
      make no commentary
on the metamorphic boulder under the briefly
      waxing moon of their hand.

A valley figure drove down the other side,
flailing at a mule, which nonetheless serves.
That pair came closer. Bent low, they will arrive,
while towering corrosions go forward
and the foreground I inhabit grows too bright –

      Let me climb down past sheds
      for fodder, no certitude
      in this rick, from handholds
      the odor of burnt workings
      seeping, this was birth also,
      and he will latch the door,

spread saplings in piles
for drying, both their breathings
uncoiling nebulae through
the lantern, and bed down.

Inattention, penetrating lyre
put by yet kept at hand, unplucked body
chorded within a frame, stretched axials
credal inside the genitals of the metal.

*

Not camaraderie
of the gunnery draftees
dozing after pint liquor,
nor the shawled widow
gesturing towards the farmer
urgently, girlishly:
No, not my husband is him,
nor was it the man's part
in winking at me, nor even
his story after the widow
also dozed on the night train
to Chiasso, a sergeant
in the Greek campaign while
his daughter and one playmate,
when my cousin waded ashore
north of Naples, were bombed,

it was not even his gaze
or my own holding his
as we plunged the tunnel,
Lei era una bella
ragazza, molto bella
and without bitterness,

and it was nothing we heard
or said or could not say,
neither metal nor breath
ringing, nor attunement
in the arm of the being
who held us and would not sleep

on the train to Chiasso,
it was the night and time
and all of us the held tone
from a throat singing in full voice,
it was that kind of singing.

*

I went over to that rise because its curve nestled
through burnt recessions the downward course of a piper,
squiggle on the hogback who skirled figurations
and was gone. But up there were graves of the shepherds.

I went though it is said we cannot get there anyway.
That we cannot even think of going back to that.
Bellies, ignorance, eyes that have not seen what blinds us
after the shield wall has gone down, sky dearly bought.
Rude stones and chisellings grass-blown, and though
barbarian there I squinted and deciphered them.

Low lips nuzzle them, they tend and mourn
the breeders who did not forget the transposed
hands in Jacob's blessing over his grandsons
and whose piping in winter, carried into the squares,
unbolts shutters but leads only again to the open.

Where had it just gone, hand cousin to my shoulder,
dripping rock ledge, fever-prickling shade? O dust.

Turning, think the cypress against cloud
as a weapon lifts towards an oath or a candle
into its heat sheath, lobe for lobe fitting
into vapor yawning from a great root. Swallows
as if pressed out shot fanning from the matched rims.
So a blind man, seeing, might scatter before day:
reaching into every corner it will not let be.

TO THE LAMPBEARER

I try to keep the vigil.
But the taste of ungathered grasses
stretches before me, a savannah
    furlongs beyond my tribe.

Turn by turn I shall keep it,
assured that its strong seasons will prove
malleable in the arc-weld, one more
    watch in the night.

The shorewatcher's house
has come with me like a loose jacket;
fennel and chervil and the waxy nerve plant
    break in surf on the hills.

But when air pulses
in at the door's crack, still I jump forward
with quickness unsponsored and inveterate
    to greet your coming.

DESCENDING TO NINFA

From the green glow-light in the clock, or was it
    from a green congregation of the dead,
        radiance streamed into the wall, their visit
thronged from behind in parallel past my head
    vise-like, diaphonous, down a stairwell
        in a tenement I must have inhabited
but had forgotten. Peered, but could not tell.
    Waited, but heard only children outside, playing
        in the still afternoon. Rome, then, the spell
of midday broken, a spinning thrust laying
    the path south. They swung to its seeking hurl
        and I was with them, their aim never straying.
Where we came was down but an elsewhere, curl
of waters under and over sandstone courses,

terraces butting the walls, roofed levels, furls
of color from the standards. There are sources
   without apparent springs, and there are givers
     of life who have lived, or will live, through hid forces
in the manifest, cloaked goings, rivers
   underground – as here there were all these things
     displayed in mortared solidity, the shivers
of its flags trilling their wavelength: gatherings!
   Stains of the plague, stench of bodies, intact.
     Not age-old, either; our own. Viral rings
uncoiling Saturn over them, whooshing, cracked
   in the sun's towers, while a thudding wail
     went trailing, crowds dispersing then repacked
around the false androgyne, female male,
   tall rays, mauve, green, pearl, blood, weaving, unlacing.
     But that smoke, the drummed night, vanished. That shale
avalanche, rasp and castanets, the pacing
   sweated shapes, flattened and faded. Out
     shot light's thrust, yet stayed, from interfacing
ashlar, glass, polymers, bent alloys, grout
   of a new make and mold; and sun rose
     yet stood among that mix giving the shout
silent and ringing which is time that goes,
   ringing and unheard which is time that comes.
     Into each head and hand, each fluent pose
caught running, volleys of spirits, with hums
   of those wings guiding me there, disappeared.
     And just as the inturned leg gradually numbs
and a step, throbbing, stinging, brings the feared
   delicious pain, so those concerted planes,
     housefronts palaces villas cleanly sheared
still half-known forms, billowing veils, new stains
   from ancient spectra, pillarless unbearing
     walls and anatomies, like easing rains
fell on themselves and through themselves, outwearing
   the steady ache of the stones, tension in steel
     and cable, and composed the place whose sharing
is instantaneous. Ninfa of the real.
   But then sweat trickling down the neck, the has-it
     has-it-not of mind. And its jab: *The Seal
lies broken!* Yet I knew: what shatters then draws it
   all the way to Ninfa is Ninfa as well.

HE, SHE, ALL OF THEM, AYE

In only a few days they will change houses,
the counselor and his wife, daughter, maid, adopted
    son,
so I work my way around their patio, momentary cousin
loosening stanchions and a green wire trellis.
Eleven o'clock, the Limmat shines below,
gulls glide to the rapids, plop in, drift down, and skim
    back,
prospecting where a trail threads budding poplars.
The consulting room gapes onto foggy sun,
a drained fishbowl, the drapes not yet unhooked.
More than half of the bolts have frozen fast.
I use the hacksaw and roll the trellis into tumbleweed.
Crows preen among tips of the shore forest.
Across the river, more poplars, then a sprawling factory,
then a multilane, and then hazy mountains.
Cloudy glass flung wide, cockpit of aid vacant,
steady cello twang of the road washing over.
A spider blows from the trellis to go the wind's way.
Don't worry, Brother Eight-legs, God cleans house without
    fussing.
The last time I did this I carried the owner's clavichord
like a fairy coffin out to the front lawn
and, weary, laid it across two chairs
to pick through the F-minor fugue by Sebastian Bach.
Halfway through the second countersubject I found
the upper voice in my left hand, the lower in my right.
May we always be so lucky. And may we only half notice.
Packing my own house, pushing our girl on her swing,
I saw in her brave face more than I thought could break
    there.
No instrument this time, but there's a river, there are
    mountains.
Facing them, the gardener walks towards the brink.
He unbolts the jagged scimitar from his pruning grip
and slips in a larger, shinier scimitar.
He swipes down through the first wiry rank of brush
to grasp the lanky trunk of a golden sapling.
The top branches wiggle, and then sway, and plunge
    over.

He descends further, another one falls like a flail,
and two crows flap up. It is nearly noon.
He takes off his red shirt, folding it like a flag,
and begins the climb back uphill, wiping his steel.
He will sit down and eat. Midday veils the mountains.
And so, tell us again: why this endless spring wind?
Why do we cross the river?

M AND OTHER POEMS
(1996)

For visible humanity is in many respects also not human. . . . Therefore, although each person is human in one sense, there are many senses in which each is not humanity.
— Proclus on Plato's *Parmenides*

The soul must lead itself to execution.
— Eckhart

WOODS BURIAL

At the rapids father and boy pitch in a young birch
    laid out by winter.

It is the March of mud roads and triggered hearts.
  That boy leaps as the limber corpse
  hurtles a chute, his father chuckles.

If they really knew what history is,
even though they're in it up to their necks,
they'd feel it, the tug, the cold tilt. They'd stand, shiver.

But how much smarter is that? And how am I better?
    It is that log I've got to be,
      shot straight, unstuck from the banks,
sluicing my wood-lice through the white gates,
        hurling home.

AUTUMN SYLLABICS ON THEMES FROM HORACE AND THE CHINESE MASTERS

Efficiency in the great round
moves darkly to completion: circling
though not returning. Its curves disperse
winds and carve bone. And yet any seized
fullness easing through grace to release
surges from springs, no tributary.
Between asperity and sweetness
gushes one water with two tastes. So

broach the hoarded wine and commit pace
to the powers, their timing,
                  achieve
  what remains by yielding what
  has already been taken
  though not given up. And much

will be given, though not much
in seeming, so be now
a taker, with your friend give over
at last what can never work.

Boughs slough their white loads and swing
into spare curves, the crow landing there
scans bluish drifts for little
footprints, one hunger gazing
after others, one velocity
subsuming the rest: the deer
drifting up defiles, the goatwalker
of gone and coming summers
gazing towards the peaks.

SO THE NAME OF THAT PLACE WAS TABERAH
because the fire of the Lord burned among them
– Numbers 11

Past Gary, to Chicago on the train,
stench from the slaughterhouses streaming east,
black bascules yawning above acid, the brain's
imbalances like yeast
tilting, spreading the hidden face of rain

in a vast scrawl along the miles-wide front,
scaling the whole expressive inventory:
lust from morning skillets for darkness to blunt,
sadness out of the story
of simple meat, sudden wars and long want,

bacon hanging in the grandparents' pantry
and thrummings of a power station at night –
biography eclipsed in the black chantry
of childhood, and second sight
in slag with its magma suns under looming gantries.

ANASAZI, ANCIENT ENEMIES

I rubbed wax crayon against blowing paper.
From the rock face footed a dancer white through red.
  My family gave me over
  to it, gone for the river.

Were I a peasant harvesting grapes near Beaune
in the last century, even, I might have dreamed
  a saint lifting off for Arles,
  Les Saintes Maries de la Mer,

and knowing about cannon in that long peace,
might have been troubled therefore that my flier
  hauled a magnum of the best
  and bloodied the west sky with it

and vanished. My fisting that loose sheet in place
was secretarial, not visionary!
  Already in that decade
  small tribes entered the void

like windows on a skyscraper when the bent
janitor makes his way. But those flick back on
  each night, costly difference.
  It is not only portents

in dream or flapping images of the gone
or the soon-to-be-going or the tremblingly poised
  that catch like undertow
  the foot in tide-rip toeing

down the singing or remembered beach.
We study populations in the forests,
  we hold the paper flat,
  mark, note, warn – the dictated

prophecies do their work, we do some work –
cut horn from rhinos so they won't be poached.
  But, to go on from there,
  one needs to stand in the doorway

some evening and feel the air as if it were fire
pulling illusionlessly, letting the draw
    of one fact heat its chain
    of links, such as, Japan

clear-cutting forests in Siberia
where tigers not already harvested
    lope their dwindling range,
    two hundred as the hinge

for their growled arc of existence, bones of the others
ground to powders for old men's potencies.
    One needs to feel the tug
    of the draft on skin, the drag

of process utterly anciently itself.
Faster, now, the pull is from birth through dwelling through
    dissolution, along lines
    streaming through us, ageless winds.

GETTING AT WHAT HAPPENS

There was a wife named Hope, who reconstructed every
stanza her husband, whizzed by the raven, could not inscribe.

Tarnish among tall gildings in the Hall of Mirrors
sinks from infiltrating sun, parquetry crackles.

Sleek carter of first fire, Apollo from Louis's fountain,
aims horsepower at plate glass cooled before the revolutions.

Losses at hand, with lined faces, what have they
to do with the grassy palace, the dwindling and combed prospects?

Doctors pulled at the splinter
of fat in her Homeric heart, but she sang the days.

If one sways with it faithfully, the pendulum
takes back what it etched with dribbled sand. The sun also.

What they talked about in the cities, what they heard
their hearts fractioning, forecasting, was not all that happened.

A carpenter, planing and sanding,
stands and unstiffens, then hears them: mice in the rafters.

They talked about what they thought revolved inside them,
and what they thought had bitterly happened to them. And talked.

There was a wife named Luna, who had to reverse her tiara
whenever light filled it, annulling her fine entrance.

The old year, crone on the back of a Vézelay yeoman,
tends goose girls in the tale, her gift is love's beginning.

Joinery combs grainy solids, toothing them, to bend planes
seamlessly, then shut them fast. Where ends the beginning?

Ah but then blood happens, unstoppably, and so
why, then, a filmy stream of counter-gleams?

Room roofed over, stanza struck and ringing, meet in
the dancer's live arm, torsions of grazed pasture, forest.

Filthy hunters through them chase throat sound with horn sound,
hugged couples in the high grasses press closure to genesis.

Lancehead corroding there to dark bread, plough and tractor
tipping it forth, guards with damp sachet the queen's bedchamber.

And so the joints lock: sadness somewhere in it but finished,
its polish smells of hair and the gilded flooring of brooks.

And begins to press past even closeness, wing not the raven's
but hers who remembers, a mind past the hours, throbbing
      both ways.

WINE OF THE SOLITARIES

Resonance in the hated process
and the despised figure, are we prepared
to hear its hum across our cherished
assumptions, and violate our course?
And so hear the new beauty in the perished?

Core amore viso riso gente innocente –
chimes at midday, shadowless, nonetheless
bang at obdurately daylit certainties
with harmonies past the obvious, they rain down
the rebuke of hard-won clarities:

in the first stanza, that bright room
of the canto addressed to his wife,
Leopardi rhymes love with heart, smile
with face, and people with innocence,
but it is like the flash of a file

in those miniature armies we have lost
with the ground beneath them, in our tilt
into the indiscriminate, all clawing
together in one slide. Like a file
catching sun gleam, then, while drawing

chinking out of the infantry square
to extend its front rank and broaden
around the opponent and wrap him in,
folding over his flanks with that long
cutting edge, backed by the rest, to win

the center at day's spookiest hour,
unshadowed apex – so that with this
brave extension of his quick means
the strategist across that fulcrum
insures that this night tureens

of soup gladdened by slaughter will pour
to his companies while in his own tent
after the officers have taken leave
he will decant the saved wine from skins
of his own goats, no one to receive

the downward narrowing of red light
within the glass's stem, that treasure
hauled in fur across the white passes,
save him alone. Turning it, his hand
finds the gleam steady, amasses

all that he brings to it fluidly
after the clanged wager and its throw
from his hand through hands not his own.
Neither blood nor victor's mantle that sheen,
nor ode's ripple, but a thing known

only from the solitude of his
stewardship in the fields, his villa
the baked focus of his gaze. And we,
massed beyond all this in the blue,
populous and impossible, at last see

the contraries escape us to enter
his seasonal efforts with the hacked vine,
battle's counter-rhyme trimmed with other steel,
as ancient as marriage, as the bed canopied
within, his arched vein at her heel.

LITTLE FUGUE

An apple paring
curled from the knife wetly
    down my thumb –
and what I had failed
to do rightly touching that life
    next to mine, wearing
late afternoon's numb
luminosity, impaled me.

371

A hunter knee-deep
in salt marsh, whom Anton Chekov
might have set there and then left,
  back to doctoring,
or choked off as too dark, wanton,
  met the steep
flailing of teal, trailed their shrill lift,
but stood only, hearing them.

  Pouring the last tea
of an evening, dark amber
alive, breathing in quintessence
  of India,
I felt limber bark
sheathing the shrub of my life's tree
with root good, but dense,
dark, local, raw there,

  and so in dark he woke,
the seeing doctor, two simple
profiles of linked characters
  in his air,
cruel, good, a pair ample, true
across that split yoke,
true to its splayed force –
simple so rare, though.

OCCAM'S RAZOR PLEDGES NO HOSTAGES TO FORTUNE

Predication is routinely outpaced by the ache of process.
Thus, possession's claim falls short, but thus too
the wholehearted outwaits all erosions to spring
in a spatter of the unexpected. Hid glories hang
unmanifest in pig iron puddled in bulbed Bessemers,
in the turned stomach subsiding and sacks lugging anthracite.
Predication! Skeptics peak early, disemboweling discourse.
Idealists secrete one late pearl and take fire in the gate's shadow.
Hara-kiri fascinates then saddens, but pale primroses
distend themselves at dusk to drink in night, lanky lamps.
The old historian staying at his desk through the uprising,
his young housekeeper, unenamored, climbing stairs with tea.
Seneca was eloquent as he entered the hot bath with

                                                    razor,
his wife after him, oratory rises over the spreading stain,
its accomplishment of coda is not to be underrated, it is *la gloire*
as the rose is, lemony spreadings of the implicate
transposing through bobbing auras the aroma
of what steps forth and then reclines like the clay couples
at their nestled banquets suspended on tomb lid.
But such is not the deed. That lay seeded long since
to drift scent through phases following, in the small hours.

MONUMENT

Wrong turn, then on rounding a night-wide lake
pink trotting feet, swerve, thump, weasel or badger:
time will suddenly differ, bent reed break,

or warbler, not across a royal hall
window to window dark to dark but veering
from guardrails just when I slowed, into the grille –

this is the edge of the entire machine
and I am back of it with my two hands,
turn wand floating beneath the dials' lit brain –

373

there is a condition, an atmosphere,
much as vacancy waiting for something like form
to fill it, that eludes impact, that's not here

yet was here a moment ago, the way tiny
people on parapets, or trudging with cattle
under low clouds, meeting the blind spot go grainy,

or turning back for a squirrel in the Val Bregel
she found it no longer twitching but laid flat
where young Giacometti through a trill

of vapor saw a walker narrow in
like the Etruscan figurines and pierce
luminous space it had filled, take bronze, and lean.

SOUNDLESS TUNE IN THE JEWEL

Horrors as underbelly to winning this
    human life, its treasure my master.
    This, then – but not its bazaar,
horror and chintz, styrene and alabaster.

Heaped along the bridge's ledges, crammed shops
    smeared muddy in Arno, Firenze!
    Stops for the trinkets at war
in wishing's cubbied darks, curbing flow's frenzy.

Not them, but neither the chorus at Delphi, a smother
    of clangs around a widow
    mother, her mind ajar
over the fife-led drums. Yet water shadow,

and one crossing beneath toothed towers and flags . . .
    memory stirs, turns a wheel,
    sags with the banners, lifts far:
revealed, the rare is plain yet something sealed

374

floating soundlessly, no bridge for that –
   revealed yet anciently clear there.
   That, then: transparent bar
in the crystal within the wave on wave breaking nearer.

FIRST THINGS

Powers, in dispossession,
repossessing their birthright past disaster!

What I am after, the original of it,
is not at the peaks, nor washed in valley rivers.

It mingles with the refugees in a camp
over from Tibet in Punjab, it takes a chair

where lamas studying
lunar eclipses with a bright blue globe
stay after class with flashlights and pencils to giggle,
rolling shadows over continents.

And leave. It stays in the corner, unobserved,
inherits the pine smell of desks, and the sweat smell,
and the sound of wind from the passes,
and enters sleep with eyes open.

VESTIGIUM PEDIS

As rain across a lake's face
chills it, leaving streaks of warm runoff
and rising current darkishly vital,
just so one day they shine clear,
mottlings across skin, spotty streaks
waiting to be bannered by flaws
of wind drifting the pocking water.
That day points to the footprint, the vestige:
dearness of revealed patterns harbored.
Yet though I trailed this shore down
into evening then back up past dawn,
finding the same litter, toy shovel,
cigarette pack, and the brave cairns,
it is one kingfisher squat on his boulder
exploding through the shower, razoring
the other shore with his black crest,
that flashes to me the mirror's spin:
discipline of all disciplines, not to
supply past likenesses for the fact rising.

FRÈRE JACQUES, FRÈRE ANTOINE

At a bus stop in Arles a fellow wounded in the Last War
winced into sunlight: *Oui, they are beating the drums against
les juifs again, and the Moors. France is an old man!*
An old pink thing lacking one eye, with his good one he gazed
through and past me to something which held his interest
and at which, after a silence not uncomfortable, he smiled.
Were I to tell this to acquaintances they would brand him senile.

Below a ridge in the Drôme, a goatherd huddled in mists.
His little carboniferous eyes glinted. He was not clean.
A kid bucked and sprang. I asked him how long a goat lives.
He stared, shrugged, and up the slope of wonder intoned,
Who knows?
          I asked how many in his herd, and discussed income.

376

I started to turn over figures in my alien mind, doing
sums and multiples on his eighty head, with calvings pyramiding
upward through geometric promise. He watched me.
He knew what I was thinking, and what I was going to propose.
Monsieur, he chuckled, *NO one needs more than eighty goats!*
And were I to relate this to the literati, they'd call it anecdote.

MEDITATION IN THE MIDST OF ACTION

It was a clear day on a full street, with
    everything for sale.

A white-hair stood by his frozen cascade of pins,
    medals for shock troops of labor,
    brooches from power stations,
five years had thrown him clear of that collapse,
    bronze horseman and bright hammers.

    This from Petersburg also,
      'Fortress of Peter' it says,
    and there rounding from blues
of young night bent a woman drawing water
in her gold bowl towards her gold flesh, N Y M P H A .

    Medea watched them also,
sword dangling – servants filling tureens
that spill along their skirts, cord over cord,
ropes of it bound me once to that low relief
    in a long hall of gazing,

long because with everyone of an age
I'd been thrown clear. Children that were not hers. . . .
The children. Not thinned and fenced, and not burned.
Metal when stroked in a reflective way
    gives water, a flowing stillness.

But cool through din and clang, rash acts, displacements.

If only we could drink it, it would cure us.

POLYBIUS

As with historians out of the Great War
for whom diligence failed to fulfill their call,
I've had to sense, no spiritual warrior,
that being out on cliffs it is not all,

or even half, to gauge the lean into wind,
to balance in it and still claim the ledge,
although that may be much, the knife's point skinned
to one crystal, grief parting down the edge.

More than much. But not enough for strange life,
long thrust unnamed. The name, staring, inherits
a stone gate with false door, high cenotaph,
dark polish showing flights as submerged spirits.

Rebirth! That I climbed to the Capitol
out of the vanquished heights perfects the pattern:
the clank of the law, its close fit in seeming full,
pays its due to the void caw of the bittern.

But the life climbing and the tearing air,
it might have been among the peaks of Chungnan,
always came to full quiet, to the pair,
one old one older, in their emptying dawn:

What is coming will shatter the categories.
So, as for your ambition, you'll be learning
it will do you no good. Mist rifting firs,
and down on the river's bend a barge turning.

ON TINY OBSIDIAN BLADES
FROM PEARY LAND, GREENLAND

No farther east, none,
nor stayed they for months or weeks:
through blackness the eye's light
chipped these, scattering black flakes,

half a finger's length
but with a tension that flings
from Bering Strait through
full north to extreme dawnings,

into the nooks most
barren and coldest to us,
star-shorn nights, and so
past even the disastrous.

Failure no measure,
they compress under some weight
not quite destiny's
because not reduced by fate,

but made small by sparse
possibilities of such
grander cohesions,
the driven hunt's trove and trash.

And are still useful:
no weeping at some image
on a screen, no fate
loved emptily, such roughage.

These, at the full stretch
of hare-tracking and fox-chase,
meet philosophy's
shattered mirror and lost face,

breath on the still air,
shrinking into the litter
of pursuit, under
day years and the wind's glitter.

Harsh miniatures!
The light most ancient, clear,
is of forgetting,
of memory without fear

and without content,
cutting no flesh, horizon
looking to the rise
of a disc long since risen

where one can drop free
of you, refound talismans
of identity,
beyond fortune and past plan.

What you are will stay
in the mind that flares, passes,
the strewn ledge, the site,
with its ice plow, its mosses.

ROMANZA

The untutored Richter showed us, but now there is this
bent girl. It is the middle of the long Andante.
The sufferer has penetrated her suffering,
not figuratively but really. One has to want to,
with the ancestors, and the race also, gathering.
She has convened them, the sign of which, hint to
radar watchers, is the shine of runoff trickling
from her hump. Its rock, concentrating into
quartzes, will show on their scanners as a searing
dot strengthening to core whiteness among scanty
blues repeating across sands of the swept ring.
She has found that part of Provence or Burgundy
in which honored ghosts abandoned a sunk dwelling,
and has poised herself on the chalk doorsill, twenty
horses champing within her thighs, and has cleared that rung
into, not space, not landscape, but their minty

lavendery cloud-mongering sandstone-levering
bed of forcings in the backmost band of mind, plenty
nor scarcity categories there, but emergence, ringing,
her elbows maintaining elevation while flinty
shoulders mass over wrists
                              from which everything
whatever its modes pours with cobalt coherence, chanty
or chorus. But there is no naming it now, only following.
She has found the chink, she has gotten through once
with the entire kit on her back, no slackening
of present actuality, its freight, and where that chance
has been taken it can be taken again, untrembling.
She has not protected herself with what the art wants
usually to shelter, nor has she done duty by fleeing
what the art in its deepening narrowness demands.
A sweaty cave has turned out into heart's shattering.
Gone landforms into future beachheads, the homelands.
Future? The rarely present, the abiding there unfolding.

TOMBEAU FOR VERNON WATKINS

Awash in grass and oak leaves calmed and then shivered,
a face of woman, or man, Chinese, or Danish,
mask set by when the play, or the actor, wavered,
its leather peaty. Treasure steeps in that tarnish!

Heroine and hero, bearers-through,
driven imaginer behind them dreaming,
have dwindled. Where I stand, though ancient, a few
moments reveal as shorespreads of the streaming

boundary, patience beside their lappings reveals
body behind, lost-vast, at ease in mind,
and in those features shuckings of the seals,
with love light-sundered gone for the dark to grow kind.

TRIO THREADED ON LINES
FROM THE PARTHIAN HYMNS

Grasp happiness with this leavetaking!

Wet strew from sycamores
shot my boot out towards the bend of Tiber
    when I was halfway down
stone risers to the embankment's mulled gibber,

    quietest lappings, and toss
of trash, rufflings of dusk-muffled gulls,
    like muted strings for the stripes
squiggled from lamps down the depth's gliding pulls,

    all this registering
in the swift tilt of the world away, rolled gap,
    as my head sought its hard pillow
and my frame slithered through that stair's loose grip.

    How much quieter there:
overhead, on all sides, the withdrawn traffic.
    Farther, the slide of dark cloud.
Dank smells, no annals, no lights. Cold flow prolific.

    Long before I learned
that Pasolini dropped to the same view here,
    stunned, I looked up at it,
two meters thin, history's glitter and fear.

    Buonarotti's bridge,
Cocles's clicking sword, the litter of bills
    from American cars on the night
of the elections: up there, on the seven hills.

    As in a kiva's hub
a gully lets the dancer burrow down
    under a trap and fling it
flagrantly back and shoot out as god, clown,

    and with his anomaly
focus the plane he returns to, so, with fury,
    jackanapes, go on up,
with innocence the blow has restored, go, harry!

you were jailed in the roaring void
and dragged captive over every threshold,

Into dens of approbation
   in the dun north
was ushered the anomalous
disturber and refiner, desolation's
allegorist who drove forth
from his south the ripe figures, scandalous –

vitalities as victims, throttled
   or trumped, or married
whitely to mortuary meats,
himself the stainer of youth, fabled mottled
stingwing to the staid virtues, ferried
for brief honoraria to the sweet seats.

The villa with dusky screening room.
   To the book signing.
The watering hole of the prize-givers.
To the seminar. Assiduously bright gloom.
He entertained their questions. Dining
quickly, he abandoned them, the long livers,

he enplaned once again for hell,
   and entered standing,
ambassador of the pierced boys,
of men who although sold out would not sell
something of a countermanding
fantasy, nourished against increasing noise,

and stupor of empty liberties,
   and garbage stenches
in their own streets, and the tiredness
everywhere, most at the heart of hot energies,
most even in the loins and haunches
of consolation, wearied out to weirdness.

And there a few of the servitors
    bashed in his skull
and shattered his hand and ruptured his heart with the wheels
of his own car, where Tiber snores
out to vastness, where the legendary null
of Hades began once, and now bright mist steals.

> *you orbited through the whirl of births,*
> *you were pillaged in all the cities.*

    Pastorals have flown
out with the probe, or in, down the cell's helix.
    Zero trajectory,
or else picnickers in the Mendelian calyx.

Between, I stretch a giddy cable.
    Towards you I balance,
Persephonèia, you said you'd return,
and so my left hand I shall let wobble
as reason, my right as dalliance,
between the infinities a rhythm to learn.

    Pastoral has dissolved
as tea swirls from leaf shred into hot ichor.
    Towards you I lean and climb,
refugee in red gown, brave with the seasons' liquor.

Flown and dissolved, while the rampart spreads.
    Perhaps a neglected
fountain burbles yet in the garden,
the weedy center. But certainly the dead
shall live, out on the unprotected
wind sag of the wire, on, where you hum them pardon.

VIATICUM

Up under waterfalls,
passing the lacquer workers over their bowls,
the air for them cleaner there
but some still going insane,
a walker towards the Alps from a lake's brief plain
took the route of the peddlers, their stacked wares.

Tin funnels, gingham bolts.
Toffees, tobaccos, spices, nails, augers, felts.
Lace for the rare body shift.
Sweated grace of exchange
above the passes, where no armies range,
where herb is heal-all but footing is no gift.

I catch it: the drift down years
backward, slipping, as if I blur the fear
that mounts in the peoples yet hovers,
that smears haze even through valleys
shadowed by the blown peaks. With the bellies
of serpents I must feel this, not eyes of lovers –

that what is thus feared is failed
for going ungreeted, or for being impaled
with a warlock's dug-up corpse,
crucifix over a stake
in the high pines. That with its old tread it will take
its winding climb through the levels that dusk absorbs.

FOR A SMALL CHORUS

The tightest square is mere event's. Around it
repetitive cities, hazed microcircuits, pile and jam,
until the pressure within it makes
vacant lots, deserts,
and chines of stripped peaks whisper of their fellowship

385

in moods of many hearts,
down chines of the ventricles.
To whom assign the blame? The altar stands unbuilt.
Ushered away from that spot
where touch crumbles, as naive
urchins get pushed from the opera, all deities.
To draftees held in departure barracks by khaki police,
five at each door, pistols drawn,
and files under guard chinking
towards transports gleaming in night,
blessings from a father
who neither scars nor devours,
yet touches: blessings from some hand!

By some Dravidian river, under bankside groves bending,
beside waters rifted with cloud, by shores untracked,
the body of giant humanity
mounded and decked,
soaked with berry, draped with plantain, branch-boned,
lies out under day's sweep
while beside it a stage
disposes actors in regalia of the gods and devils,
miniature gestures
of men and women their score.
And like a huddle of preschoolers beyond that shape,
the watching generations time sceneries of truth.
Near one of the interior rivers
it stands clear, shines out
in cloth and bangles, voice drift
volleying over dust.
It steps forth. And animals
watch from verges of forest.

AVE

Not quite the god who lies back in milk's ocean
out of whose reveries curdle the worlds, not, then,
like island hands breaching then sleekly gone;

nor yet an orant from the catacombs,
linen her seamless length, her rosy palms
lifting a semaphore in the tiered tombs;

though somewhat these. More like seeing hands
of the support dancer reaching up, not tense
to be filled, yet filled before the other lands,

or on a Munich ivory Peter's hands
at the back (while forward Thomas's grope the wounds) –
floating, starting to curve like window blinds

reefed gently as their puller takes in day,
they pause along their rise, foresails one ply
of paleness across the glow, fluttery,

or shining like the palms of the Elgonyi
wet with spit to greet breaklight, ebony
leathery from the hunt, or the grainy

handprints of a painter held at attention
among herd animals and through commotions
of the chase down a rockface, or Asian

palms of an Eskimo into sunrise
after he has puffed on them, and across glaze
greets that day as long as a season. Like these

rather than a crook's dropping his gun,
or spookball from another planet, or thin
stalker cornered, hands up in unison

within a folktale flooding through little eyes
    from page or screen, the gaze
    passivity's or fury's

down each miniature fate holding it:
those all swim in and out, anticipate
dear phony real life minute after minute –

but when in the tub a girl rolls the sheen of atolls
from her wrists, or his arms float under swells
as brother in the hot soak beside candles

their father has set on the enamel rim
slowly lifts a hand and watches steam
banner off in the half-dark, there is some

earliest opening breathing, Vishnu with Peter
bracketing it, the hunters, too, in utter
balance. And she is quiet. And he knows better

than to say anything, think anything
as the heroes disappear, as their gleaming
colors go. Something far older there, smoothing.

FROM THE HEADLAND AT CUMAE
People expected that the evil would finally drain away.
– Aleksander Wat, *My Century*

Faded and baked here to a tawny grit,
spills of blood and seed from humanity
called from it for its crimes against mute earth
gully in footpaths, dribble down to the sea,
payment now and forever drawn from birth
through flesh's sunny darkness. Light yeasts in it.

And if I find the slope to crumbled temples
of that light's god dragging at me through heat,
shallow degrees of slant up to remnant stone,
then something more than burnt air, or the repeat
of weight known as time, pulls heavily in this zone,
something the bone brings, terrible though simple.

Phoibos, slayer at distances with shock,
sower of plague and arrower of healing,
tension of bright-dark beyond spanning, love
will not quite cast out evil while revealing
your fissionables. The raven was your dove.
Heavy isotopes hum with crickets in rock.

Neither woman nor man, my driver laughed
when his lights torched writhings down the far shoulder,
cross-dresser in the night beyond Naples, huge,
sinuous, crooning as we shot past. Life seems older
in its variant forms, drawn by the centrifuge
to the rim and swinging, swayed in time's dream uncalfed.

For the vast thrower, shafter of quivering force,
sex was filigree in whoever served.
Pythoness, yes, wombed keeper of those coils
in the wet cellar where tongue darted and swerved.
But her own throat when it swelled with voice knew toils
past a man's strength, torqued bulging from the source.

And that young man fitted with bone and thong
and membrane from his withers by his father
the maze molder, when he climbed into flame
itself in the high nucleus, dripped as slather
down the sky's maw. Union there, with an aim
at the center, crisped on a central soundless gong,

sizzling from his overreach extended
back on itself and down, the soundless hurry
of the sea far below minutely riven,
trembling in place, diamonds in blue slurry
nowhere disturbed yet flecking everywhere, driven –
all this a boy's cry endlessly thin, suspended.

The sybil when at last her throat disgorged
its burdens rumbled like a pawing bull,
or the bull-fiend on Krete, and shrilly warbled.
Birds ride the bull's hump in stone graphs, that full
barbarity at poise piercing now the garbled
clang of Ikaros, over us tensile and forged.

This in the crumpling whistle of shells and frags
in their close arc. Philosophy gets precise
when it turns practical. This in our background whir.
Archimedes, old Fermi in your eyes,
naked, ecstatic with theorems that assure
conclusion, your city falls, your hacked flesh sags.

There was a sprig which, if you bore it in hand
on landing here, your pilot drowned and your herald
crushed in the surf, would bend and seem to listen –
there was a branch that trailed her voice through imperiled
corridors to throats of the dead, and glistened,
then brought you back to your breath near shining sand.

And there was pelt from the solar scavenger,
its blond mane tossing with your workings, turning
catastrophe to triumph, lion crud
strewn now on waves, coat of the charger burning
obsidian cobalt platinum and mud
in craters of the shaker and avenger.

Eroded skull of this squat promontory,
nubbled shrine over cave by surf hypnotized
before deeps enameled with fire's mosaic,
you are the structure lucid though pulverized
behind the logics, and the omens prosaic
in their spelling out, and the blaze of story.

Give me your light! I am the darkened thing
seeking it. Give me your fire and your cry!
But hood me from sulfurs she inhaled when she twisted
over the fissures, give me your hand from the sky
we have fallen into. Give, yes, what you insisted
she utter, rasped uncoilings of your spring!

And then release me to the animal
shy of speech yet steady in ecstasies,
your cousin the outsider's gaze through life,
the drink of it down, and finally mind as frieze
eternally in metamorphic strife
released, sea stone and cloud infinitely small.

And there the migrant and his wanderers
may find the new land, and their future wars
may roll, exhausted in hissing foam, to sink
over the fish spines, and the blunderers
of fulfillment stare at samsaric wink
of ocean, stare and find sleep that dissolves the curse.

MEMORANDUM

I have begun this many times and shall not finish,
nonetheless! Hsuan-tang rendered into our tongue
the sutras he lugged across
ice ridges from India,
and coaxed forth a pagoda
in the capital's lower quarter of sunrise
to shield them from storm and fire.

Those who passed their exams
brushed their names in the arches
that surveyed empire unblinkingly
from four high outlooks.

Along these curving registries of ambition
visitors saw geese climbing into autumn.

Also he had been ordered to set down
a record of his travels, which became
an era's hangout, lovable
master-tattle, all-fathering novel,
anything that any mind found scrutable.
Whereas his sutras lay out schemas
of the orb onlookers peer into
but do not see through: all-mind.
The one world as one mind. And then?

Following their ordeal, during a good decade
examinees took up assignments in every
reach of the bureaus, each more remunerative
than that posting in Philosophy to the lycée
at Le Puy for fledgling Simone Weil.

Through-sight lifts from the sill, webs tucking under,
it leaves insight safe there. Only it
goes on out. Visitors began to call this temple
Pagoda of the Great Goose.

The ninth-month flocks trailing
their navigators aim
at the sun, however obliquely, as in those Vedas
lisping orientation towards Le Puy
eras before Gautama spilled like Caesar
from his mother's side.

Madame Professeur took her pupils past the babble
of the agora, into the Platonic abysm, then turned them
to face the acetylene torch of Pythagoras
and the fusion-orb of Parmenides afloat in night.

It is the human privilege to hang a gleaming
necklace of labored fashioning, *kosmos*, around
the neck of the universe, and wait for compliments.
Unvarying shiver of onset, rolling shifts of glissade:
    pine wind and fire wind.

Tu Fu inscribed his name under the arch coping

                                                    then

fashioned a quatrain about gosling-diplomates
streaming off towards day's furnace door
and screaming, *Where will I rest?*

    All this by way of reminding you:
we must promote implementations,
rephase the proposals but stay on schedule,
but dump the tapes from their bunkers, shoot
no more bullets ferrying Bach past Arcturus.

Most of the signatures are gone,
only pomposities from the snot-nosed
Ch'ing great-grandfathers of the reborn revolution
hang on above the spring peonies.

How old, those aromas? That is perhaps
not the most penetrating question.

My own recommendation: become arrow, meet the bow,
requisition platinum for the thumb ring,
but snare this with roundabout nets, rely only
        on collateral agencies.

Where the mind perhaps opens
past where mind has definitively stopped,
there hovers the next proposal, the pulsing chinook.

To the code team: scratch contingency plans
for restitutions, scotch all apocalypses.
For they creep back into the galvanics
of fresh feeling, they twitch there. We have ignored the fire
before any judgment, prior to undoings, its coals present.

Read the unwritten and inhale.
Climb to the four outlooks, graduate to dawn's flare.
Sleep not. Still the heart. Study.

RELAY OCTETS

*

If sound, then why not the full reach of mind,
and if that cantilever then why not the whole
keyboard with its totality of partials?
But then one meets the dragon, pipes up a bright
disciple, *whose two dramas, lieber Meister,*
are suicide and the founding of the state.
My name is a household word, writes the hid teacher
to his ambitious aspirant, *in my own household.*

*

Three, three, and two, the comeliest proportions
in twice four, carols a bobolink at midtree,
the golden sections of sight flap nostalgic for sound.
But of touch there is no ratio, there are only
gradient, ascent, compression, easing,
and space evacuated, not yearning; filled.
Therefore, Belovèd, middle is neither midmost
nor at the squeezed core, but where breath resumes.

*

A man who had killed in order to save life,
and had left his clan to guide the foreigner,
never went home. Or, home was what he came to.
The girl who knew that something before and after,
of which no one spoke, was always brimming now,
came to his corner, knitted, did not speak.
What had striven in him and was seeding in her
gazed out over the harbor, through white sails crossing.

*

Simply because temple and trave rise framed
like verse of the Silver Age, it's not dreaming back
to loop out with those curves on sunflower faces –
points on their net, widening, hold tight
in casts of fishermen, fowlers, and high buds
leafing stone along the load-bearing wall.
Lighthouse beacon sweeps over, that arm bends,
star swirl releasing the torch to a dark cycle.

*

The beginning of the third Razumovsky quartet
sets one in midstream doubt, amberish dam
for joy's spillover: true beginning starts late.
Slaying the interlopers, he has only just
told her he must go off again, she accepts,
neither climax nor close is the end in their lightning.
And the shaft of it shearing down, it is steadily
here, and the clamor in it is calm, its roar a vast silence.

FROM THE 1990s

INCIDENT NEAR VICENZA

Bright, yes, but this is the floor of the crypt,
where Adam was told to scratch a groove with his foot
when cloud printed it –

though you would have me lose
even that bare grasp of my law
and the law of heat-shimmer over rock, Termia,
though you meant to veil
every rupture, you cannot bar
my stumbling fall towards the unpredicted
sanctum, its explosion
in furnaces of the dust.

     And so
it was not worth your while trying to stop
the hill road from sliding under
or the crest from descending and leveling out:
behind me you were not,
nor before,

     and through my plodding
it wasn't worth tallying
the count which your heartbeat's mimicry
pad-padded in sliding shadow's
meeting of each downstroke
on earth, sweetish solar
talcum and the angels'
improbable residue –
in them there, sounding! Your rhythm, meetingless
greeter, boundaryless mapper, counterfeited
the burden of appointments
missed and never to be made, and canceled
relief where mass grew mighty
at last: from far, from within,
from every side to the one point
declared past all law by geometers
of the furious inch and spearing
light-year, it was neither of us
who took on substance there,
but rather that which everywhere stands, fleshless fire

able to score its own sign, its gash
of crushed squirrel in the rut
beneath three swooning lupines, and below them
a severed mountain's gleaming
quarry of chalk.

ENCOUNTER ABOVE STRESA

Were I to have modeled the flights of doves,
Venus's as God's, from the belly
of Mary's effigy
swung open in procession,
by feathering my fingers along your flesh . . .
Were I to have mimicked
truth born to earth
by tripping touch down your breasts, those repeatedly
ghostly tractions would not have
drawn milk from glands of the light. Nor by
tunneling *in cava*,
thrusting there with love for the dead, Termia,
would I have aimed into
my darkness with knowledge of the dark.

Threadbare terms needing our blood, yet even
replenished they do not draw down
the wealth itself, being – for
the small frame shatters.

Selah! The harmony
sustains curves of the hand but is never the hand.

The clear thing turns encoded
when it rolls in on itself
for the plunge towards birth; the encoded
revolves that spasm which rolls a bawling life
into the clear, baroque
agony of a renewed triumph. Yet you would
persuade me that these yoked

400

emissaries are enemies. For your veil
with each wind thrusts your breasts'
aureoles yet drapes separation, while your name
promises an end without ground. Through your gaze,
thus, the perpetuation of worlds
necessary rather than possible.

Still, I bore the belly and lugged the womb:
a spark swelled down in, and blood broke
crowning my drained thighs and creasing the pearled
caul as it crested.
In my hale stupor I confused you with that – and thus
I was drawn down
in that lake descent with you,
where nothing of our release
to islands hugging the near shore
gave or could have given
that thrust of what will not be denied this clay,
rammed earth of the walled moment
widening.

Even for the confused
may the snug frame crack where
release rises! For down
to the boats' diesels and then
tunneled streets, down to the hall
rearing its mottoes, drilled our mere
foragings. Borromeo
of the gold, of the black,
congealed in one dome one resolution
confronted by cypress and tiered stone gods as
witnesses of snowy peahens and peacocks,
and not long since of the booted strongman
hoodwinking premiers and ministers,
feather-dancing the states to a fine stasis
before his long-withheld
cymbal crash.

Peahens, privet, gods, and the dousing fountains
sustaining a suspension –
let the caul break!
                    Fire in the mortal cave

401

when doused mounds down to such hills, their moored
monasteries strung with pleasure boats
by gossamers of extinguishings.

How your eye glazes and your touch floats –
yet why did I turn
as across fields stubbled and sun-leveled
unless to warmth of the ripped furrow? But that
is the termless earth's. There when
my days are given they reel out
in cable, nor could the strongest
downstroke axe through them. And such cord I must pay out
only to those I've scarred in holding
and children generous before the fact:
those who abide with those
who carry the seed, a tattered
parade thin and gleaming
through beetfields towards bessemers
flaming with early distances the late gate.

Should the enforcers come for us too one day,
then you would have to wake
to the flame sealed within you, and follow her
your stifled igniter, working the hidden stream,
its cascades. And stooped Maillol
would take us in at his homestead,
and Vierny his model
would lead up through his vineyard and point us to
the Catalan heights. By then we should have seen
the whole art. Nothing but what we carried,
and everything we could, if you'd climb there.

The clear is the encrypted
stripped and scoured forth,
cresting among bright lichens and blown rocks.

Through it the order of companions
cadences, lofted yet not weightless,
dragging their share. But not one rung of our
descent carried, unless it was when, turning,
I caught your look from up there suspicious, assessing –
guarding the reserve

of dead distances, the gold
of a vocation bound to remove you:
gaze in which I now read
a birth that fearingly
the decades are dragged into, drawn
up with the entire
icon your eyes must have framed there: flecked shores
and the towns, boats plowing, hill-shoulders
nestling an upper lip
severe on the axial face, its lower sensuous;
trafficked hands at last
deposited on the bench of knees, their blur
of acquisitions dispersed, the one
fascist pogrom at their base as if absorbed –
the whole in all its registers
ranged through an innermost
eye dead at last to claims, judgment, the whole
poised wholly, gowns of the lifetimes
swirled across its repeating core
so that it may slide
stacked and arrayed to the tongued
forceps, gliding
forth at last, given.

The Spring Festival on the River   This Vietnam-era poem borrows
its title from the venerable Chinese vernal celebration of
Ch'ing-ming or Clear-Bright, which is also pictured in the
medieval scroll which I render in 'Colophon for Ch'ing-ming
Shang'ho T'u'. The attack remembered here is the one on
Chungking by Japan in 1937.

In *The Broken Blockhouse Wall*, 'Lucien', 'Refinding the Seam', '*Am
abend . . .*', 'Bounds', and 'To the Allegheny' are set in the
Pittsburgh, Pennsylvania region. 'Ground Observer Corps' is
set north of there in Cambridge Springs.

Cussewago   names a creek in northwestern Pennsylvania.

Let Us Call this the Hill of Sotatsu   honors a Japanese painter, and
is a close cousin to section four of 'March Elegies', both from
the Vietnam era.

In *Poems and Translations of Hĭ-Lō*, besides Zurich and its districts
such as Hottingen and the Adlisberg, several place names are
also Swiss: the Val Verzasca in Canton Ticino, the Val Ferret in
Canton Valais, the Grisons Mountains, Herrliberg and Rappers-
wil in Kanton Zurich, Baden, Sankt Gallen, the Isle of Ufenau
in Lake Zurich, and Einsiedeln in Kanton Schwyz, birthplace
of Paracelsus and site of a prominent shrine to the Black
Madonna. I am indebted to the late Franz Jung for the finder's
technique in *Fifteen stars . . .* , and to the late Mary Briner for
the glimpse of Furtwängler in 'A Gross of Poems. . . .'

Four Ancient Poems   The third incorporates bits from Ch'en Lin,
Ts'ao P'i, and perhaps Cai Yong. The first line returns in 'A
Gross of Poems. . . .'

Ditty for Mayor Fu of Freiburg im Breisgau   This city was 'exempt'
from air raids until 27 November 1944. The Philosopher Paul
Shih-yi Hsiao reflects on the behavior of the monitory duck,
memorialized in bronze by the lake, in an essay which dis-
cusses his collaboration with Martin Heidegger on the trans-
lation of Lao Tzu. Heidegger's version of two lines from chap-
ter fifteen of the *Tao Te Ching*, based on Professor Shih-yi
Hsiao's rendering, underlies the last stanza here.

Forged Heart Blade   puts on display what recent Swiss archaeology has retrieved.

Tally Stick   'Even in / an age . . .' translates the first half of Saigyō's *sue no yo no*, which itself transmits a dream voice (the administrator Tankai to the poet Shunzei). The decline which is the subject of Saigyō's poem is not literal but spiritual.

A Sash for Wu Yūn   Wu Yū (d. 778) failed the imperial examinations on Confucian topics but passed them on Taoist ones, and spent a brief period at the court of the late T'ang emperor Hsuan-trung. Both Wu and Li Po, whom Wu introduced to the emperor, became members of the Han-lin Academy, which, including physicians, diviners, writers, and entertainers, served the ruler directly. Both men, however, were hounded out by the court eunuch Kao Li-shih (here 'Cow Leasher'), and Wu spent the long remainder of his days as a recluse. – Both the abbot and the prior at White Cloud Monastery in Beijing, the Monte Cassino of Taosim, were murdered by their own followers in 1948, shortly before the Guomindang surrendered the city to Communist forces. Within two years, the new regime edited and reprinted the Taoist scripture *T'ai-ping ching* or Book of Great Peace, while extending no such preferment to other classics. – The end of this homage echoes a poem by Wu Yūn (Kyoto no. 46748), in which he approaches the immortals by climbing out of the cosmos towards blinding light.

The Death of Yuri Andropov   Alexander Solzhenitsyn reported the remark by Swiss radicals in 'Our Pluralists', *Vestnik* 1983 (*Survey* 1985).

Rhyme Prose Three   The final panel draws on the Adamic iconography of Golgotha, Hill of the Skull.

Clam Shell with Hunting Scene   alludes to an actual object (though not to its specific details), one of many such archaic Chinese ornaments.

Osip Mandelshtam in the Grisons   Mandelshtam studied for years in Paris and Heidelberg (1907-1909). Gleb Struve and Arthur Lourie maintained that Mandelshtam never made his brief visit, or visits, to Italy, but Nadazhda Mandelshtam confutes them. The poem alludes to 'Notre Dame', 'Canzone', chapter sixteen of 'The Noise of Time', and 'The End of the Novel'.

Wind under Sash, Val Ferret *Hǐ-Lō* includes a translation, not collected here, of Borchardt's 'Underworld North of Lugano'.

Rhyme Prose Four This painting by Rüegg belongs to the Kunsthaus Zurich.

Seventh Moon The ancient tale alluded to with Turnip and Nīladhi, the *Maudgalyayana*, was recovered among scrolls at the caves of Tun-huang.

A Gross of Poems Linked in the Mixed Manner The two groups of poems that are inset enter for archaic reasons: the whole poem is a cauldron or *t'ing* with flaws set in the rim to permit the spirits free passage. The first group, beginning at 50A, alludes not only to the ancient 'long wall caves' poem but also to strikes that were brutally suppressed during construction of the alpine rail tunnels. In no. 35, line two renders part of Wu Wenying's 'To the Tune of *Mulankua* man'. Nos. 64-65 refer to the Basel exhibit by Joseph Beuys. The house in no. 120 became a hotel. No. 133: an early professor of medicine at Zurich, Dr Moleschott proposed that 'one is what one eats'.

from *Rhyme Prose Six* The vignette of Johannes Bobrowski tallies in part with his 'Novgorod: Coming of the Saints', translated in *Hǐ-Lō*.

The Cells at Tun-huang The cave-like cells at this Buddhist desert monastery were built over several hundred years. The fresco showing episodes from the ancient tale of the golden stag, in the *Ruru-Jataka*, was painted circa AD 500. One of the episodes is rendered in stanza seventeen of 'Sorting Straws'.

Honan Folksong The original is filled with the playful homophony which I reproduce here.

Folksong I.ix . . . Present here because it is the only item omitted by Ezra Pound, I believe, from his *Confucian Odes*.

Single Seal Quodlibets through *Barometric Reading* These four poems draw on materials selected from Bernhard Karl-gren's revision of his own sinological monument, *Grammatica Serica*. Karlgren offers compendia of archaic inscriptions, incised in all sorts of materials including the most perishable, alongside the traditions of their interpretation; these supply me with staging-points for westward raids from eastern outposts still shrouded in mist. The marriage in these ancient inscriptions of concreteness with openness to multiple reconstruction – particularly exploited in 'Age of Gold' – permits projection to play across *faux*-traditional screens.

Liu Xie . . . This writer's maturity coincided, in the early sixth century, with a peak phase of literary innovation. His position in debates between ancients and moderns is represented here. 'Writing' is *wen*, 'patterns' of every kind, from macrocosmic to psychological; and with his braided rope he may be recalling the fact that in the transition from prehistory writing replaced 'government by knotted ropes'.

from *Twenty-three Poems about Horses* This selection from the suite emphasizes its main theme, the misuse of good men by corrupt administration during the Late T'ang. I am indebted to Mrs Susan So for wise counsel.

Weeping for Ying Hao The original is a quatrain. In this rendering I aimed at suggesting what English cannot very well reflect from a tonal language: the sheerly phonic play of its tones, hinted at here through repetition and variation.

Orphic Fragment From an inscription on gold leaves used in the Dionysos cult practiced in southern Italy.

Poem on Divine Providence This long poem was attributed by Migne in the *Patrologia Latina* to St Prosper of Aquitaine. The mis-attribution puts one in mind of context, for Prosper compiled an anthology of Augustine's work, the readers of which would have found that the calamities described as remote in *The City of God* were on their own backs. Orientius was a Pelagian Christian. He brought his experience as prisoner of war into the poem, alongside a confidence in spiritual survival which Hï-Lō's selections do not translate.

My Country Weeps: 1636 'Das Rathaus liegt im Graus . . .': *Graus* may double for both rubble and fear. – 'Conduits of blood': Shakespeare.

Rawlinson Two-Step The poem by Gottfried Keller translated here was memorized by members of the resistance movement against Hitler because they regarded it as prophetic.

Novgorod: Coming of the Saints Part of 'Rhyme Prose Six' sketches the compositional background. Within the poem, Bobrowski has encoded Russian folklore into the second stanza, whose imagery recapitulates early testimonies about how certain Russian icons were discovered caught in the roots of river-bank trees – much as the child is found in a tree, where it hides in order to be found.

Century and *The Last Centaur* Ion Barbu, Professor of Mathematics at Bucharest, was called Romania's Mallarmé by his compatriots. 'Downpressings', not included here from *Hĭ-Lō*, curtly lambasts 'Moscow heaven, pitchforking air'.

Yu-Vu Songs of the Na-khi Such folksongs by shepherds, about suicide pacts among lovers from this Tibetan and southwestern-Chinese tribe, were drawn on briefly by Ezra Pound in Canto CX. The particular ballad-like cycle rendered here, with formulaic repetition removed, was first translated by the scholar to whom we owe our knowledge of this people, Joseph Rock ('The Romance of Ka-Mā-Gyu-Mi-Gkyi: a Na-khi Tribal Love Story', *Bulletin de l'École Francaise de l'Éxtreme Orient* XXXIX, 1939). Imported Chinese marriage customs made these pacts common, and the Na-khi developed a ceremony for the propitiation of spirits lost in suicide, the 'sway of the wind ceremony'. The lovers are believed to join the mountain winds of the high groves and meadows in which they carry out *yu-vu*. The songs are typically improvised by young shepherds on triple-reed Jew's harps, in lines of five syllables sung in syncopated rhythm.

Argura This title corresponds to no single Latin word, but rather to elements that derive from roots shared among several terms.

–

408

Interleaved Lines on Jephthah and his Daughter As its title indicates, this poem combines independent strands in alternating fashion. I composed it as an experiment in bi-hemispheric dialogue, writing one strand left-handedly and combining the two threads, not tampering with the combined result.

Six Stanzas in Nine Lines The Benedictine monk and poet Strabo of stanzas two and four, one of whose epigrams appears in *Hī-Lō*, also figures in 'Reichenau Afternoon' in *Selva Morale*.

Times Passing the Breakwater In the third section, mention of the Christ and his following derive from an early legend.

Boat near the Capo Miseno This headland north of Naples marks the legendary landfall of Aeneas.

Zurich, the Stork Inn My title alludes to a poem written by Paul Celan for Nelly Sachs.

June Fugue The little that is now known about the Etruscan Feronia enters into play here. Quoted lines distribute most of an anonymous Middle-English lyric.

Cento Biblioteche Italiane As with 'Interleaved Lines . . .', so here: alternating lines array interleaved strands, each internally consecutive. One of these explores the Medea myths while the other rummages through libraries and archives in Italy, a few known at first hand but most of them glimpsed in the pages of a mid-century Italian photographic volume which gives the poem its title. This title also puns on the genre of the *cento*. Serious personal folly led me to comedic treatment of these myths, a treatment which ends with convergence; the organized chaos which is a library meets the myths proper through the pictographs chiselled into walls of the Valtellina and Val Camonica, sites which overlay Medea's last stop in her story. This convergence turns molecular and the scale becomes atomic. My slant on the great solar princess does not lean towards the most interesting variant of the tale, the one favored by Christa Wolf, according to which Medea does not murder her children. The italicized lines translate from a chorus in Euripides' *Orestes* that follows later in this collection.

Animula 'O little one' (little soul) translates the title, a venerable topos from Hadrian to the present.

Kayak Island   includes a version of lines from St Augustine's commentaries on the Psalms.

Rhapsody for the Gatekeepers   'The barrack-allée of winter poplars': Dachau near Munich.

Report from Mendrisio Station   Mendrisio is in the Swiss Ticino, Foligno in Tuscany.

Riddle of Peace   incorporates a version of the anonymous ninth-century Irish 'Inten bec', translated in *Hĭ-Lō* but not collected here.

Frieze from the Gardens of Copenhagen   While I stand by the whole suite, experimentally here I omit sections 2, 4, and 8. The tale in section 10 stems from Isak Dinesin; the *Akedah* in section 11 stays open to Isaac's actual sacrifice, in this respect following the Hebrew tradition.

Round   The endura mentioned in passing was a fatal ritual cocktail among the Cathars.

In a Railway Compartment near Glarus   The named town is in central-eastern Switzerland.

Never You . . .   The title comes from Stesichorus's palinode to Helen.

And Fresh Cuttings . . .   This title borrows from Plato in *The Republic*.

Selva Morale   I borrow this title from Monteverdi's *Selva Morale e Spirituale*.

Archeus Terrae   Mentioned also in *Sing and sing me again*, this term comes from the renaissance physician Paracelsus, spanning in its meanings our own senses of the Aristotelian entelechy and Bergson's *évolution créatrice*.

Lakeside   The doctor here I have compounded with one other informant-survivor who stays behind the scrim. The castle museum: at Rapperswil, Kanton Zurich. This poem kicks a door open in one more American's inevitable tendency, after a long spell of work in Europe, to identify himself with his nostalgia for the cultures so long rooted there.

I Struck the Name 'Provider'. . . 'Israel': Wilfred Israel, the Berlin mercantile heir who pioneered a Jewish children's exit-rescue network through his frequent business trips outside the Third Reich.

Vigil of Parmenides treats a medieval legend. The seventh line borrows from Tolkien's rendering of *Sir Gawain and the Green Knight.*

Conductus Albinus The phrase 'after temptation' comes from a personal prayer of Muhammed.

Stars over Evil Dwellings takes its title from a painting by Paul Klee, and was written during First Citizen Bush's Gulf War.

Tree of Life The inverted tree form is Vedic.

Autumn Syllabics . . . *Wind and bone* translates a traditional Chinese formula about poetics.

Anasazi, Ancient Enemies Anthropologists have rendered 'Anasazi' as 'the old ones', but by this name the Navajo mean 'ancient enemies', the original dwellers in the Four Corners region of the American southwest from the twelfth through the fourteenth centuries.

Getting at What Happens 'Hope': for example, *Nadezhda.*

Vestigium Pedis This phrase once stood as a reminder that existential forms point beyond themselves.

INDEX OF TITLES

INDEX OF FIRST LINES

424